@ 6⁰⁰ 2/13

SWAMI
ANANTANANDA

WHAT'S ON MY MIND?

BECOMING INSPIRED WITH NEW PERCEPTION

D0973678

SWAMI
ANANTANANDA

WHAT'S ON MY MIND?

BECOMING INSPIRED
WITH NEW PERCEPTION

A SIDDHA YOGA PUBLICATION
PUBLISHED BY SYDA FOUNDATION

---— ❀ —---

DEDICATION

for Gurumayi Chidvilasananda
with gratitude for everything

Published by SYDA Foundation
371 Brickman Rd., South Fallsburg, NY 12779, USA

ACKNOWLEDGMENTS

This book has benefited greatly from the loving and skilled
attention given to it by the following people in the following ways:
Jonathan Shimkin and Peggy Bendet, who edited the manuscript;
Jim Drobnick and Jennifer Fischer, copyeditors; Valerie Sensabaugh,
who offered editorial assistance; Cheryl Crawford, who designed the
cover and text; Stéphane Dehais, typesetting; and Osnat Shurer
and Sushila Traverse, who oversaw the production of the book.

— *Swami Anantananda*

Copyright © 1996 SYDA Foundation.® All rights reserved

No part of this book may be reproduced or transmitted in any form
or by any means electronic or mechanical, including photocopy, recording,
or any information storage and retrieval system, without permission
in writing from SYDA Foundation, Permissions Department,
371 Brickman Rd., South Fallsburg, NY 12779-0600, USA.

(Swami) MUKTANANDA, (Swami) CHIDVILASANANDA,
GURUMAYI, SIDDHA YOGA, and SIDDHA MEDITATION
are registered trademarks of SYDA Foundation.®

First published 1996
Printed in the United States of America
00 99 98 97 96   5 4 3 2 1

Library of Congress Cataloging-in-Publication Data
Anantananda, Swami, 1940-
    What's on my mind? : becoming inspired with new perception /
Swami Anantananda.
      p.   cm.
    "A Siddha Yoga publication."
    ISBN 0-911307-47-8 (alk. paper)
    1. Spiritual life — Hinduism.   I. Title.
BL1237.36.A48   1996
294.5'44—dc20   96-9267
                                                 CIP

The paper used in this publication meets the minimum requirements
of the American National Standard for Information Sciences —
Permanence of Paper for Printed Library Materials,
ANSI Z39.48-1984.

CONTENTS

Foreword

IN THE SPRING OF 1994 at Gurudev Siddha Peeth, the Siddha Yoga ashram in Ganeshpuri, India, I was asked to give a series of talks on forgetfulness and remembrance — of our own true nature, the inner Self. They were talks on how we live in forgetfulness, on different obstacles to remembrance, and what remembrance is. *What's on My Mind?* is a further evolution of those talks, and it is a distillation of many things that I have been taught and have discovered during twenty years of Siddha Yoga practice. Its purpose is not to be an exposition of the basic Siddha Yoga teachings but to answer questions and offer guidance to help one deal with the kinds of issues that can come up on the journey to Self-knowledge.

Once I began walking this path, I found that while grace and the practices — such as meditation, mantra repetition, and service — gave me many experiences of inner steadiness and bliss, much of my day remained filled with emotional swamps, habits, confusion, and anxiety. The contrast between the inner states that Siddha Yoga meditation was giving me and what my mental and emotional habits kept putting me through impelled me to try to begin unraveling the mental net in which I struggled.

So I worked with each issue and habit that came up in the flow of living — and most of them kept on arising many times. In the meanwhile, grace and the practices continued to supply me with experiences of the independent well-being and goodwill that characterize idenification with one's true Self. These experiences have had their own purifying impact and have empowered all my other efforts.

In short, *What's on My Mind?* is about sadhana — life as spiritual practice. Siddha Yoga sadhana has as its foundation the awakening of one's spiritual energy, which happens through the grace of a Siddha Master, a perfected teacher, such as the head of the Siddha lineage, Swami Chidvilasananda, and her Guru, Swami Muktananda. As Swami Muktananda once said, "The power of the Siddha's grace cures one's forgetfulness. Then the awareness of the all-pervasive Consciousness arises automatically."

Yet our old mental and emotional habits keep pulling us away from this awareness and clouding our perception. Being caught in old patterns of thought and feeling, identifying with the products of our mind and circumstance, is the condition of forgetfulness. And how we relate to our thoughts and feelings is a key factor in overcoming this condition.

In psychology, there is a great emphasis on analyzing our emotions and thoughts to understand the intricacies of personal history behind their contents. This focus works on the *contents* of our thoughts and emotions, to see what they reveal about the unconscious or subconscious patterns from which the contents arise. Then these patterns — brought to awareness — can be changed. For two decades, I took this approach both formally and informally, and learned a great many helpful things about myself.

What's on My Mind?, however, takes a different approach, which comes from a profound tradition of wisdom that is many centuries old and very effective. This is the yogic practice of *dropping* thoughts and shifting to Witness-consciousness. In these pages we will examine this process. We will look at what to do when we find an opening, a "window of opportunity" in the flow of our daily awareness. For in such moments, yoga shows us, we have the chance to recall the all-pervasive and ever-blissful Consciousness that is our true Self. Then we see ourselves and our world through new eyes. This is a stance of equanimity, of detachment and joy; this is the stance that the scriptures of India call *sakshi bhava*, Witness-consciousness.

What keeps us from the independent happiness and clear perception of Witness-consciousness? The texts of yoga identify a profusion of tendencies and traits by which we are bound to our limited identity and thus kept from Witness-consciousness. These are such things as anger, greed, and infatuation. Known in yoga as the "inner ene-mies," these tendencies all receive their power from forget-fulness, from our being out of touch with the inner Self. *What's on My Mind?* examines nine of these inner enemies, and presents various ways they can be dealt with.

When we see the world as a composite of separate, different people and things, this is the dream of forgetful-ness. When we fully remember God, within and without, we see and experience the same world as the body of the one divine Self, which we also are. Cultivating Witness-consciousness is a basic step in this process. May it be an intriguing, fruitful, and liberating adventure for us all! ✤

———— ❧ ————

One's own thought is one's world.
What a person thinks is what he becomes —
That is the eternal mystery.
If the mind dwells within the supreme Self,
One enjoys undying happiness.

— Maitri Upanishad

A Note on the Text

For simplicity, Sanskrit and Hindi words that are commonly used in Siddha Yoga courses and publications are printed in the text in roman type. Less familiar terms appear in italic. For the interested student, all Sanskrit terms are also presented in the Glossary according to the conventions of standard international transliteration. A Guide to Sanskrit Pronunciation accompanies the Glossary.

Chapter 1

Witnessing
in the Moment of Choice

*You must stop your mind from wandering here and there.
If it begins to wander to a place ten miles away and you
try hard to stop it, it may at first go only nine miles. The
next time you try, it may go only eight miles. Eventually
it will go only one mile, and finally the day will come
when it will remain completely still.*

— Swami Muktananda

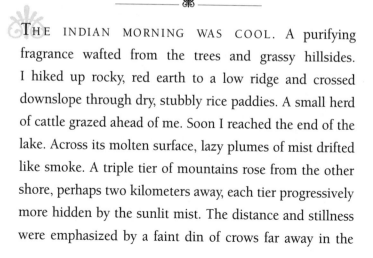

THE INDIAN MORNING WAS COOL. A purifying
fragrance wafted from the trees and grassy hillsides.
I hiked up rocky, red earth to a low ridge and crossed
downslope through dry, stubbly rice paddies. A small herd
of cattle grazed ahead of me. Soon I reached the end of the
lake. Across its molten surface, lazy plumes of mist drifted
like smoke. A triple tier of mountains rose from the other
shore, perhaps two kilometers away, each tier progressively
more hidden by the sunlit mist. The distance and stillness
were emphasized by a faint din of crows far away in the

forest. I crouched by the water's edge and gazed across the lake toward the mountains. What vastness!

Suddenly the distance and stillness triggered a corresponding spaciousness within me. There was an inward pull on my attention. Closing my eyes, I let go of looking at the outer scene, and I felt its immensity expand within me. When my eyes opened again, I saw the whole scene, including myself, in a detached, quiet-minded way. There was no separation. I was part of the landscape, spacious and still.

Consciousness is astonishing. It brings the outside inside, and makes the interior workings of the mind manifest in the outer world. And when we have learned to still the mind, or to let it go still, we gain access to the blissful fountain of Consciousness that is the mind's source. The chattering mind, with all its careful delineations of who we are and who we are not, of how we should feel and how we should not feel, is but one facet of Consciousness. To see and experience the world only through the filter of one's chattering mind is to live in cramped isolation from the present moment's infinity and joy.

How often have I stood on the shore of a lake or the crest of a ridge, grasping at the view — trying to squeeze out another drop of the peace and well-being it had evoked in me? How often have I thought the glimpse of spacious timelessness within me came from "out there"?

But union with the timeless present, the sage Patanjali tells us in his *Yoga Sutras*, comes not from grasping harder at the sense impressions and ideas that flood into the mind but from the *stilling* of the modifications of the mind. That union is the source of the joy and aliveness we are looking for.

The understanding in yoga is that behind the veil of our thinking mind and behind the unconscious lies an eternal wellspring of natural happiness, intelligence, and loving kindness. This wellspring is the ocean of pure Consciousness from which all our feelings, thoughts, and their meanings arise. That Consciousness is our true Self. That Consciousness is the joyful Witness. Yet we experience the true Self only fleetingly. Why? As Patanjali wrote over sixteen hundred years ago, our attention and identity get tied up in the contents of the mind whenever it is active with chatter and moods. By stilling the mind, he said, this identification with its contents diminishes and we rest in the Witness.

Then we are no longer identified with our ego and its personal history, although it is still there. Instead we are identified with our eternal Self, that greater Consciousness.

In this identity lies peace and independent joy. This is why yoga aims at stopping our mind from wandering here and there.

I remember walking down the crest of a mountain ridge lined with eucalyptus trees, in Hawaii in 1993. My time in Hawaii had been devoted to the concentrated study of Swami Muktananda's books and the practice of meditation. By this particular day, I had been pursuing this practice for several months. It was late afternoon, and the sunlight was gentle on the valley forests to the right and left. At one point, I began to spin into a familiar inner emptiness that always ended for me in emotional impasse and pain. In moments like these, the content of my thoughts was often despair about the environment, the population tidal wave, and the damage done by cultures that seem bent only on growth and consumption. But underneath these thoughts, and fueling them, was an anguished personal urgency: "I'll never make it." To what? I didn't even know.

On this day, armed with a clear perception of the nature of my mind's flow — a perception that the past three months of intensified meditation had empowered me to use — I intervened at the edge of my precipice, saying, "I do not have to follow out these thoughts; I do not have to enter that pain." With that assertion, my awareness suddenly resolved into clarity, like a camera lens finding its focus. And it did not waver. I continued down the ridge, fully present to the moment at hand, in a state of utter equanimity.

⚜

HOW DO WE STILL THE MIND? How do we free ourselves from the habit of thinking and living behind the veil of our own preoccupations? Are there moments when we can choose to bring our attention back to the present and give the mind the chance to be completely still? To answer these questions we need to look at the moment-to-moment working of the mind as we experience it in normal waking consciousness. This simple flow of the mind happens again and again, all day long, every day of our lives. This flow is very familiar to every one of us. Once we become conscious of its pattern, we can use this awareness to work in harmony with the mind instead of being at odds with it. This everyday process of the mind can be described with an example as follows:

You may be chopping onions in your kitchen, brushing your teeth, starting a car, or listening to music. You are there, fully present and naturally aware of what is happening with you and around you. In that simple moment you are quite content and unself-consciously happy. Then, without being aware of it, your mind wanders into a train of thought — "These onions are so strong! . . . Aunt Isabelle used to say if you put matches in your mouth your eyes won't water. . . . The first time I played with matches was in 1947. We lived in Catonsville, Maryland. Halloween there was like living with the Addams family. . . . Oh. Here I am chopping onions."

What happens in a cycle like this? First, our awareness is present to the situation at hand (including ourselves). The mind is basically still. This might be for a fleeting moment, or for quite a long time. Then, our mind wanders into thoughts without our really being aware of its wandering, and our attention goes with the thoughts. A few moments later we become aware that we have been thinking. Immediately thereafter, we are aware of ourselves and the scene around us once again.

No matter what the content of any moment might be throughout the day, and no matter what thoughts and feelings the mind wanders into, these steps in the flow of awareness are what happens. You can count on it. The final step (awareness of oneself and the surrounding situation) is the same as the first, thus creating a cycle of the mind's process.

In this cycle, the moment when we become aware of our

thoughts and ourselves again is the moment of choosing. This is the moment when the mind can be stopped from wandering here and there. Awareness empowers us to make use of these moments of choice, which occur again and again throughout the day. How we respond to this moment of awareness is the key to stilling the mind. Instead of fighting with the mind to make it be quiet, we befriend its natural flow and turn knowledge of this pattern to our advantage.

❈

HAVE YOU EVER NOTICED that we do not just have thoughts and feelings, we simultaneously have thoughts and feelings *about* them as well? We are rarely just sad, for example. Instead, we're sad or angry about being sad — or we *like* being sad. When we are in love, we're rarely just in love, we're *happy* about being in love — or scared, hopeful, excited, or all of these (and more)! Take the example of feeling well after a bout of the flu. Few of us are just well again. Instead, we have a reaction to being well, such as gratitude or relief.

Or consider the strange case of how we frequently respond to ourselves when we remember something. You'd think we would be happy about it and go on from there. But whenever we remember something, an astonishing number of us get upset with ourselves that we had forgotten! We've just remembered something, yet we react by getting upset that we had forgotten it! People are always forgetting things and then remembering them again. So the issue shouldn't be that we forgot, but that we remembered. If we'd just stop and notice what we're doing to ourselves by criticizing ourselves for having forgotten something (when we've just remembered it), wouldn't we change our reaction? Wouldn't we want to enhance our chances of remembering things by thanking ourselves when we do? Of course we would. But habits die hard, particularly when they aren't even noticed.

So, not only do we have thoughts and feelings, we also have thoughts and feelings about them. We can be angry that we are upset, ashamed of being jealous, delighted with desire. The possible combinations are practically infinite. However, most of us have developed habitual patterns of response to our own thoughts and feelings. For example, we are either sad about being sad, or we relish being sad. In the state of forgetfulness, our reaction to a spontaneous thought or feeling is so habitual that we rarely have a different reaction. Indeed, we may think it's impossible to — or odd. But becoming aware of and then changing the habitual judgments and reactions we have to our own thoughts and feelings is a key way for us to step free from them.

In that moment of self-awareness, if we choose to let our thoughts go instead of reacting to them, we can return our awareness to the breath, or to our mantra, or simply to awareness of ourselves and the task that we're doing. Each time we make *this* choice, we strengthen our capacity to stay with stillness; we further our spiritual life. This choice is an act of remembrance. We cannot stop the geyser of thoughts, but we can — and do — choose whether or not we shall react, pro or con, to our thoughts, thereby continuing to think about them, or let them go.

When Baba Muktananda's book *Where Are You Going?* came out in 1981, I read it eagerly. It is a beautiful introduction to the Siddha Yoga teachings. Each chapter begins with a quotation from a scripture or great being. One of them struck me as "containing the key." I kept returning to look at it again and again. It rang so true. The passage was from the *Maitri Upanishad*:

> One's own thought is one's world.
> What a person thinks is what he becomes —
> That is the eternal mystery.
> If the mind dwells within the supreme Self,
> One enjoys undying happiness.

Thus I saw why it *does* matter what we think, and why
it is useful to repeat a name of God, a mantra. This quote
convinced me that every thought has creative power, for
good or for ill, and our repeated thoughts make us who we
are. There is, in short, no such thing as an idle thought.
Furthermore, the Upanishad promised that if the mind can
come to dwell in pure Consciousness, the Self, one would
enjoy undying happiness.

I remember the day, in Ann Arbor, Michigan, when I
decided to take up mantra repetition as a regular part of
life. I had been walking in the Arboretum, an area of wood-
lands and meadows that forms an apron around the town.
As usually happened on such walks, my mind had wandered all over the place. Two blocks from returning home,
waiting to cross a street, I remembered the mantra. Up to
that point in my sadhana, I had repeated the mantra in
meditation, but not on the street nor in the midst of activities. Baba Muktananda, however, had said that one could
repeat it everywhere! With a sense of awe at the recognition
that I actually had this option and could direct my mind in
this way toward God, I began repeating the mantra. It felt
like an adventure. I had never before established such a
conscious relationship with my mind as a whole, asserting
what I wanted from the relationship. In staking out my

requirements and expectations, I knew I was crossing a frontier in my whole mental life. I still see the winter tree and the cloudy sky behind it that I was gazing toward when I began repeating *Om Namah Shivaya* instead of following my thoughts and feelings wherever they would lead. Of course my mind continued to wander periodically during the rest of the walk, but there would always be moments when I remembered and felt I had a choice again. Again I would repeat *Om Namah Shivaya* several times. Having a single thought that I returned to made the moments of choice in my mind's flow visible to me for the first time, and it gave me tremendous hope. I *could* shape what I would become! Joy and capability arose in me as I completed the walk home.

Baba Muktananda wrote about the nature of thoughts in his book *Meditate*: "The dog, the horse, and the camel that appear in your mind are not made of anything material; they are made of Consciousness." So when we think of a dog, it's not a dog that will bite us if we ignore it! It is a thought. This is obvious. Yet how often do we spend time either running from our own thoughts or running after them — as if their contents were physically real! No matter what the content of a thought is, Baba Muktananda points out, it is still only a form of energy. Therefore, in the cycle of the mind, whenever we become aware that we are thinking, we can practice the understanding: "Regardless of its contents, that is only a thought, a temporary form of Consciousness — like a wave on water — and I do not have to think further about it." That is, we can drop our thoughts and stay *present* with our Self.

※

EARLY IN 1976, A FEW WEEKS AFTER I'd met Baba Muktananda, I went to the Oakland Ashram for his darshan and evening talk. In terms of handling old habits, it had not been a good day for me. When I knelt before Baba in darshan, he immediately turned his head aside with a frown. I waited and waited for his customary smile and the brush of his peacock feathers. Other people came and went, exchanged greetings with him, and were brushed with his wand, but Baba studiously avoided me. Finally a hall monitor asked me please to move on. When I protested that Baba hadn't greeted me yet, he said, "Can't you see he's not going to?"

I returned to my seat halfway back in the hall in the midst of a large crowd. Darshan ended and Baba began to speak. I had never heard him talk with such intensity. He looked right at me and began: "You must avoid bad company." He continued for several minutes on this theme,

looking directly at me again and again. With amazement, I
recognized that this is what Baba's refusal to greet me at
darshan had been about. "He knows what my day was!" I
exclaimed to myself, feeling a combination of consternation and joy: consternation at being seen so thoroughly,
and joy at how intensely Baba cared that I take care of
myself and stay on the sadhana track. At this point he said,
"And I don't just mean *outer* bad company; I mean inner
bad company as well: like anger, lust, jealousy, and greed."
In my heart I replied, "Baba, I want to avoid bad company;
that's not my problem. My problem is that I don't know
how. *How* do I avoid bad company?" Interrupting his own
sentence, Baba paused and said straight to me, "At a distance. You avoid bad company at a distance." Then he went
on. A few moments later, he ended his talk. A bad day had
become an invaluable encounter.

"At a distance" stayed with me. I began to see how we set
ourselves up for meetings with outer "bad company" (whatever its form may be for us), often hours or even days in
advance of the actual event. For example, we find all kinds
of reasons why we have to go to this place or see that person. And then when we're there, our hidden purpose leaps
out and ensnares us in a sequence of events we often feel
dismayed about afterward. Armed with the awareness of

when I actually make decisions to seek out bad company, which I disguise from myself with other supposed purposes, I found the situations easier to avoid.

But "at a distance" with regard to *inner* bad company was more challenging. As a friend once said, "It's hard to fight an enemy who has outposts in your head." How to get distance from them? The resolute return to repeating the mantra in the moments of choice between thoughts turned out to be a major help. So did the detachment and inner contentment that arise from Witness-consciousness, particularly with regard to witnessing thoughts and their accompanying feelings.

Witnessing our thoughts is different from not having them at all. Many thoughts may be there, particularly the spontaneous trains of thought that just geyser up and then subside, but we are not caught in them. With detachment, they fade to the background of our awareness, and the present moment comes to the foreground of our attention. As our tedious and repetitive mental chatter subsides because we do not give it attention by reacting to it, we experience an inner quiet that is both restful and spacious. Released from the cobwebs of mental preoccupation, we are present to the situation at hand. Then we can respond to it according to our highest values and goals.

Clouds come and go in the sky all day, but it never occurs to us to *identify* with the clouds. Imagine if we did! What trauma we would feel as they dissolved; what distress we would feel if clouds that we did not like arose in the sky. We would tie up all our attention just noticing what was happening with the clouds, which clouds were "good" and which ones were "bad."

Just like clouds, our thoughts come and go in the sky of our awareness. Why couldn't we be as detached from the thoughts that come and go in the mind as we are from the clouds that come and go in the sky? Clouds are many. They come and go. The sky is one, and remains unchanged. In the same way, thoughts are many; they come and go. Their Witness is *one* and remains unchanged. The fact that we are not as detached from our thoughts as we are from clouds is a habit of perception, not a necessity. The yogis tell us, change your perception, then you'll be free. Or as Baba Muktananda used to say: "Change the prescription of your glasses."

Witnessing means detachment. It also means moving beyond blame and excuses — with anyone: ourselves or another person or even God. And it means moving past the hope that someone else or some new situation will "fix up" life for us while we remain the same person inside.

There is a gift that comes with this responsibility for our own experience of life. If we want to make the change, no one can stop us. And while it is our responsibility to make the change — because only we can — the freedom and the power to do it are also ours.

Witnessing is not suppression, nor is it denial. To witness something, you first have to recognize it is there — and *allow* it to be. Allowing something to be does not mean indulging in it, however. It means watching it arise and dissolve without either struggling to make it go away, on the one hand, or acting it out on the other. Does a mirror resist some images and try to prolong others? The detached Witness is like a mirror.

Yesterday, walking downstairs from my office toward the garden, I got caught in an idea and feeling of being left out. Dismay rose in me. The stairwell looked empty and blah. I saw it absentmindedly as a backdrop to what was "really" going on, which was my inner world. When I was on the threshold of developing many conclusions about my unworthiness, up came a moment of choice in the flow of my mind. It was like a small window in the wall of thoughts. Through it, so to speak, I *saw* myself thinking and feeling left out. And in that moment of spontaneous detachment from identifying with my thoughts and their feelings, I stepped aside from them by affirming with conviction, "I am not these feelings. They exist and I am not them." With this release, the mantra rose within me of its own accord and with its own joy, naturally detaching me from those previous feelings. Anchored in the mantra, I watched the whole mental drama of being left out evaporate. For the first time, going down the stairs, I was aware of the fresh air pouring up the stairwell from the garden. Details of the steps and walls lost their tedium. The familiar was new again.

Witnessing is remembrance. Witnessing is the act of letting go. Once we let go of struggling to make a feeling go away — and let go by turning toward the Self in the moment of choice — the feeling *does* go away.

"Oh nonsense," you might think. "How can a reaction evaporate just by thinking 'I am not this feeling' and letting go?" That was my initial response to this approach. The first several times I heard Baba Muktananda say that the way to get over a feeling like anger was simply to "drop it," I thought, "That's impossible. How do you just 'drop it'? If I could do that, I would have done it long ago!"

Sadhana, spiritual practice, gives us the experience that not only is it possible to drop thoughts and feelings, but dropping them really *is* an effective way to be free. Gurumayi Chidvilasananda has said, "Love doesn't solve

problems; it dissolves the situations in which they occur."
Witnessing is a form of self-acceptance and love that
dissolves the situation in which a problem occurred.

❋

WHY WOULD ONE CHOOSE the path of forgetfulness,
the path of getting tangled in one's thoughts and judging
oneself for having had them? Why wouldn't one choose
the path of remembrance: letting thoughts go in the
moment of choice and returning to awareness of the Self,
the remembrance of God?

The basic reason for forgetfulness is what Kshemaraja,
a tenth-century Master from Kashmir, called being "poor
in *shakti*," that is, having a lack of inner spiritual force. In
The Perfect Relationship, Baba Muktananda writes, "You
cannot find the path by clever thinking; thoughts are not
sufficiently subtle. As long as you do not give up your
mental cleverness, as long as your thought-waves do not
subside, you will neither recognize nor experience the
bliss of That. This is why one needs the Guru's help in
order to find the way."

The fundamental help the Guru gives is *shaktipat,* the
awakening of one's inner spiritual power. In yoga this
power is called the *kundalini shakti.* When this subtle energy
of spiritual transformation is awakened within one by the

Guru's grace, *then* the seeker gains access to an abundance of *shakti* and has the capacity to overcome forgetfulness. *Shaktipat* is the basis of lasting awareness of the eternal Self within, of lasting Witness-consciousness.

Without the direct experience of pure Consciousness within ourselves — an experience brought about by the bestowal of grace — we never have an alternative place to stand; we never have an experience of selfhood other than the limited one created and sustained by our thinking and our personal history. The grip of our memories, beliefs, and self-descriptions on our identity is so strong that we cannot experience remembrance of the eternal Self except in fleeting ways. The grace of a Self-realized Master, one who himself or herself has completed the journey of self-transformation and lives as the Witness, awakens us to the alternative sense of Self and gives us lasting access to it.

This awakening gives us the force to detach ourselves from the grip of our thoughts and emotions, for such detaching takes more power than we typically have available. When we are poor in *shakti*, every vagrant thought or emotion can drag us into its web and pull us down; but when we have an abundance of *shakti* coursing through us, we have the alertness and strength to step out of the thought's way and to experience the Self beyond thought.

At the end of 1975, I first met Baba Muktananda. It was outside his ashram in Oakland, California, when he was returning from an afternoon walk. The moment I saw him, the world stopped. That is, everything looked motionless, as in a photograph. The traffic on San Pablo Avenue, the people walking along, Baba Muktananda himself, and my own body, all became still. Everything stopped — except my mind. This suspended moment kept lasting. To this day I have no "scientific" explanation for it, and need none. Something else was happening. As we stood there, motionless, my heart said, "Bow!" and my mind objected. Again my heart told me, "Bow!" And again my mind balked. The third time my heart said, "Bow!" my mind created an excuse. It said, "You don't know the customs in India; perhaps it's rude to bow." So I did not bow. The moment I made this decision, the world began moving again, and Swami Muktananda went into the ashram.

Suddenly, I could not believe my refusal; I was filled with dismay. I had just met someone whose mere presence had changed my experience of reality, and I had denied my heart's response! Caught in my regret, I gazed absently at where he had been. In a second-story window across the street, in my line of sight, there was a poster with an image of Swami Muktananda. Aware that anyone who saw me would think it weird, *and* that they would forget it in a day or two, while I would remember this moment for the rest of my life, I bowed deeply to that photograph. Then the doors to the ashram opened for the public program, and I went inside.

The meditation hall was quiet and dark. A few dim lights offered minimal sight. It struck me that there was no furniture. An ashram resident invited me to sit on the floor. He said the lights would soon come on. Then the evening program with Swami Muktananda would begin.

I had long been uplifted by the understanding that life, the world, and the universe are *one*. Ecological science was the university major I chose because of its vision of oneness in nature. From it, I understood intellectually that the biosphere is one and that one energy underlies all phenomena in life and the environment. However, I had never experienced that oneness. Except for fleeting moments of surprise or breathtaking beauty, there had always been two: "me" and "the environment." For twenty years, this experiential split had been the source of much frustration and dismay.

When I sat down in the meditation hall and felt its stillness, the sensation of separateness disappeared. I was steeped in peace. I was fully aware of my body and myself, but there was no longer any felt boundary between "me" and the other items in the room. Everything was the flow of one experience. Astonished, I closed my eyes. Now swirls and pulses of sky-blue light arose in me where there had always been darkness before. I watched that soft light. Everything, including me, was forming from and dissolving into this light. For the first time, I was immersed in an experience of the oneness that I had studied for so many years. The experience continued effortlessly. There was no impulse to grab on to it, no need to try making it last. This state was completely new and completely familiar at the same time. Next, waves of love rolled over and through me, love that had no reason and no object. It simply was. Scientific thought had never hinted at this blissful quality of the "unified field." When the lights in the room came on, I opened my eyes. A Master's grace had given me new life.

In many cultures, the Guru, the Master who can awaken *shakti* within others and then guide them to their own lasting experience of the Self, has been honored by some and maligned by others. Whatever people's responses may have been over the centuries, a true Guru's gift of grace is nonetheless the *sine qua non* of spiritual life.

The descent of grace, or *shaktipat*, that I experienced on that day was not a one-time event, like a flash of lightning.

For grace took up residence within me as the awakened *kundalini shakti*. Twenty years later, it is still a miracle. Nothing in my studies had ever told me about grace, nor had I ever heard about the transforming power of this inner energy with its joy and quality of revelation. In Swami Muktananda's meditation hall, I awoke to a new dimension of reality.

Other traditions give the *kundalini shakti* other names: the Holy Spirit, Shekinah, the inner *ki*, or the inner *chi*. For millennia, it has been honored and treasured as *the* key to spiritual life, to the realization of God within oneself and others. A comprehensive and straightforward examination of this sacred energy and its awakening through the bestowal of grace can be found in *The Sacred Power* by Swami Kripananda.

The transmission of grace is a mystery in the classic sense of that word: something one knows in silence, within.

Shaktipat alone, however, does not guarantee liberation in this lifetime. One has to support the process of spiritual transformation by doing sadhana. Sadhana is spiritual practice coupled with understanding.

❀

ONE OF THE SIDDHAS' greatest gifts to sadhana, to spiritual life, is the gift of a *chaitanya* mantra. When a true

Guru gives his mantra, his sacred Word, to a seeker, it too is infused with grace. By repeating it, the seeker opens further to grace. Through repeating the mantra, the seeker's thought, speech, and perceptions are purified. Then she or he becomes increasingly attuned to the wisdom in the soul. Therefore, during the moments of self-awareness that occur in the ongoing cycle of the mind, repeating a *chaitanya* mantra strengthens the bonding of one's heart and mind with the highest Truth. Such a name of God is alive with the vibrations of pure Consciousness, the Witness of all. Repeating such a mantra turns our mind's habit of thinking into a tool for moving *beyond* thought. As we repeat the mantra with love, the experience teaches us how to repeat it effectively.

A fundamental understanding is given by Baba Muktananda in his book *Meditate*: "One who wants to attain the power of mantra, who wants to merge in mantra, should have the awareness that the goal of the mantra is one's own Self and that there is no difference between oneself, the mantra, and the goal of the mantra."

When we repeat the mantra, it is important not to fall into the feeling that the mantra is about an "other." One way to avoid this pitfall is to maintain awareness of one's pure "I-feeling" while repeating the mantra. What does this mean?

For a few moments, think the word "I" — all by itself. Contemplate the feeling-space evoked in your consciousness by holding just the thought "I" in your mind. This I-sense is the pure I-feeling. Alongside this pure I-feeling, everything else we think about ourselves is personal history, i.e., ego.

This I-feeling is not hidden. It is very familiar. It's what our first experience is whenever we think the word "I." It's a feeling of presence. Another description of this pure I-feeling is to say that it is the sensation you have when you are aware that you are aware, while still seeing everything else that you are usually conscious of: the room, your body, and so on.

Baba Muktananda wrote, "We all have the awareness of 'I.' It exists naturally within us, and it is pure. If we leave that 'I' as it is, that 'I' is God. But we always add something to the 'I,' and as soon as we do that, it becomes ego and causes all our troubles."

Thus, the pure I-feeling is a talisman of the one Self. As we repeat the mantra while maintaining awareness of this I-feeling in ourselves, we overcome any sense of separateness from the mantra or its goal, the experience of God. This act of dedicating our consciousness to the remembrance of the Self in the midst of being aware of everything around us is an act of devotion to God. Practicing mantra repetition this way, we begin feeling the bliss and equanimity of the Self.

Yesterday I was contemplating a teaching of Gurumayi Chidvilasananda: "Remember, love and respect must be renewed with each dawn." I saw that an inner dawn occurs every time we wake up from our limited identity, from a train of thought and emotion that we have hooked in to. Every time we come to the moment of choice and are self-aware once again, we stand at a dawn in the flow of consciousness. In that moment we must recommit ourselves to love and respect, instead of rushing on with our fantasies or criticizing ourselves for having had them.

This love and respect has to include ourselves; it cannot be just for an other — or even for all others — leaving ourselves out. Each time we remember to include ourselves as an object of awareness in our picture of the situation, thus making the picture *one*, we shift away from the feeling that "self" and "other" are separate. The feeling of inclusion — that we have included ourselves (our body and presence) as an object of perception in our picture of the moment at hand — is a hallmark of Witness-consciousness.

Shri Shankaracharya, the great Siddha and Master of nondual Vedanta wrote in *Viveka Chudamani* ("The Crest Jewel of Discrimination"):

Just as you don't identify with your shadow, with your reflection in water, with the body you have in the dream state, or the body you assume in your imagination, stop identifying with your physical body of the waking state.

Identification with our own body and person causes us to go "unconscious" about our true Self; in contrast, when we witness our body and thoughts, we are aware of our Self at the same time. In witnessing our own body, it's not that we "stand outside" ourselves in an "out of body" experience and see our body from another vantage point. Our awareness is still centered in the body. We see our hands, arms, legs, and torso from the same vantage point that we always do, i.e. through our eyes, and within ourselves through our kinesthetic sense. In Witness-consciousness, we still can't see our own face, the back of our head, and so on. But our *experience* has changed. For we witness both our body and our being with felt detachment. They are objects of awareness. For example, our hands and forearms appear to our sight somewhat like the hands and arms of someone else. Habitually, we think that our consciousness is in our body. One of the secrets of Witness-consciousness is to practice the opposite awareness: that our body is in our consciousness (which, incidentally, it is). Thus we see our own body as part of the whole picture, along with everything else.

Baba Muktananda used to tell the story of the ten pilgrims who came to a river without a bridge. The river was in flood; the torrent was rushing by. With trepidation they agreed that they would hold on to each other's shirttails and wade across together in a linked chain. This they did. And when they got to the other side, their leader gathered them in a circle and said, "I'll count to make sure that we're all here." There were ten of them, so he counted, "One, two, three, four, five, six, seven, eight, nine. Oh my God, one of us is missing! Where is he? *Who* is he?" Another one of the band said, "I *know* we're all here; let me count," and from his position in the circle, he also counted one through nine. "Oh no! You're right!" he cried. "One of us *is* missing!" He began to weep. This procedure of counting went on and each pilgrim counted nine. Soon the whole group was wailing in grief for the missing one, whomever it might be.

A man came by on horseback, and from his vantage point, he saw ten people standing in a circle, wailing away. He asked what the problem was, and they said, "We were ten pilgrims, and we crossed this river and lost one of our members. Now we're grieving for him."

Realizing what must have happened, the man on horseback said "Let me count." And so he did, pointing his hand at each pilgrim as he counted — one through ten. As he said "ten," the pilgrims' faces lit up. "Oh joy! We're all here! How wonderful!" They were so relieved. They were so excited.

Baba Muktananda used to say that this is why we suffer: we forget to count our own self. "First count yourself," he said. So when we look at life, we must include ourselves as an object of perception in the world. Then we get the whole picture. Then we are a Witness.

The same is true of our thoughts and feelings, of course. We must include them in the world we witness, instead of identifying with them while "witnessing" everything else. Whether we witness our thoughts or not, they will still come and go. But the subjective experience of having those thoughts is so different when we let ourselves not identify with them, when we witness them as phenomena that are happening in awareness just like every other thing. Our thoughts and feelings can arise and be there as part of our awareness-field in just the same way that our hands can be, or the sight of a tree. We neither struggle to make our thoughts go away (when we don't like them) nor to keep them around (when we do like them). Instead, we let both the negative and positive thoughts run their course. They exist, true, but they are not us, and we are not them. We stay anchored in Witness-consciousness, aware of awareness itself. And in this detachment, we are free.

Each return to self-awareness in the flow of the mind is an opportunity to practice allowing ourselves to be carried toward liberation by remembering the presence of God, our own pure "I," the felt presence of our own awareness. It's an opportunity to drop the thoughts and judgments that trap us, the thoughts and judgments that maintain our small selfhood, our selfishness. In these moments, in a nonjudgmental way, we can rest our awareness on the whole situation at hand, including our body, our thoughts, and our awareness itself. This is Witness-consciousness.

Witnessing one's small selfhood as part of the picture, instead of identifying with it and feeling that the rest of the world is separate, is as normal as watching a prairie sky on a summer afternoon, or walking on a beach with the wind and the surf. Not only is everything else in place, so are we. In Witness-consciousness we are profoundly and simply settled in the Self. Then we are not bothered by the pairs of opposites, such as heat and cold, honor and insult, "me" and "not-me." With great serenity we live as a Witness of everything. ❀

Chapter 2

Dealing
with the Inner Enemies

*There is the mother called Maya, and she makes you forget
everything. She has six children, who keep you away
from God all the time. These children are: desire, anger,
greed, jealousy, pride, and infatuation.*

— Swami Muktananda

THINK OF THE CHARACTER TRAITS you struggle
against and lose out to. They're the issues of your personality that keep you going round and round on the carousel
of hope and despair. Sometimes one or another of these
traits so consumes you that you are aware of nothing else.
At other times, it pops up and derails a great moment. Or
it simmers along as a low-intensity drain on your energy
and joy. You become preoccupied with how you are, and
how you are not. Traits like these can make you apologize
for even being. Or they open the trapdoor of loneliness and
you fall in. So much of our life is spent trying to manage
these tendencies and dealing with their consequences.

All the vagaries of human consciousness that stem from the experience of being a separate, limited, mortal person are known in yoga as the "inner enemies." Having made the fundamental "mistake" of identifying ourselves not with our eternal and all-pervasive awareness but with just a few of its contents — the body, the mind, and our personal history — we then suffer an array of feeling states or attitudes stemming from that mistake. Whenever we experience ourselves as being incomplete in ourselves and as being fundamentally separate from each other and the world, we are in Maya's thrall. Then her children happily take up residence within us.

These children of Maya — greed, anger, pride, and so on — carry a lot of energy and keep us far from the awareness and experience of God. They become such a constant element in our experience of life that we even lose awareness of being in their grip. One's own pride, for example, can be very hard to see. Or they are so much part of the way we relate to the world that we cannot conceive of life without them. One man defended his chronic anger by saying, "If I weren't angry, how would I get my work done?"

Jealousy, anger, desire, infatuation, greed, and pride are the six classic enemies that Baba Muktananda cites in the passage at the start of this chapter. Other familiar enemies include fear, worry, delusion, cynicism, and the sense of unworthiness. Some people struggle with sloth, others with melancholy. Gluttony, carelessness, and habitual dishonesty lock still others into combat with themselves and the world. The inner enemies put a pall over our joy, and they consume us from within. These dust clouds in our consciousness keep us in manipulative, conditional relationships with the world and ourselves. No wonder they keep us "away from God all the time"!

These particular attitudes and feeling states, which make us forget God within and without, arise in conjunction with thoughts. Sometimes the feeling is foremost in our awareness, and the accompanying thoughts take a back seat. Sometimes when we're out of touch with our feelings, we're very much aware of our thoughts but in a state of denial about the feeling.

We deny ourselves awareness of our inner enemy because we have judgmental reactions to it, which we are struggling either to fulfill or to overcome. For example, we may have a judgment that "anger is bad." Or we may be out of touch with an enemy because we're trying to obey a command that we were given regularly, such as "don't be sad." Or it may be that we learned from experience that some feeling states were dangerous. Feeling desire led to punishment, for example. Hence we react with fear when we become aware of desire. This fear, in turn, causes us to repress our awareness of desire or to suppress its expression. The inner enemy is there, and we're pretending — sometimes desperately — that it is not. This kind of control is very different from yogic self-control. Authentic self-control is an act of freedom and has the feeling of easeful mastery to it, like all learned arts and skills.

Some of the inner enemies, like anger and fear, are emotions. The literal meaning of the word *emotion* is "motion outward" — *e-motion*. So an emotion is an up-rush or an out-flow of psychic energy. Suppression and denial of an emotion ultimately result in an explosion or in constant "leakage." With leakage, a suppressed emotion is expressed through things like nervous habits, recurring dreams, attitudes of mind such as sarcasm or indignation, physical ailments, bad digestion, and so on. Other inner enemies, like pride, envy, and infatuation, are not emotions as such, but they also have the quality of "motion outward" — and its consequences.

When James Watt, who invented the first truly practical steam engine, was a young boy, it is said that he took a teapot, filled it with water, plugged all the openings, and tied on the lid. Then he put it on the fire. Of course, as it got hotter and hotter the steam pressure rose, and the teapot finally exploded. This is what happens when we try to suppress or deny an inner enemy; it explodes into expression.

What is this explosion? It is indulgence in the inner enemy. We may suddenly get an outburst of rage or jealousy, or we may have an out-of-control desire: for food, to go steal, to gamble, whatever it may be. It is such a relief. We feel so alive. The dismay, embarrassment, despair, or self-hatred about what we have done comes later.

Neither suppression and denial nor outbursts and indulgence work as long-term solutions. We are still completely caught on the yo-yo of the enemy's energy. Suppression and indulgence *together* keep us tied to the world of forgetfulness, which is the world of not remembering God, the world of limited identity and underlying distress.

When we indulge an inner enemy we may feel temporarily satisfied. Our restlessness *does* go quiet. We feel content or justified — for a moment. But it's a pyrrhic victory. For what we have done is strengthen that pattern of attitude and behavior. We have strengthened the grip that the enemy has on our lives. Indulging an enemy like anger in order to get over it is like trying to eliminate a hole in a piece of cloth by cutting it out! The hole *is* gone, but what do we have left? A bigger hole! So we may ask:

"What *does* work?"

Ultimately what works is grace combined with effective self-effort. Baba Muktananda used to say, the bird of sadhana has two wings — the wing of grace and the wing of self-effort — and both must be employed in order for the bird to fly. Grace-filled spiritual practice is the foundation of all effective self-effort. Siddha Yoga practices include meditation, chanting, mantra repetition, contemplation, and selfless service. Their basis is grace, the awakening of one's spiritual energy, the *kundalini shakti*. Starting with this foundation — of grace and steadiness in one or more of the spiritual practices — one then makes self-effort to develop skill regarding specific issues in life, such as dealing effectively with an inner enemy.

In the sections that follow, we will look at ways to deal with nine of the most widespread inner enemies: desire, anger, greed, jealousy, envy, infatuation, pride, fear, and worry. These discussions, which can be read in any order, are not exhaustive or definitive treatments of each topic. They are seeds of new perception. Their purpose is to open us to new possibilities in relating to these inner energies. ❀

Desire

Desire is the craving for things, people, events, and experiences. We want this and we want that. In English, the verb "to want" has two main meanings, and both of them apply to desire. First, "to want" means to desire something. Second, "to want" means to lack something. This sense of lack is what gives desire its drive.

My struggles with desire have run the characteristic gamut from its outright repression into the unconscious on one hand, to willful self-abandonment on the other. For a while, I even lived by the ethos: "It's only a temptation until you give in to it — so the sooner the better." Neither extreme worked. One day it occurred to me that desire itself (apart from its contents) is a *shakti*, an energy of being. One should therefore be able to focus on that energy without reference to its target, and through this focus, I thought, one should even be able to experience the Self. I practiced it a few times, and it seemed to work. Instead of focusing on the object of desire, I would turn my attention to the feeling of desiring. Its energy would at first increase as I stopped blocking it; then it would dissolve — because I was no longer feeding it by focusing on the object of desire. I would end up in an energized, peaceful state.

This approach seemed to be more effective for handling desire than struggling to suppress it had ever been. However, I wanted some guidance. So I wrote to Baba Muktananda and asked him whether or not this focus on the feeling itself was on track. His reply came quickly, and it said simply, "Read the *Vijnana Bhairava.*"

The *Vijnana Bhairava* is a scripture of Kashmir Shaivism that gives 112 *dharanas*. These are ways to use the energy of situations in life to still the mind and experience the Self. *Dharana* number seventy-five says:

> When a desire or knowledge (or activity) appears, the aspirant should, with mind withdrawn from all objects (of desire, knowledge, etc.), fix his mind on it (desire, knowledge, etc.) as the very Self. Then he will have the realization of the essential Reality.

Commentator Jaideva Singh further elaborates: "When the mind is withdrawn from the object of desire . . . and is fixed on the desire . . . as the very Self, as a *shakti* of the divine, then the mind is rid of *vikalpas* [thoughts] and the aspirant has the realization of Reality."

Desire is an energy within us. In the flow of the mind's cycle in the moment of choice, we become aware both of the feeling of desiring and the object we want. You can test this for yourself. Think of a desire you've recently experienced. Try to put yourself back into that moment so that the object and feeling are very present. Now shift your focus from the object you want and rest it on the feeling of desiring itself. The *object* you desired may have been either an object of thought in your mind or an object outside of you in the situation at hand.

In this moment of choice, when we shift focus from the object we desire to an awareness of desiring itself, we have stepped back, and instead of being *in* the desire, we are looking *at* it. This is Witness-consciousness with regard to desire. The object becomes the background, and we stand in a state of awareness we can call "desiring without an object." It is desire as an inner, free-floating energy. A remarkable change happens when we shift our focus to this energy within us; the mind goes relatively still. The compulsive preoccupation with the object that we want goes away. We feel inwardly balanced. The object or objects of desire may still be there, but they are astonishingly easy to ignore. The "electric charge" in our awareness of them is gone.

There is another crucial step. In the state of witnessing this desiring energy itself, remember God. One way to do this is to repeat the mantra. By repeating the mantra while witnessing the energy of desire, we consecrate this moment of desiring and make it support our sadhana. Then there is nothing we have to *do* to make the "attack" of desire go away. Haven't you found that struggling to get over wanting something actually makes the desire stay and intensify? But left to itself, no longer fed by continued focus on the object of desire, any specific "attack" of desire energy fades. Then equanimity returns, not as an inert state of dullness due to suppression, but as balanced alertness.

"Desiring without an object" manifests itself differently within us at different times. Sometimes when I focus on the feeling of desire itself — instead of on its object — I experience its energy as a subtle fire rising through my body. Sometimes I experience it as a balanced spacious awareness above my eyes. Simply by watching our experience, we can become familiar with all the ways that the energy of desire-per-se manifests in our being.

Freedom from focusing on the objects of desire means we are present. We are self-aware. We are no longer on "automatic," being led around by our attractions and aversions. We have become conscious. This freedom is also freedom from the consequences of desire, such as the anguish of not being successful, the disappointment of being let down, the anger of being blocked in succeeding, and the pain of grasping for an object. The state of completeness and ease we are looking for, ironically enough, is found by letting go of the objects of desire. In this freedom, there is the freedom to choose our actions, to choose our focus, and dharma, kindness, and love.

Clearly this approach does not mean we stop enjoying company, enjoying food, enjoying activities, music, nature, a good book, shopping, and so on! Throughout this section, we are talking about situations in which our desires cause inner conflict, pain, and distress, or preoccupy us to the detriment of other parts of life.

Sometimes attraction to an object of desire becomes so deep-rooted that it feels like a permanent part of our character, and we despair. We believe that we could no more give it up than we could jump over the moon. Again and again this desire and its behaviors surface. Again and again we pick ourselves up from it only afterward. Again and again we find ourselves preoccupied and debilitated by this obsession. It defines us to ourselves. No amount of self-criticism or number of "techniques" serve to help stop or avoid this compulsive, repetitive behavior.

Perhaps this kind of desire is what Saint Paul wrote about when he spoke of an affliction that kept him humble. Such strong, habitual desire patterns are something to live with and to work around. Sometimes the attitude "At least don't make it worse" becomes the best we can do — and sometimes we can't do even that!

Only two approaches have ever helped me in such situations. And they have to keep being applied, because the desire keeps recurring. The one approach is: In the midst of allowing the desire energy to be, I turn unconditionally to God and say, "I am out of control, Lord. Please be with me through whatever happens." I don't say this in order to get over the desire. For it is not a bargain with God or a ploy to keep control. I say it because I am already defeated and in desire's grip. The struggle is over, and I have lost. The only thing left to me is to remember God for the sake of remembering God. It's as though I say, "If I am going to be possessed by this octopus, then let me at least remember God in the midst of it, whatever else happens." The pride "I can handle it" is gone. The relief of ceasing to struggle can be immense. Then a very interesting thing happens. In that instance, at least, I am relieved of this affliction. It's like being a swimmer who is in deep water, struggling toward shore. At the moment of giving up, my feet touch bottom — with my head safely above water! God's mercy is infinite when we let go into remembering Him unconditionally.

Of course, just a few minutes after remembering God, another attack of desire may erupt. In fact, if this kind of behavior is familiar to you, don't you find that as soon as you feel you've regained your footing and you relax your remembrance of God, the desire is quite likely to emerge again? This is particularly true for me when my relaxing contains some pride of "Hey, *I* got out of it!" Whether it's desire for a cigarette or liquor, an impulse to check out a beautiful person, to snack on something we know we'll regret afterward, to explode in anger, or to gamble — to name a few — the moment we say "Hey, I got out of it!" the result is "Here we go again!"

This is why such an affliction *can* become a great ally in the remembrance of God. In this moment of defeat, remembering God in a non-bargaining way is the only thing we have left in life. It's no longer up to us whether or not we stay out of the clutches of the inner enemy that we have come to dread and even to despise ourselves for. However, while the outcome is out of our hands, remembering God for the sake of remembering God is not.

The other approach I rely on is to analyze the situation arising and ask: "If I took this desire all the way out to its logical conclusion, what result would I be hoping to obtain?" I've found that there is a moment right after this question when my whole being not only fleetingly imagines the full behavior, it also feels the *inner* result I'm seeking from that behavior. If I let myself stay in that feeling of fulfillment instead of discounting it as imaginary, I find myself released from acting out the desire. To make this practice work, I must have the understanding and conviction that the ultimate result that a compulsive behavior seeks to obtain is an inner experience: of contentment, well-being, fulfillment, whatever. As well, I must remember that because I am looking for an inner state, it is inherently available from within me right now and does not depend on the outer circumstances that my personal history tells me are necessary to it. These perspectives help me validate the feeling of fulfillment that arises, and I let the feeling have its releasing effect.

This approach also has to be practiced repeatedly, in each instance that the desire arises. For how long? Does it matter? For rather than struggling to get over this obsessive desire, I've turned my attention elsewhere. The first approach is a practice — unconditionally remembering God — that I want to do with my life anyway, whether I experience attacks of desire or not. The second approach is an exercise of wisdom: the result I seek is a feeling state which is already available to me directly, from within. ❀

Dealing with Desire

❧ *To experience shifting your focus from an object of desire to the feeling of desiring, sit quietly and settle your posture.*

❧ *Think of someone, something, or some place you desire. Bring the object of desire fully to mind, and let yourself feel your desire.*

❧ *While continuing to be aware of the energy or feeling of desire itself, let go of thinking of the object. That is, shift your focus of attention from the person, place, or item to the feeling of desire itself.*

❧ *Simply watch it and allow the feeling to run its course, neither suppressing or combatting it on the one hand nor feeding it with images and thoughts on the other.*

❧ *In the midst of this state of desiring-without-an-object, remember God just to remember God.*

❧ *Notice the inner equilibrium this exercise brings.*

Anger

None of us needs to be told that anger that is not dealt with effectively is physically, psychologically, and spiritually damaging. As Baba Muktananda said, we are the first victims of our own anger. We burn in it and it clouds our thinking. Anger distorts our perceptions. The *Bhagavad Gita* tells us: "From anger comes delusion, the inability to discern our true nature, and from delusion loss of memory." Ah, forgetfulness! And so, anger itself keeps one far from God. We think, "Oh, a little anger here and there, no harm done." And yet . . . each moment of anger keeps us from God.

What is the source of anger? The *Bhagavad Gita* explains it beautifully, saying:

> When a man thinks of objects, attraction or aversion
> to those objects arises.
> From that attraction or aversion, desire is born.
> And when desire is thwarted, then comes anger.

So anger arises from thwarted desire. We want something to happen that's not happening, or we want something *not* to happen that *is* happening, and out of that thwarted desire comes anger. So, consistently handling desires in the way the *Vijnana Bhairava* recommends, as we saw earlier, is one way to reduce our times of anger.

We can also use the wisdom of Lord Krishna in the *Bhagavad Gita* to handle our anger more effectively, thus freeing ourselves from its negative physical, mental, and spiritual effects. Because of the relationship between anger and desire that Lord Krishna describes, one of the things we can do when we become aware of feeling anger is to use that awareness as a signal to stop. Stop — and ask this question: "What do I want from this situation that I'm not getting?"

When we ask ourselves this question, it creates an immediate detachment or distance from the anger — because it changes our focus. In that detachment, we find that we're looking *at* anger instead of being caught *in* it. This is a moment of Witness-consciousness with regard to anger. Then, as soon as we know what is not happening that we want to have happen, we can ask ourselves: "What other way can I achieve this?" Often it's surprising how quickly a successful alternative plan of action comes to mind. And then we can follow that plan, instead of just hitting our heads against the frustrating situation.

Have you ever watched a bee or a fly bang again and again at a windowpane trying to get out? If the insect would

simply pause for a moment and back off from the windowpane, it would see that there's an open window merely three
feet away, and it could change its course of action and get
what it wants. When we are angry and don't ask ourselves
the question, "What do I want in this situation?" we're like
the bee or the fly, just banging our heads against the glass.
When we stop and ask ourselves, "What do I want?" we
back off. It's like pulling away from the windowpane and
seeing the open window nearby. Or, if there is no open window, from our new perspective of detachment we can still
move away from the impasse.

Another way to handle anger effectively is to take the
experience to another level. After we've asked ourselves the
question, "What do I want from this situation?" and an
answer has offered itself, we can then ask: "What did I want
from getting *that*?"

If the phone rings while we're trying to get out of the
office, and it's a colleague who has done something really
stupid that has caused a big problem in our area of work, we
may feel the urge just to let him have it. If we were to stop
and deal with him now, we would have to skip that news-
paper and coffee break before our next meeting. (Please
plug in your own scenario!) It might feel good to blast him,
but a wiser part of us knows it would only make the situa-

tion worse. Can we stop and think forward quickly to the end result we want in this situation? At first we might think, "I want him to disappear from the planet, that's what!" Even then, we can ask, "And what do I want to get from his disappearance from the planet?" By then, part of us might even be laughing. "No stupid error to have to deal with," we might say. "And from *that*?" — "Peace of mind and the chance to get on with my project." Ah, peace of mind and the chance to get on with the project — okay. The miracle is that just by having seen that desire consciously, we are in a much better position to speak on the phone in a way that most effectively guides us — and the other person — toward that now consciously preferred goal.

When we ask this series of questions ("And what did I want from getting *that*?") with regard to any frustration we have, ultimately what is wanted is an experience of happiness. Independent happiness is the hub desire, a goal fulfilled from within. At this point, we reap a little harvest from our life of spiritual practice. We handle the outside situation in the most effective way possible at the time, and internally, the mere remembrance of our ultimate goal — the Self — brings us contact with that happiness. As Swami Muktananda said: "If you do *arati* to your desires all the time, you will never be able to get rid of them. However, if you keep remembering the inner Self, which is beyond all desires, you will certainly go beyond those desires."

❧

SOMETIMES IT'S NECESSARY to admit to ourselves that we *like* getting angry. One man told me that he used to periodically blow up at his employees. He would get great satisfaction out of it, a tremendous sense of power and freedom. Yet he was also mortified by this. He struggled to control it and often did. Still, there were times when he would just let fly. One day a friend was visiting him at his workplace, and one of these blowups happened. The friend knew how to wait. He let it happen. But right afterward, when he was alone with the man, the friend said to him: "I know it feels good . . . but it does not work."

These words penetrated the man's heart. His habit of explosive anger fell away from him like a ripe fruit from a tree, and that was the last time he indulged in it. He said later that what made the difference was that *before* his friend told him that blowing up did not work, the friend had acknowledged that it does feel good. That acknowledgment opened the man up to hear the second part of his friend's message.

At other times anger flares up so fast it catches us completely by surprise. Haven't you found this to be true?

You don't have any time to go through a list of questions about what you want! At this moment, detachment is not a likely option. What to do?

One person told me that his anger would flare up unexpectedly in a sort of white heat when somebody would grab his arm to talk with him and pull him off balance. He said that the only way he had learned to deal with this kind of anger was to turn abruptly away from the situation and walk away. *After* he had cooled down, *then* he could come back and deal with the matter.

It took humility to do this. Often when I'm angry like that, it is compounded with self-righteousness. I want to make the other person admit *they* were wrong. It's pride. My pride. Turning away in a moment like that means we have admitted that solving the anger is more important to us than being right or making the other person wrong. That takes both forethought and humility.

Humility is an ally of Witness-consciousness. All of the six enemies, or children of Maya — jealousy, pride, anger, desire, greed, infatuation — feed each other. So if we are stuck in pride, it is much harder to handle our anger. Humility says: "These things happen. I do not have to get caught up in it even when it is a criticism of me." Humility helps us witness what is happening. Pride identifies with being the "offended" party, and it demands compensation. Thus it ensnares us in the web of forgetfulness.

Sometimes a person can misidentify another feeling or energy as anger and be caught in a treadmill regarding that energy because of this mislabeling. One woman, for example, said she felt a chronic low-intensity anger for years. It would come up daily for her, over and over, usually when she was alone and merely thinking about the situations of her life. And often it was just there, as background "noise" in her day. As she progressed on the spiritual path and her awareness became more subtle, she began to recognize that she had misidentified several feelings and was therefore reacting or responding to them ineffectively.

One of these mislabeled feelings was one that she had always called "sadness." Once, while away from her friends and family for several months on a work assignment, she received an unexpected phone call from some of her good friends back home. As they talked, her heart flooded with love for those friends. When the call was over, she suddenly burst into tears. Her whole body was crying and her heart felt wide open. In the midst of this initial rush of feeling, very clearly in her mind she heard a command: "Don't be sad." Instantaneously, as if someone had pulled a plug, she stopped crying, and her feelings shut down. However, during the months of meditation that she had engaged in after receiving *shaktipat* from Baba Muktananda, she had developed a sense of the detached Witness. And in this moment, the Witness was watching her thoughts and feelings take place. A recognition occurred: "It is *not* sadness; it's *love*." With that her heart reopened, and she reveled in this new discovery.

Similarly one day, feeling angry in her familiar, undefined way, she decided to meditate and to do some breathing exercises to help side-step her chattery mind. As the exercises took effect, she entered a gentle, dark inner spaciousness. She watched the anger again and the initial reaction of shutting it down. However, she was detached enough to let go of her suppression. When the so-called anger unfolded, it metamorphosed into a vibrant power, rising through her body like a fountain. Her whole body became energized, but not with aggressive anger. In fact there was no reference to anything or anyone outside herself. This power was the energy of her life. Her mind tagged it with the words "personal power." Again, as had happened with the so-called sadness that turned out to be love, this new label — which indicated to her the energy of being itself, and her capacity to act from inner strength — was a revelation and it changed her relationship to this energy.

After the meditation, as she was preparing breakfast and then walking to her job, she felt a light of capability continue to rise through her. Instead of combatting it as inexplicable anger, she accepted it as her own power. Now it was available to her for work and interactions with people. Over the next several weeks as this new relationship with that energy took root, her "problem" with chronic, generalized anger dissolved.

We have choices regarding our treatment of anger, and any feeling for that matter. When a couple had an exchange of angry words over breakfast, and the husband left for work without it being resolved, his wife found herself stewing over the argument — as she had done so many mornings before. Suddenly, in a moment of self-awareness, she saw how miserable she was making herself feel. She looked ahead and realized that if things went "normally" she would have three more hours of misery before noon, at which time she would drop the whole issue and get on with the day. Later she told me, "A light went off at that moment. I thought, 'Since I am going to drop it by noon anyway, why not drop it *now*, and save myself the three hours of misery?' So I did. I just turned my attention to other things, and I had a great morning."

When we are feeling angry over something that has

happened, going over it in our minds is not going to solve it. Our anger will only increase until it wears us out and we finally suppress it or let it go. Furthermore, when we finally *do* get a chance to resolve the situation with the other person, we will have made such a "federal case" of it within ourselves, we will not have the presence of mind to handle the opportunity. So why not do what the wife did? Drop it now. If it also has to be outwardly solved, we will be in a better state when the opportunity arises and much more likely to do the effective, right thing. ✺

Dealing
with Anger

* *First, get in touch with a situation in which you felt, or still feel, anger. Let the feeling of anger be there and acknowledge to yourself that you do feel it.*

* *Now ask yourself, "What did I want in that situation that was not happening?"*

* *Listen for the answer. Just be open to it; it may come very quickly.*

* *When the answer comes, ask yourself: "Well, what did I want from getting that?"*

* *Repeat this question with regard to the most recent answer as often as necessary.*

* *When you reach the answer at the end of the line, rest in the feeling of completion it brings and offer your gratitude to the Guru and to God.*

Fear

Fear, like anger, is an *e-motion*, a motion of energy outward. When we allow fear to happen and witness it, it helps us solve the situation in which the fear arose. It helps us to do the right thing in a tight spot. But when we fail to relate to fear effectively, then fear can paralyze us and make us lose touch with our common sense.

Most of us have one or both of the following responses to our own fear. Do you recognize yourself in either of these pictures?

First, we avoid facing the situations in which we habitually feel fear, and therefore we leave many things undone. We attempt to solve the issue of fear by avoiding the situations in which it arises. These can be very innocuous situations, like avoiding using a phone or getting on a crowded bus.

Second, we try to solve the issue of fear by struggling not to *feel* the fear, or we try making it go away. Often we try to hide our fear so no one else will see. With our energies tied up in these ways, we cannot *use* the fear's energy to our advantage in the situation in which it arose. I remember once being very anxious about a presentation I was going to deliver. I was beginning to go numb so I wouldn't have to feel the fear. A professor of mine said, "When you feel anxious, *act* anxious. Then you will calm down. If you try to act calm to hide nervousness, you will stay nervous." So before I went to class, I took the risk of letting my anxiety out, hopping around and cowering in fear in the privacy of my own home. I fairly shook with fear. Of course this immediately changed my relationship with the fear. Instead of struggling to control it under a mask of calmness, I had let it "have its day" in a situation where I was willing to risk experiencing the damage it might cause. And it worked! After a few moments of agitation, the energy was dissipated and I calmed right down. My problem had been less the presentation than my attempt to bottle up the anxiety!

The main difficulty with fear or anxiety is not the fear itself. It is our reaction to it. For example, sometimes we *fear* fear. This reaction is particularly paralyzing. Out of fear, we try to deny fear by pretending it is not there. Or we may feel ashamed at having fear. We regard it as something a "big boy" or a "brave girl" does not feel, and we are ashamed that we feel it. Or we may react with anger in order to hide our fear: both from others and from ourselves. None of these reactions helps.

One way to change our reaction to fear is to redefine fear. Think of any time you were excited. It may have been on a roller-coaster ride, it might have been riding a horse bareback very fast across a field, or meeting someone who was important to you. You felt anticipation and excitement, not fear. Whatever it was, by looking closely at the feeling, we can see that the excitement was actually a form of fear. Yet this fear was not paralyzing, because we experienced it in a way that let us get into whatever activity was happening. When we redefine an instance of fear as excitement, we can stop fighting the fear. Then we can use it to enhance our experience.

The next time you feel nervous or anxious in a situation — like talking with someone whose approval is important, giving feedback to a work associate about a habit they have, or leading a meeting — you can draw on these perspectives. First acknowledge to yourself that you *do* feel nervous, anxious, or afraid, and then treat it as excitement. In all kinds of situations we can practice feeling fear as excitement. We can let it *move* us, as an outward motion of energy, an e-motion, and see what it does *for* us when we do.

What do the sages tell us is the root cause of fear? It is the sense of "self" and "other," the experience of duality. The Upanishads say, "Assuredly, it is from experiencing a second entity that fear arises." Any perceived "otherness" is a second entity. From this splitting of our field of experience into "self" and "other," fear arises.

The most fundamental duality or split is the sensation of separateness from God: "There is me, and there is God. That makes two of us." This experience is accompanied by fear. In fact, the *Taittiriya Upanishad* has something fascinating to say about this: "To the man who thinks himself learned and yet knows himself not as Brahman — Brahman, who drives away all fear, appears as fear itself." This is an astonishing insight. When a person considers himself to be separate from God, it is God who appears in that person as his fear.

What if we changed our reaction to fear by practicing *this* understanding? What if we recognized or remembered that our fear is a form of God's energy within us? What if we remembered that when we stop fighting off this energy called fear, we stop fighting off God? Then God is there with us as an *ally* in the situation — not only as an ally, but as our own energy! No longer blocked, the fear floods through us as *shakti*, the energy of God, and it gives us the power with which to handle the situation. ❀

Dealing
with Fear

❀ *First, breathe in and out at whatever pace settles you. Allow your breath to penetrate your whole body and let your body adjust itself in response to your breathing.*

❀ *Now become aware of a situation in which you felt fear, anxiety, or worry. It is more effective not to start with a high-intensity situation.*

❀ *Once the situation is clearly in mind, focus your awareness on the feeling itself. It might be mild, or it might be intense. While allowing that feeling of fear to be in your awareness, look at it with the understanding, feel it with the understanding, that it is shakti, the energy of God rising within you.*

❀ *Allow yourself to let go of resisting it. Allow the fear's energy to be.*

❀ *Bow to this energy of fear and offer the mantra to it.*

❀ *Staying in touch with your fear in this new way, let yourself go through the fearful situation in your mind again and see how the released energy of fear guides you through it. Pretend you are in the situation again, with the exception that now you have the energy of fear as an ally, as God's power within you.*

Greed

Ah, Greed — the spouse of dissatisfaction. With greed, our heart wears a "lean and hungry look." Greed fuels ambition and yet goads us so that we cannot enjoy whatever we *do* achieve. For greed is actually not about having or being something. It is about having or being *more*. Naturally, then, caught in greed we are never satisfied, always restless, and perpetually discontent. No wonder our heart feels starved.

With regard to spiritual life, greed makes sure that whatever experiences we have, say in meditation, we discount within moments of their occurring. There is always the ambition to have something *more*. The truth is that the mantra by itself, for example, is more than abundantly enough. So is the fact of grace. But greed will not let any experience be enough, so we doubt all the experiences that we *do* have. In the grip of greed, we want an overwhelming experience that — by its sheer magnitude — will finally still our doubt, our dissatisfaction, and the chronic sense of being inadequate or being cheated by life.

Greed also leads to extremes — to our constantly overdoing things — with regard to food, company, money, travel, curiosity, whatever. For greed is insatiable. As long as we think we won't have enough until we have more, we are on a treadmill to nowhere. Greed leads only to excess, disappointment, and bitterness.

How can we free ourselves from greed? First we have to listen within and hear the language and beliefs that fuel our discontent: for example, the voice inside that says, "You are never satisfied!" It is meant as a sarcastic instruction to *be* satisfied. But of course, when we learned this description of ourselves, we did not hear it that way. We simply heard that we are never satisfied, and the tone told us that there is something wrong with us because of it. Then, in obedience to this description and attempting to please, we faithfully fulfill this portrait in spite of the pain it has caused ever since.

Perhaps our inner judge says, "Enough is enough!" Since this statement is a tautology, it gives us nothing with which to gauge our behavior until we have well overshot the mark. Or we do not stop until someone else stops us — which is how we learned the sentence "Enough is enough" in the first place. And by then it really meant "Too much!" Or perhaps the inner stance that shapes and directs our greed is the conclusion: "I'll never be good enough." When we operate with a self-description like that, nothing we accomplish will ever make us good enough. And, lo! an unhappy over-achiever is born.

Of course, it is very likely that our greed is supported by several beliefs in combination. By becoming aware of them and consciously experiencing their connection to our greedy feelings and behavior, we gain the option of stepping aside from them in the moment of choice.

The second aspect to overcoming greed is this: in the midst of striving for more, we have to recognize that the actual amount of what we have (of anything) is not to blame for our discontent. In meditation, for example, the experience that we're having is not to blame for the feeling of distress, the need to do more, and the "hunger" for more experience. No, our dissatisfied and restless striving for more is due to our belief and conviction that we do not have and cannot have — or are not and cannot be — *enough*. This idea is the enemy, and this idea we can drop. In the moment of self-awareness, instead of either being driven by this idea or reacting against it, we see the idea and turn our attention elsewhere: to the Witness, to the mantra, to gratefulness. In the moment of being conscious of greed's grip, we have to affirm, for example: "I *am* enough." We can assure ourselves that we are enough and then thank God for this feeling and understanding.

Our attachment to *more* and our belief that we do not have or cannot be enough will keep us from experiencing the peace, equilibrium, contentment, and silent expansiveness of the Self. In meditation, we might be experiencing the velvety black void. But as long as the windowpane of attachment to more stands between us and that inner spaciousness, we will not *feel* its gift of inner peace. This is why Baba Muktananda said the inner enemies keep you far from God.

Baba also said, "You can overcome greed only through renunciation. You should think seriously about the consequences of greed and then give it up." Renunciation, a practice and virtue in yoga, is not so much about giving up things as it is about giving up the greed for things. "God has created this world for us to love," Baba said. "He has not created it for us to reject and hate." When we renounce greed, our appetites are contained naturally by a built-in feedback system: the contentment of the Self. When we are in touch with the energy of our own being, we become aware of the inner signals of what is actually enough: enough water, food, clothing, space, enough contact with another person, land, money, and power, to name a few targets of greed.

Greed's only measure of satisfaction is the sensation of having obtained *more*. More is an attribute of comparison. So the moment we acquire something and experience it as having the quality of being more than we had before, there is a sensation of satisfaction. However that sensation, like all sensations, quickly fades. Then what we have no longer feels like more; it is just what we have. So greed sets in again. This cycle is endless. In it, no actual amount of anything will ever be enough.

With attention and kindness, greed can be overcome. We have to assure ourselves that we are enough and have enough. Enough is our very nature. The true Self is an unending source of well-being, and it is already us. It is okay for us to bask in the feeling of being enough, no matter how much or how little we are. It is okay for us to trust that we are all that we need to be. ❧

Dealing
with Greed

❀ *After reading the following exercise, sit quietly and close your eyes.*

❀ *Assuming that you are greedy about something in life, what is it? Bring a situation to mind in which you characteristically feel greed. It might be greed for food, attention, or money, for example.*

❀ *It might be marked with the glee of the exclamation, "Mine, all mine!" or with embarrassment that you'll be caught taking more than your share, or with anxiety that if you don't get more, you won't have enough.*

❀ *Watch yourself in the situation. Be aware of the feelings and actions that indicate your greed.*

❀ *Now, keeping yourself mentally in this scenario, intervene by having yourself affirm in the scene: "It's okay to feel content with what I have and am. God loves me. I already have and am enough."*

❀ *Let the feeling of this permission pervade you. In this feeling state, allow the scenario to continue, and see how the feeling of having and being enough changes the outcome.*

Envy and Jealousy

Envy and jealousy are first cousins. Envy is coveting another's wealth, position, fame, looks, physique, house, car, intelligence, health — you name it. In envy, we resent a person (or group) for having more of something or being better at something than we are. We want what they have and dislike them for having it. Sometimes envy strives just to deny something to the other, without necessarily obtaining it for ourselves. Jealousy is a particular form of envy that involves a third party. This third party gives the attention that we want to someone else. We are jealous of that someone else because he or she got the attention we wanted, whether it came as a gift, a smile, time spent with the third party, or in some other form.

In envy, one wants the *item* the other person has; the item's source is incidental. In jealousy, one wants to have been given the item *by* whomever it was who gave it. We are jealous of the person who received the attention instead of us. The item's *source* is what counts, and the item is secondary.

Jealousy of someone can be expressed as anger at them, as scorn, arrogance, fear, or dislike. Or jealousy can take a reverse form of expression: buttering up the person because she or he is closer than we are to the person from whom we want attention, companionship, or approval.

Envy and jealousy are based on the wrong understanding that what we need in order to be happy comes from outside us, and someone else has it. Envy and jealousy are forms of poverty-consciousness. They have nothing to do with how much or how little of something, including someone's attention, we already have. The dynamic of envy and jealousy is that as long as someone else has more of something than we do, we cannot be happy and do not have enough. Sometimes it isn't even about the other person's having more. We can be envious or jealous of them if they have *any*! Since that is always going to be the case, we are in for a long and painful ride. Yet even were we to obtain that possession for ourselves, envy and jealousy would not rest. They would cause us to start looking around for someone else to resent for what *they* have, or are.

To get out of envy and jealousy, we have to admit first of all that we are in their grip. Again, this takes humility. Pride will prevent us from acknowledging to ourselves that our pain is not due to the other person's good fortune but to *our reaction* to it. As long as we insist that the problem is either the other person or what they have, jealousy and envy will wink at each other and laugh.

After we acknowledge that our jealousy or envy is the problem, then we can step away from focusing on the other person and their possessions. We can ask, for example, "What do I want their possessions *for*?" That is, "What will those possessions get for me that I do not have now? What would having them do for me?" When we know that, we can ask, "Is there another way for me to achieve that result without being jealous or envious of someone else?"

Swami Ram Tirth, a great being who taught math in a boys' school at the turn of the century, drove this lesson home to his class with an exercise on the blackboard. Once when the boys were competing with each other by putting each other down, he drew a line with chalk on the board. Then he said to them, "Here is your challenge. Without touching this line that I have drawn on the board, without changing it in any way, make it shorter." Caught in the paradigm of envy and jealousy, the boys were completely stumped. Each one invariably broke the rule of "Do not touch the line in any way." They were unable to resist erasing part of it to make it shorter. Finally they all stopped and sat still. Then Ram Tirth said, "Let me show you," and he drew a longer line alongside the original one, thus making the original one shorter. To have what we need to have, to become what we need to be, we do not need to take anything away from someone else.

A jealous person cannot even enjoy the attention she or he *does* receive, because there is always the danger that someone else will come along and draw the attention away. Jealousy leads to some bizarre and painful attempts to possess and control the life of the person whose attention we want. That of course makes them less eager to give it. Jealousy also leads us to outrageous plots to discredit and shut out the rivals. What a painful way to live, so focused on the threat of loss that what is received can never be enjoyed!

Jealousy makes another mistake. It is focused entirely on *getting*. Giving is not part of its nature. Therefore, giving *is* part of the solution! To the other person — the so-called rival — we can give our goodwill, our best wishes, even pleasure at their good fortune in their relationship with the third person. And we can do the same for the person whose attention we seek; we can delight in *their* delight in our so-called rival.

Their gift of attention to another is as much in our awareness as any gift of attention to ourselves. Only our narrow, limited identity prevents us from enjoying it. An antidote to jealousy, then, is to consciously wish and act with goodwill toward the recipient of the attention we want. We can witness ourselves doing this. When we know this and practice it in the moment of choice, that is, in the moment we become aware that we are jealous, then our goodwill becomes genuine. Our willingness makes it genuine.

Gurumayi Chidvilasananda has said, "What you need is your own contentment, not the contentment of another." There is a profound secret in this. Contentment comes from within, from contentment with oneself. It is independent of circumstance; it knows that one's worthiness does not depend on what one does or does not receive from another. The moment one enters Witness-consciousness and sees oneself — one's body and presence — as part of the picture, contentment is there, even if different thoughts and emotions play through the mind. Witness-consciousness touches eternity in the moment at hand, and one is profoundly and compassionately willing to "let it be." ❀

Dealing
with Envy and Jealousy

❊ *Settle yourself to do an exercise. Adjust your posture and breathe in and out consciously several times.*

❊ *Think of someone you envy or are jealous of. Let yourself feel the envy or jealousy. Now shift your focus from the other person to the feeling itself.*

❊ *Let yourself be aware of your jealousy or envy as if it is another "you," the you who feels jealous or envious. Allow him or her to be there in his or her pain and hunger. Simply allow and watch. Let yourself continue to breathe.*

❊ *Regard your jealous or envious self with kindness, and with kindness say to him or her: "I am here and I love you. I will be with you every time you need me to be."*

❊ *Rest in this stance until the panic of jealousy or envy subsides of its own accord. Give thanks to God.*

❊ *Repeat this act of kindness to your jealous or envious self every time he or she arises. In this way, your love for your jealous or envious self will dissolve the inner situation of neediness from which jealousy and envy arise.*

Pride

The poet-saint Kabir said that one's own pride is as hard to see as a black ant in a dense forest on a moonless night. For me, it took a dream to shed some light on pride. In the dream, I was coming down a trail with a group of people. We were near the foot of a mountain. As we hiked, we fell in with a woman who came up the trail every morning. In the brief, chatty conversation I had with her as we walked along, I said that I had spent time in the upslope meadows thirty years before. And then I added a phrase that was superfluous in the conversation: "when I was working on my Ph.D." As I uttered that phrase in the dream, I woke up. "Pride," I exclaimed, switching on the light. "Wow! Pride." I began to write. As the next hour unfolded, I saw pride everywhere in my life.

Pride is the inseparable companion of forgetfulness. When we live *as* our small selfhood, pride is automatically there. The ego and pride are basically synonymous. For this reason, we often confuse "ego" with "being proud of ourselves." In fact, ego has a broader meaning. It is the sense of limited selfhood, of identification with our body, thoughts, feelings, personality, and personal history.

Because ego has this broader meaning, so does pride. It

means we can be proud of *anything*. Each member of all the pairs of opposites is something that someone somewhere is proud of being or having: poverty or wealth, health or illness, winning or losing, and so on, through all antonyms in the dictionary. National pride (or embarrassment), personal pride, pride (or embarrassment) about family, education, wealth, length of time your family has lived in town . . . everything is fair game for pride.

Pride is distancing. It makes us want to show off our little (or large) accomplishments when they are irrelevant to the situation. We tell a story about where we grew up and find ourselves slipping in details of the house or the car, details that "just let people know" how special our upbringing was. In that moment, a little jockeying for position has taken place, or a little reconfirmation of our (limited!) identity.

How many conversations have you been in where there was an unspoken competition to establish who had the most wonderful or awful thing happen to them? Have you ever told a story or recounted an event and had someone say, "That's nothing. When I was . . ."? Have we ever said that ourselves? Pride. Of course, this is such *crude* competitiveness! See how pride even takes note of the skill or clumsiness with which one person puts another one down!

Pride can also express itself as indignation. Have you ever said, "How could they make such a mistake?" — your whole tone implying that *you* would never do such a thing!

Indignation even disguises itself in the form of concern for a third party's well-being. We say to someone, "How could you treat your teammate that way? Don't you know how valuable he is?" Or we say, "Don't you know she is sensitive to that issue?" It's our indignant tone that gives our pride away. Indignation reveals that our purpose is not to correct an injustice or insensitivity; it's to show off *our* justice or *our* sensitivity.

Every one of us has things about our personal history, our appearance, or our position that we are proud of because they set us apart. That is pride's function: to set us apart, to define our limited selfhood.

Sometimes pride takes a projected form, too, and we become very conscious of someone else's arrogance. "How dare he!" is an exclamation about someone else's pride that signals the presence of our own.

Complaints about others also come from pride. We complain about another's liberties or his disregard of a rule. For example, "He made that decision without consulting me, or even Tom!" Or "Look at him just walk in there. Can't he read the sign; it says 'Do Not Enter'?" The key word here is "complain." In the case of the decision, for example, it may be that in fact they should have consulted either myself — or Tom for that matter. Not only is it part of a useful procedure, but Tom and I had information that would have saved everyone a lot of grief had it been part of the decision-making process. But when we complain, we're not just pointing that out and going for a solution, we are *complaining* about it. Through that whine, aren't we jockeying to put the other person down? Aren't we expressing our wounded pride?

Pride's favorite word is "me." If it is sophisticated pride, it never uses the word "me" directly, of course. It finds subtler devices. And so we can have pride in the good manners of our pride, in the "pleasantness" with which we assert our individuality. Other people, however, are proud of the opposite trait. They "pull no punches." They "tell it like it is." They assert themselves with a bludgeon instead of with a stiletto — or is it "with a rapier if you please"? After all, stilettos are for thugs.

The compulsion to explain something about oneself can also be an expression of pride. A little spider bites me under the eye at night. There's a bit of puffiness on the left side of my face. When I come to work, the first thing I do is explain to people what happened last night. It's not just

that it is an experience I had. It is also pride. I am embar-
rassed that my face looks "funny." The truth is, people have
to look at it intently to see what I am talking about: "Oh,
yeah; it's there." But for them, this appearance is not something to worry about. For me, it is a matter of pride.

Shame is a form of pride, too, because any feeling state
or attitude that creates or maintains our sense of separateness is an expression of pride. Thus, pride permeates all
our *identification* with our thoughts and feelings.

Pride is also a mechanism behind claiming turf. The turf
can be physical, like a car, a computer, a house, or a city
block. Or it can be qualitative — as in the newest car in
town, the fastest computer, the most strategic block, or the
most expensive house. It can be reversed, too: the junkiest
car, the most battered up computer. Furthermore, pride can
also make us say that if we do not have these things ourselves, we know the person who does!

Comparative differences per se are not only *not* the problem, they make the play! Hooray, in fact, for differences.
But do we see it as a play? Where is our identity centered?
Do we remember our shared divinity regardless of our role
or position in the play? Or do we forget and live as if the
differences are who we really are?

Baba Muktananda would tell a story called "The Lords'

Club" in which all the members were children of lords. In order to make the club function, they all took turns filling the different roles: from footman to cook to president. However, they never forgot that they were all equally the children of lords. In telling this story, Baba would conclude, "No matter what work we are doing, we are all children of the Lord. This world is the Lord's club. No matter what position we hold, our awareness of being the Lord should never change. The supreme Truth is within every person. . . . A person should not think, 'I am this,' or 'I am that.' These kinds of feelings are transitory. They are short-lived. When you are playing a certain role, you have a certain name, but it is not the ultimate Truth."

Pride is about comparisons made in forgetfulness. They are comparisons laced with believed-in judgments of "better" and "worse." Both positions, "I am better" and "I am worse," are positions of pride, of limited identity. Even sentences like "No one is as down and out as I am," "No one has the troubles I have," and "No one could be clumsier than me" are statements of pride. Pride is all-pervasive wherever our identification with limited selfhood survives.

Whereas pride hardens distinctions, draws lines, and then goes to war to sustain them, humility lets them go.

Not that the distinctions are made to vanish, but they are contained very naturally in a greater vision: that we are all members of the Lord's club. Felt and grateful dependency on God is also an antidote to pride. Having such humility is like being an ocean wave that is aware of the water, or an apple that is aware of the tree.

The first step in overcoming pride is to admit our pride to ourselves, even if its forms are still invisible. We can pray, "Pride exists in me; please let me see it, Lord." We can also assume that any judgment that we make and energetically hold on to has a component of pride. A stance of indignation is a particularly strong clue. In his book *Ashram Dharma*, Baba Muktananda tells us to "see innocence in others' failings." This practice alone is a great step toward freedom from pride. In the moment of choice in the mind's flow, we can let go of our judgmental reactions to ourselves and to others, and presume innocence instead of malicious intent. We can turn our attention to the mantra, to the present moment, to our breath. "Without a backward glance" is a great way to step away from pride in the moment of choice.

It is a matter of values. Which is more important — being right (or wrong), or being happy? Which is more important, being "somebody" — or "nobody" as the case may be — or remembering God? When we really see that all identification with limited selfhood is painful no matter how much "above" or "below" others we may be, we begin to let go and give it up, resting in awareness of God in the moment of choice. Then we know that it is the same for everyone. That is, no sense of limited selfhood is better or worse than any other. Every limited self has its isolation and its pain. So why the pride?

This sense of ego — of separate, limited selfhood — was described by Shri Shankaracharya as *aheya*, "that which cannot be given up." When this is the case, becoming free from pride is ultimately not in our hands. It is in the hands of grace. So we can turn to God in our powerlessness and — owning up to our inability to free ourselves from pride — we can say, "I cannot do it, Lord. Please see me through the situations where my pride is running the show, and please never let it keep me from remembering You with faith and gratitude." It's not that we become totally dependent on God with this prayer, for we already were. It's that we recognize and acknowledge our dependency and go from there.

The *Sama Veda* says: "Just as the stars, along with the night, disappear on seeing the all-illuminating sun, so in the light of the knowledge of God, the seer of all, the thieves of the heart — like lust, indignation, avarice, anger, and pride — disappear." As our small-selfness dissolves in the light of the Self, like a star's light at dawn, pride dissolves, too, and we step free, into the humility of God. ❧

Dealing
with Pride

❀ *To uncover pride, pray for the grace to recognize it in yourself.*

❀ *When you begin to see it, notice all the specific ways it manifests in your thoughts, attitudes toward others, speech, and actions. Make a study of your own pride. Let yourself neither deny or suppress it on one hand, nor defend and justify it on the other.*

❀ *Let yourself watch your pride — and that of others — with detached amazement and goodwill. No commenting is necessary.*

❀ *Thank God for the gift of this perception and the change in your relationship with pride that this practice brings.*

Worry

How often do we say to each other, "Don't worry!" Since it's so easy to say that when someone else is worrying, you'd think we could say it to ourselves as well. For when someone else worries, we see that their anxiety is a frame of mind. We see it is not necessary to the situation. We know that the topic of worry is not the cause; it is a person's habit of worrying that is. *Our* worries, of course, are different! They are "real"!

Whenever I am in a worrying frame of mind, I experience *any* thought that I have through that lens. So if I try solving my distress by thinking even more intensely about the content of what I am worrying about (for example, an exam I have tomorrow, how I will get a new work assignment done, or how awkwardly a meeting might go), all I do is more worrying! Even when I tell myself "Don't worry," I add to the problem since now I am not only stewing, I also find myself unable to stop it. This makes the worrying seem out of control. What to do?

The cycle of mind continues. That is the mind's nature. This means that — even when we are worrying — there comes a moment of self-awareness, a moment of choice. Such moments happen several times in the course of a few minutes. In those moments, when we are temporarily free from our thoughts, we are conscious of ourselves worrying. Many times we then react to this awareness by commanding ourselves not to worry, by suppressing the awareness that we are worrying, by distracting ourselves with some ice cream or a television show, or by justifying and escalating our worry. Sometimes we even contract our body to try to stop worrying.

The moment of self-awareness gives us an opportunity to make other choices, too. A classic one, which Gurumayi Chidvilasananda suggests, is to turn our attention away from our thoughts and toward breathing. Can we just watch our breathing as it occurs? Can we give our attention to its steady, unfailing presence? In the silence of that awareness, can we become conscious of what is arising in our heart? Our breath is such an ally in the moment of choice. It constantly gives us an alternative focus in place of our thoughts and feelings. Yet how often we dismiss this choice as mere technique. Not so. *Spiritus*, as the Romans called the breath, means "breath of a god."

In his book on the spiritual nature and power of the breath, *I Am That*, Baba Muktananda explains the essential and traditional practice of watching the breath. *I Am That* is more than an explanation; it is an initiation. The mental fog of worry cannot persist in the face of such awareness-filled attention to our breathing. In the moment of choice, when we turn to watch our breath, we step away from worry.

Another way to drop worrying is to observe worrying itself. In the moment of choice, labeling our state of mind automatically creates distance from the content of our thoughts. It makes us aware of the frame of mind in which we were thinking and puts us outside that frame. Now, instead of being *in* worry, we are looking *at* it. We have entered Witness-consciousness in reference to our worried frame of mind. It is like noticing the water instead of the waves. As soon as one does this, the worried state of mind diminishes.

Isn't that amazing? As soon as we look at worrying itself, for a few moments at least we are no longer worried, and our worried thinking stops. It is like being let out of a cage and getting a breath of wonderfully fresh air. The change in our state of being is "like night and day." At this point, we can thank our Self and thank God.

To be in a worried frame of mind, focused on the contents of our thoughts — that is forgetfulness. To be looking *at* our worried frame of mind and no longer thinking thoughts through that filter — that is remembrance. We stand in Witness-consciousness with regard to worry. No one else has to tell us when we have made this shift. We feel the difference. The cycle of the mind's flow is always giving us the chance to step out of worry, or to stay in it.

In the moment of choice, another approach to overcome worry is to affirm "I refuse to worry." When a person's will has developed, he or she can feel the worrying frame of mind get stopped cold. However, for habitual worriers, a subtle form of self-sabotage can then creep in! Once I was practicing this refusal to worry. Several times I relished the experience of watching my mind start to leave its stillness and stop before crossing the line into worried thought because I affirmed "I refuse to worry." But after a few minutes, when my vigilance had waned, I came back to myself from a train of thought and saw I had been immersed in the clutching dread of worry once again. When I tried the assertion, "I refuse to worry," it had lost its punch. "Why?" I asked myself. In the next few moments, I saw that I was worried that I was worrying!

At this moment, an old Taoist saying came to mind: "When walking, just walk; don't wobble. But if you wobble, then *wobble*!" When thinking, just think; don't worry. But if you worry, then *worry*! Right on the heels of this, up came the affirmation: "I refuse to worry about worrying." Whether I was worrying or not was not going to worry me! That did it. My worrying frame of mind dissolved and did not come back.

Sometimes, even though I am looking at my fear or worry instead of being caught *in* it, I find I am still anxious. In these cases, I acknowledge to myself that I am scared or worried. (That in itself is a big step!) Then, addressing "the worried one in me" by the name I grew up with, I let him be and reassure him with kindness. I tell him things like "I am here, and I am taking care of you," "God loves you," and "It's okay for you to breathe." Whenever I am kind to myself from the position of Witness-consciousness, I relax. Then very naturally, a clear perception of the situation comes to mind. The joy of gratitude also arises: gratitude to the Self, to God, and the Guru.

When you think of it, doesn't this make sense? Whenever we are harsh with ourselves, judgmental and critical, or we refuse even to acknowledge our worry and fear, very naturally we feel the turmoil and distress of that self-rejection. So why wouldn't compassion for ourselves have *its* effects as well — and also increase our capacity for kindness to others?

❀

IN THE PROCESS OF LEARNING to step away from worry, another way to change our relationship to worry is to ask ourselves: "In my life, what is the purpose or function that worrying fulfills? What result is it meant to achieve for me? What problem is it solving?" Since habits have purposes, they are not just randomly fixed behaviors. Habits fulfill their purposes to a greater or lesser degree. And — as we all know — they often produce undesirable side effects as well. The habit of worrying certainly does.

Acknowledging that worry does something for you helps to loosen its grip. Then you can see if what it does is still something desirable, or is it something to let go? And, if you want to keep the result that worrying is meant to obtain, is there an alternative way to achieve that result without worrying?

Simply by accepting the notion that our habit of worrying does have a positive intention behind it, we may trigger insights and new ways of relating to the act of worrying that help us step free! When we have been leaning hard on a door to close it against a fierce wind, and the wind suddenly pauses, we can slam the door shut. Likewise, when we change our relationship to worrying, there is sudden movement in our former impasse regarding it, and we may slam the door on worry.

What possible uses could worrying have? One way to become aware of the purposes that worrying achieves is to affirm "I *like* to worry!" (with enthusiasm and conviction!). The time to do this is in a moment of self-awareness when you see that you are worrying. In this moment, if you affirm that you like to worry and let yourself identify with that part of you that has indeed chosen to worry, you will suddenly have access to the purposes you worry for. Or you will find yourself laughing in the recognition that it's true: part of you does like to worry. The least this exercise does for us — and it's quite a lot — is to free us from a "helpless victim" stance toward our own worrying. Then we see that what we have chosen to do, we can also choose not to do.

Contemplation is a great tool for uncovering the purposes that worrying fulfills. We can say "I worry in order to _____" and leave the end blank. We keep our attention from wandering away and listen for a "fill in" of the blank, a response from within. That is, we remain aware of the blank without having thoughts about it.

What is this practice? When we practice this "fill in the blank" contemplation on the thought, "I worry in order to _____," we think the first five words of the sentence and then hold our attention on the blank. If you hold your awareness on the feeling of incompleteness and listen to it, you will hear, see, feel, or know a response from deeper within.

The response varies from person to person, of course, and is different at different times for the same person. One time, the response could be that one worries in order to "get sympathy from others." Another time, it might be to "have an excuse in case I fail." Or one might recognize a hidden belief behind the worrying, like "It's dangerous to feel safe" or "Every time I feel safe, there's trouble." So one worries to avoid feeling safe. Whenever such a belief is revealed, we can counteract it directly, for example, with "It's *safe* to feel safe."

Another example of a belief that sustains worry is "I am no good" and all of its variations. Here, a different intervention is possible: finding the key word and changing *it*. For years I inattentively thought the key word in "I am no good" was "good" and I had whole patterns of struggle about being good.

Once I was contemplating "I worry in order to _____," and the contemplation changed spontaneously to "I worry *because* I am no good." It was the first time I had seen the connection between this belief about myself and my habit of worrying. Suddenly, I recognized that the key word was not "good" but "no." With conviction and light-heartedness, I substituted the word "all": "I am *all* good." For the moment that "all" replaced "no," the old self-description went away, and so did its attitudes, feelings, and over-compensating acts. Now, whenever the thought "I am no good" arises, I intentionally counter it with "I am *all* good." Amused delight replaces gloom.

In every case, when an answer (whatever it may be) arises to the contemplation "I worry in order to _____," I feel a shift in my mental state or a shift in how I perceive the situation. For contemplation is not just thinking about something. It *changes* our state of mind. As we practice contemplating, it has a cumulative impact on our character.

When I looked at all of the results that worrying supposedly achieves for me, I came to several realizations. One is that these purposes were all archaic and no longer worth the pain and paralysis that worrying brings. Another is that worrying ironically increased the probability of failure in a situation, thus creating more "need" for the so-called safety net that worrying was meant to provide. Third, I saw that in my life, worry is an expression of pride. By worrying, I was trying to protect my limited self's image, safety, and position against possible attack. This is clearly forgetfulness. I had mounted an anticipatory defense called "worrying" to protect something that I am not (this ego), against some criticism that might never happen — and which would not be about *me* even if it did!

It is not necessary to blame ourselves or someone else for our worrying. Nor do we have to justify ourselves, or fix and get over, the reasons we worry. Why not? Contemplating our reasons for worrying changes our relationship to worrying itself, and that is enough. When we change our relationship to worry, we are no longer locked in to one way of responding to it, nor are we locked in to feeling victimized by it. A Taoist saying advises, "Once the rabbit is caught, you can let go of the trap." Once we have changed our relationship to worry, we can drop the "answers" we did it with. The whole point is to see that we are not the helpless worrier we thought we were. Since we chose to use worry for purposes of our own, we can choose not to.

One morning, while drinking a cup of chai in the cool pre-dawn darkness of the dining hall at Gurudev Siddha Peeth, I became aware of the contracted, weighed-down sensation of worry in my brain. When I looked at it further, I saw that this worried feeling was a mode of relationship I was having with my own mind. I was "on my guard" regarding my mind; it was a subliminal anxiety that I might not be able to handle whatever might arise.

In that moment of self-awareness, I saw myself like an anxious kid with a furrowed brow who isn't sure he is going to get to school on time. Then a benign thought came to me as if from a loving person: "It is okay to smile at yourself." Inside myself, I smiled. Then my mouth and eyes involuntarily smiled. What a difference! The burdened feeling was gone. Instead, I was smiling kindly at my mind, open and happy. I felt affection for my mind. The inner frown had dissolved.

In the next few minutes, several other sentences came to mind; each added a dimension to this new relationship I was having with my mind. In turn, I smiled *within* my mind, *about* my mind, *to* my mind, *with* my mind, and *for* my mind. When I left the dining hall for the morning's *Guru Gita* chant, it is no wonder I was in a completely different frame of mind!

During the chant, I found myself letting a smile be in my voice as I sang. It floated out from me. There was no gravelly drag in it any more. How wonderful!

After the chant, I continued allowing myself to smile *at* my mind with affection and *with* my mind in delight. Then a new aspect of this changed relationship revealed itself. Indignation was gone. Someone had crumpled and tossed aside a wrapper on the path I was walking on. I did not get indignant; I just picked it up. Yet how often I have spent time shifting back and forth between worry and indignation. I saw that for me, indignation is an aggressive side of worry.

Now, whenever I am smiling within myself, I cannot muster up indignation about things; instead I just handle them.

All of us who worry know that worrying is one of the most debilitating habits a person can get into. It is merciless. Every possible topic is grist for its mill. Good fortune and bad fortune are equal targets as far as worry is concerned. Some people with good fortune even hope that something bad will happen, because then the suspense will be over. Worry's omnivorous appetite is proof that it has nothing to do with the contents of what we are worrying about.

Therefore, we can use the moment of choice to step out of that frame of mind. We can witness our worrying and make it dissolve. By refusing to worry — even about worrying — we get on with life. Pausing in a moment of self-awareness, we can speak kindly to ourselves, watch our own breath, or smile affectionately within our mind. Simple contentment and the clarity of mind to make the best of a situation arise in the heart when we step away from worry in the moment of choice.

There is one topic that I've found I just cannot worry about. Whenever I think of trying to, I end up laughing. So it is often a shortcut to not worrying. When I become aware I am in a worrying frame of mind, I tell myself, "If you are going to worry, worry about God. God has so much to do." ❀

Dealing
with Worry

❋ *The section on worry contains several practices for changing our relationship with worry. They can be used in any combination.*

❋ *The key step in all of them is to acknowledge to oneself that one is worrying, and to shift one's focus from the contents of the current bout of worry to the fact of worrying itself. Witness the feeling of worry, and while doing that, further change your relationship to it with one of the specific exercises, such as contemplating "I am worrying in order to _____" and listening for the response. In the midst of the release that the exercise brings, in your own chosen way give thanks to God.*

Infatuation

For human beings, infatuation is like a streetlight at night for a moth. We get caught in its glow, and only the rising of a brighter sun can set us free.

We all know what infatuation is. Someone walks into the room, and you are *riveted*. You say to yourself, "Who is *that*?" You become very focused, and you arrange, casually of course, to meet them. Or you try to get in their way, whatever your approach may be.

As the infatuation deepens over time, you think of the other person a lot, and you begin to measure the worth of activities in terms of whether or not they will be there. Even the most tedious task is no problem when that person is there, and even the most interesting and uplifting activity is empty when they are not. They give life its fizz, and if they are not around it's flat. This is infatuation.

Whenever you run into this person, you are charming and charmed, or you are so infatuated you cannot talk to them. Every move they make, everything they say, every attitude they have is proof of their intelligence, compassion, purity, beauty, wisdom, strength, and whatever else you would like to add to the list.

In infatuation, we measure a day's success and failure by

the interactions that we do or do not have with this person. We are pleased when we hold our own in a conversation and they laugh; the pain of a miscommunication is so intense, whether it is real or imagined, that we are driven to go find them to correct it. Or we think about it again and again until we figure out what to say to them the next time in order to fix it, and then we make sure we do.

What is infatuation? Fundamentally, it is the act of unconsciously projecting our own desirable qualities onto somebody else. And then, not recognizing them as our own, we seek to possess these qualities indirectly through association and relationship with that person.

Infatuation can happen through romance, through friendship, in relationship to a leader, in any kind of relationship. And no one does it to us. The person we are infatuated with is not making us feel that way.

When we wake up from the sleep of infatuation, we see the other person clearly and with detachment. They may, in fact, be a very fine person, but their superhuman glow is gone. The truth is, it was never there. It was illusory. The glow was in our own psyche; we were looking at our own greatness, our own beauty, our own purity, our own wisdom, our own gracefulness, our own strength.

But waking up from a particular infatuation is waking

up only part way. In order to get free of this inner enemy, one has to wake up from the habit of becoming infatuated. Infatuation is particularly hard to recognize and awake from because we do not want to. It is like a drug or wine; it seems to bring the juice into life. And it can be almost constant in life because the world is full of people. There is always a new object for infatuation.

Infatuation does not respect boundaries. It makes a person shameless. To infatuation, it does not matter if people are married or not, whether they have children, or even if the children are present during an interaction. Infatuation does not see the other person as he or she is, but as the person we want them to be, and therefore, infatuation does not truly respect the person we are infatuated with. It doesn't respect their privacy, their time, their attention to their duties, or their relationships with other people. Infatuation is jealous and possessive. Infatuation will consume everything in its path, including, first and foremost, oneself.

The person we are infatuated with may in fact be very admirable, with great qualities. Getting over the infatuation does not mean that we then think they are plain, ordinary, bad, no good, and awful. As a matter of fact, if that is our reaction, we did not get over the infatuation, we just flipped over to its negative expression. If we are angry, hostile, or disgusted with a person that we were formerly positively infatuated with, we have not stepped into detachment, we have not yet woken up.

Getting over an infatuation results in two things: experiencing in ourselves the good qualities that were projected onto the other person, and seeing the other person as he or she is.

For a person caught in the habit of infatuation, it becomes a way of life. There are infatuations that last for a moment or two, and others that last for years. Releasing oneself from infatuation takes vigilance and a whole new stance toward living, because one thing must be understood: infatuation is not love — the streetlight is not the sun. Infatuation is an inner enemy; it will keep you from God. Gurumayi once said: "Don't make a friendship into more than it is. Convert that good feeling into just pure friendship. Do not let the high of infatuation keep you from your responsibility. Turn that good feeling toward your responsibilities instead of letting it be something that takes you away from them."

Infatuation with the Guru also takes place. This is not devotion; it is a counterfeit of devotion. Infatuation with the Guru makes one run and push for a "good" seat in darshan; it makes a person stare intensely at the Guru while rising from a *pranam*; when the Guru walks by, one melts into a parody of devotion, with a fatuous grin and folded hands. (*Fatuous* and *infatuation* are the same, incidentally. They come from a Latin word meaning "foolish.") And if the Guru does not look at us or speak to us, we get pouty and anxious, and wonder "What did I do wrong?" or "Why is the Guru so cold?" The Guru is not cold; the Guru just did not get hooked by our projection. In the process, we abandoned the Self. By sliding into infatuation, we robbed ourselves of the chance to feel true devotion, which is strong, in touch with awe for God, full of gratitude, and not grabby or anxious.

So how can we free ourselves from the hypnotic clutch of infatuation? How do we get free from the streetlight's glow?

First we have to acknowledge and recognize that the pleasurable feeling of infatuation is an enemy, not a friend — that it keeps us bound, that it prevents us from getting on with our lives. We have to admit to ourselves that the experience of infatuation has a hook, brings pain, and leaves us empty of our Self. For a moth caught in the streetlight's glow, these things are very hard to see. Second, we have to know that all the beautiful qualities that we are seeing in the other person are our own, and that we can fully experience them only when we own them ourselves.

Third, in the midst of an infatuated moment, we have to catch ourselves and reclaim the projection. And fourth, in the moment of wholeness that follows, we have to remember God with gratitude.

How do you reclaim a projection? A simple technique can be used whenever infatuation is experienced, whether you are with the person or simply thinking of them. Whatever you are doing when you become aware of feeling infatuation, continue that activity — sitting, standing, walking, eating, whatever it may be — as the other person. Take on the feeling that your body and being is that other person. For as long as it lasts, which may be a second or two, adopt the attitude and the feeling that you are the person you admire so much.

What happens? Automatically, without having to name or list them, you take back the qualities that have been projected onto the other. You feel whole and still. The pain of separation from that person evaporates. You feel contented and grounded within yourself. Automatically, you will have let go of the other person and will be centered in yourself. By "being" them for a few moments, you have not become the person as they are, you have become the person that you were projecting them to be. In that moment, you also see the other person truly and with detachment, respect, and an affection that is not hungry. A moment later, you might be completely infatuated again. In this case, just do it again, be that person for a second or two. Remember, it is part of *you* that is reclaimed through this exercise.

�֎

A HABIT LIKE INFATUATION takes years to develop. As we get older, we become more and more skillful in enmeshing ourselves in infatuation. So it is not going to disappear overnight; it is something to work on.

Blessedly we have grace, which gives us access to that brighter sun, the knowledge and experience of the inner Self. If we honor grace by remembering God every time we recognize we are infatuated, then we will open ourselves to perceiving the sunrise that will really set us free.

Infatuation glitters, and we think it is gold. That's what makes it strong. When we are in it, so much seems right; we feel so alive. We have such conviction that this person is finally the one. But wherever there is attachment — and infatuation is full of attachment — inevitably there will also be pain.

Often when we confront the pain of an infatuated relationship, our response is to "try harder." For some confused reason, we believe that if we are in pain while standing and talking with someone, it is just lack of effort or skill on our part that we are not able to overcome it. "I should be able to stand in this fire and not be burned," we say. But that's an impossibility. Fire burns. In the same way, infatuation creates pain.

Sometimes we try to avoid the pain by not having the feelings while still having the situation that triggers our infatuation. But without Witness-consciousness, this is impossible. Can there be "water" without "wet"? Can "fire" exist without "heat"? What should we do?

Infatuated thoughts and feelings, or jealous ones, are old, strong mental habits. The mind is bound to keep falling into these well-worn grooves, which have been nurtured intentionally for many years. So why get discouraged by the arising of these thoughts and feelings? Their presence does not mean failure. It simply means there is an automatic habit of thought and feeling that has to be worked on. Those thoughts and feelings are not you; you are their Witness.

"Sharp as a razor's edge is the path, and difficult to pass," says the *Katha Upanishad*. On one side of this sharp path is indulgence. That is a pitfall. On the other is suppression or denial. That also is a pitfall — one which usually results in an explosion of out-of-control behavior. To stay on the razor's edge, an approach to take is to notice and acknowledge the feeling of infatuation when it comes up. Then neither denying it nor contracting, deliberately turn your attention elsewhere.

At least initially, the goal and measure of success is not the elimination of infatuated thoughts and feelings. Success means not paying attention to them, either "pro" (by getting caught up in them) or "con" (by struggling in discouragement or shame to make them go away). Instead, by leaving them alone they will dissolve, like all thoughts and feelings, back into the ocean of Consciousness from which they arose. Eventually — given a steady practice of remembering the Self — the *shakti* will "roast" the *samskaras*, the seeds from which such habitual thoughts and feelings sprout.

There is yet another approach to changing one's relationship with the thoughts and feelings of infatuation. Let us say you are interacting with a person in an infatuated way. It is wonderful. You are elated. This is what makes life worth living. In that interaction, there come moments of self-awareness. Right then you have a choice. The choice we usually make, and it strengthens the infatuation, is to credit the other person for the good feeling we have. We totally connect him or her with that glow. Then we try to increase our thrill by focusing more on the other person. (This process can also happen when we are in a euphoric reverie, and the friend is with us only in our mind.)

This choice of crediting the other person with being the source of our good feeling, ironically, leads to a painful result. In order to sustain the feeling, we have to keep escalating the intensity of the interaction. While the delight may increase for awhile, the instability of the situation (due to the over-escalation that is so typical of infatuation) will lead to some kind of painful crash, if not that day, then the next, or the next. And haven't you found that often the pain is already right there, all along, side by side with the elation?

Once we are in an interaction or a reverie, and the euphoria of infatuation is already at work, another tack to take is to practice the traditional *dharana*, or centering technique, from the *Vijnana Bhairava* that was cited in the section on desire. In the moment of self-awareness, when we have a choice, we can turn our inner attention away from the object of feeling (that is, turn it away from the other person) and inwardly focus on the glow of infatuation itself, without reference to its supposed cause. We can do this even in the midst of a conversation with the person, for it is an inner shift of focus.

What happens? Soon the good feeling reaches its own natural level. It might even subside. However, in its subsiding there is an inner peace. The belief that infatuation's good feeling comes from outside has been weakened, however subtly. By practicing this *dharana*, we can become free and reclaim our own life.

One simple proof that this good feeling represents our own *shakti* is that we have had this feeling on many different occasions over the years, while its supposed cause has changed many, many times. In fact, we may not even remember who some of the "causes" were, or we may have developed quite opposite feelings of dislike for some of them. And yet, that good feeling still wells up in us, unimpaired. Why? Because it is *ours*, not another person's.

WHEN WE WANT TO DROP an infatuated interest in someone, we often try to exert willpower. That is, we try forcing ourselves not to be interested. But the fact is, part of us *is* interested, not only interested but quite determined! So we end up pretending to ourselves that we are not interested and struggling to control ourselves. Finally, when the effort gets to be too much, we say "What is the point of all this struggle?" and we just go for it; either that, or we succeed in hammering ourselves down to a constricted peg and then walk around like a mechanical device. Neither of these alternatives contributes to a life lived abundantly.

All of the struggle, the battle of will against wishes, comes from identifying with our infatuated self and then struggling to control him or her, like an unbroken horse. An alternative is to drop identifying with our infatuated self and let it be an object in our awareness. We are, after all, not that infatuated self. We are its Witness.

The more we sustain awareness of our awareness while going about our daily activities, the more we will be able to continue detached Witness-consciousness when we are in the company of someone we have been infatuated with. Then we interact with love *and* respect — freely, within limits that are appropriate and easy to accept. Being the Witness of a situation means that we also see our own body and personality as part of the picture, with detachment. Thus our actions and feelings are naturally contained in a larger view.

The person who forgoes infatuation, who forgoes attachment and aversion, gains a far greater relatedness in exchange. Anyone who has experienced even temporary release from an infatuation — whether in a classroom, at a party, or in a work situation — can verify this.

In all our living, wherever there is attachment, there will also be pain and loss. There is no way out of this fact. There is, however, a way out of the suffering that is happening, and that is through admitting the loss, opening ourselves to the loss. It is a moment of grief. In that moment, one lets go of hope with regard to this or that friendship, job, or whatever external activity is considered to be essential for happiness. Those friendships and activities may have been accompanied by much happiness. Even then, it was *our* happiness, and it came from within. The friendships and activities will end as surely as the sun sets. As long as we maintain hope in any infatuation, we cannot know the release that comes from grief.

Grief does not have to be long or dramatic. It can be a second long, or several minutes. It has a natural structure that does not have to be invented. In the moment we let go and let ourselves experience that the overwhelming hope we had in a relationship will never be fulfilled, that this euphoria cannot last, we experience a moment of intense inner loss accompanied by connectedness with our own soul. Right afterward there is peace. We might not recognize this inner quiet as peace. We might just think we are stunned into stillness, like a child who finally falls silent after a full-out cry. But that stillness means we have grieved, and the grip of the attachment has been broken or reduced.

Grief is not a melancholy posture or sadness. Nor is it neurotic posing as a sufferer. And it can never be a technique for getting over the pain of an attachment while still keeping the attachment! Grieving is part of waking up from delusions in which we have invested ourselves.

One may have to grieve again and again in brief moments to free oneself from the grip of different attachments. We have so many. Yet if hope is attached to anything other than God, it dooms us to pain. This is why it is so important that we continue our practice and continue to turn to God, even in the midst of feeling that we would gladly give everything to possess the relationship instead. Even when we say, "To heck with overcoming infatuation; what's the use?" couldn't we maintain our faith in God?

Such faithfulness to our own higher Truth will be rewarded — from within. Twenty years from now, looking back, we will see how much our soul matured, how much our wisdom deepened, because we were faithful to the highest in ourselves. And we will see that the discipline of this effort was a forge in which the dross of infatuation was burned away, revealing the gold of compassion and love. ✽

Dealing
with Infatuation

❋ Whenever you think of the person you are infatuated with, do not dwell just on him or her. Include the thought of yourself in the picture. That is, witness yourself.

❋ This does not mean making up fantasies about the two of you. It means simply being aware of the presence of you both in your mind. This awareness is called "thinking of" as opposed to "thinking about." Whenever you think of someone or something, it is simple remembrance of them; they just come to mind. "Thinking of" is awareness of the existence of someone — without thoughts, images, fantasies, or memories about them.

❋ By including yourself in your awareness this way, you stay grounded in yourself instead of becoming lost in reverie or mental stewing about the other person.

❋ And a wonderful thing happens. By thinking of yourself whenever you think of the other person, your mind goes quiet. You find yourself feeling whole and filled with well-being.

❀ This exercise of self-awareness works equally well when you are actually with the person with whom you are infatuated. In fact, no matter whom you are with, it is a freeing practice. The moment that you pull back from the situation mentally by thinking of yourself as an object in your awareness, the hyper energy of "trying to connect" goes away.

❀ With this self-awareness you just are in the situation. Now the sunrise of unconditional love can occur, causing the streetlamp of infatuation to lose its hypnotic pull.

❀ Plainly put, the practice in this exercise is this: whenever you become aware that you are thinking about the other person, think of yourself at the same time. And whenever you are with the other person, do not be aware only of them; be aware of yourself at the same time. Keep returning to witnessing yourself in the situation. This self-recollection is remembrance, and it sets us free.

Conclusion

In the crisp winter dawn of western India, I went walking through the hills. The dry grass was tawny under the young teakwood trees. A dirt track led through the narrow vale, topping out gradually at an overlook. Valleys farther on were filled with winter mist and wood smoke. As I approached the crest of the ridge, I was suddenly caught in familiar despair, an anguish with no name.

Turning to Witness-consciousness, I stepped free. When I reached the rock where I sat and watched the hills, I wrote about this response in my fieldbook:

> Instead of identifying with the "you" who despairs and is anguished, project him in front of you in your mind, as an object in awareness. Automatically you will relate to him with detached love and compassion, and your pain (and his pain) will be gone.

When I had done this a few minutes earlier, the anguish had left and a song of praise had arisen in my heart. I was at peace. It came from *witnessing* despair instead of struggling *inside* it. My mind was still. The dawn light increased. I continued writing notes on what had happened:

Hold your sense of self in your mind as an object of your attention, and with that, repeat the name of God. Instead of being *in* your personality, hold it in front of you with your attention, like a raised hand. In this way, stand back from it. Then you are looking *at* your limited selfhood, your felt sense of self, instead of being identified with it. This is Witness-consciousness.

As I sat on the rocky overlook, my mind rested in the present, not creating worlds of thoughts and images for my attention to get lost in. Although my feeling of self-hood was invisible (as our thoughts are invisible), it was an object of awareness like everything else. With this witnessing relationship to my "daily self," compassion arose: for myself and for others.

Com-passion means "to experience and undergo with." It arises in us when we see ourselves as someone who is in the play — just as everyone else is. To live in Witness-consciousness is to live with compassion. In that state, our drive to be right or okay is gone.

A few days earlier, I had been part of an interaction that caused pain and distress to two people. Afterward, merely thinking about the next time I would see them, I felt defensive and awkward about my part in the situation. Mentally, I tried the gambit of justifying myself. That didn't work (of course). And I didn't know what I would do or say when I saw either one of them. I was afraid I'd make a wrong move, strained and artificial. Fearful pride had me in its painful grip.

Sitting on the rock at the top of the ridge, I suddenly witnessed myself in the situation of meeting them again, and I felt compassion for myself and them. It was compassion for people who get caught in estrangements, compassion for the pain of feeling distrusted and for the pain that self-righteousness brings.

The seesaw of defensive self-justification and *mea culpa* apology was over. Instead I felt empathy for all three of us. Even though I had played the opposition role in the original incident, I was now with the other two — somewhat in the way a sports team can recognize that it is playing with the team it is playing against. I was no longer defending my position. In my mind's eye, I saw myself clasping their hands wordlessly — with the feeling that all of us had undergone the situation together.

Later, when I actually did run into each of them, one at a time, I took care to step into Witness-consciousness, including myself in the picture. It was intentional. Very naturally, then, I moved *with* each one, attuned to the appropriate "dance" of interaction. By witnessing myself in these encounters while in the midst of them, I could sense with my heart our mutual wish for the rift to be healed. And I moved with that, from my own heart, instead of being defensively right or hypocritically nice.

Compassion is indivisible. That is, it is not for an other; it is for all of us. It comes with Witness-conciousness, where we have included ourselves as one of the players instead of pretending (to ourselves) to stand apart as a non-participant judge. The state of compassion contains acceptance of what is. At the same time it gives one the capacity to perceive and relieve suffering in oneself and others.

I had paused in my writing and thought. The climbing sun splashed copper across the forest and fields. The birdsong of dawn was dying away. Before I stood up, I wrote once again:

> To experience compassion, project yourself forward
> and out in your mind's eye, feeling your selfhood as
> an object of awareness. Then, maintaining awareness
> of yourself in your mind like this, greet the other
> person. This act of witnessing yourself while interacting
> with others is one way to fulfill Baba's teaching:
> "The greatest religion of mankind is to welcome
> another person with love and respect."

Release from the inner enemies requires self-effort: the effort to step aside from our judgments, to step aside from staying caught in the mind. The key step toward Witness-consciousness, in the moment of choice, is to shift the focus of attention from the content of our thoughts to the feeling or attitude in which we are thinking. With envy, for example, we first admit to and then focus on our feeling of envy itself, as envy-without-an-object. When this has happened, *then* we take another step back in our consciousness by becoming aware of awareness itself, the felt presence of our pure and constant "I."

By this point merely a few seconds have passed. The original target of our envy, desire, anger, or whatever has faded from the foreground of our attention, and we are very much aware of the present moment.

❀

IT IS AN INHERENT QUALITY of consciousness to be aware of itself along with everything else. We are not learning something new; we are enhancing a capacity. Every time we practice it — even with regard to unimportant or low-voltage situations — our capacity to witness is strengthened. Then we can step back effectively in more emotionally charged situations.

All the children of Maya are inherently insatiable. Like

aggressive parasites, they only rest when they have destroyed their host. No wonder they keep us far from God! God exists in our feeling, and these enemies obscure it, like bad static on a radio. As Baba Muktananda has said, the inner enemies pose as friends. We think they are helping us through life. We think that fulfilling their drives will get us what we want and make us happy. This is forgetfulness. When they are active in us, we are their first and ultimate victims.

In the grip of these inner enemies, we might wreak a lot of havoc around ourselves. But throughout such a life, and in the end, we are the ones who live in their little hells. With God's grace and self-effort, we can free ourselves from these enemies, every one of them, and live on Earth in paradise. ✤

Remembering Your Purpose for Being

If you don't have time for the inner search that will take you to the highest levels of consciousness, what is the point of just eating, drinking, and living in the outer world? If you don't make time to work for your spiritual growth, what is the point of your human birth?

— Swami Muktananda

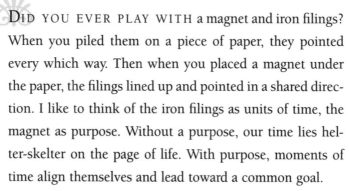

DID YOU EVER PLAY WITH a magnet and iron filings? When you piled them on a piece of paper, they pointed every which way. Then when you placed a magnet under the paper, the filings lined up and pointed in a shared direction. I like to think of the iron filings as units of time, the magnet as purpose. Without a purpose, our time lies helter-skelter on the page of life. With purpose, moments of time align themselves and lead toward a common goal.

Luckily for us, each soul has its purpose even if we do not know what it is. But if we do know it — and cooperate — how much more joyful and meaningful our journey through life is! We even have a chance of achieving our purpose. Otherwise, it is unlikely. The *Bhagavad Gita* says that we are born again and again until we reach our soul's destination.

For achieving our purposes, we can set goals. One type of goal states a desired outcome. These are achievement targets, so to speak, with a specific completion date. For example, such goals could be:

1. "By January first of next year, I will be able to still my mind in meditation."

2. "When I complete my stay in the ashram, I will have mastered my bad temper."

We need to further define how we will know and by what measure we will determine whether or not we have succeeded.

A second type of goal is about how we want to live, about day-to-day discipline — for example, "I meditate every morning." Of course these goals also have results, but we are not predicting what the results will be nor when they will happen. In these goals, the process of living is the focus.

The two types of goals are related, and both kinds are

used for enacting purposes. If we want to know the *Guru Gita* by heart in a year's time, for example, we live each day in a way that makes it happen.

The yogic scriptures point to several fundamental principles about setting goals effectively. The first principle comes from the *Maitri Upanishad*: "What a person thinks is what he or she becomes." Therefore, in an effective goal statement, focus is placed on what is to be achieved (not on what is to be avoided). For example, "I do not eat junk food" (however defined) focuses on what to avoid. "I eat only health-giving, wholesome foods" (however defined) focuses on what one wants to achieve. "What a person thinks is what he or she becomes."

The second principle of goals comes from a text called *Shiva Drishti*, "The Outlook of Shiva," written in the ninth century by Somananda, a Siddha from Kashmir. It says: *shivena shiva sadhana*, "Do the sadhana of becoming Shiva by being Shiva," which means to act as if you already embody your goal. This is why it is good to phrase goals in the present tense, not as statements of future intent. For example, not "I will chant the *Guru Gita* every day" but "I chant the *Guru Gita* every day."

When stating something in the present tense that the conscious mind might regard with some disbelief (perhaps we have not actually been chanting the *Guru Gita* every day), it is important not to let doubts cause us to waver and abandon our goal. The *Shiva Sutras* tell us: *vitarka atma jnanam*, "The unwavering awareness 'I am the Self' constitutes knowledge of the Self." In other words, we must affirm our goal with confidence and conviction. Then even if there's a time lag, our being aligns itself with our intention and the goal becomes manifest.

Just as self-doubt can undermine our sustaining and achieving a goal, so can the skepticism or even the envy and ill will of others. Have you ever told someone about a plan you had, and he laughed or raised an eyebrow in disbelief? Did your confidence waver? Therefore, it is important to tell our goals only to people who understand the value of consciously chosen goals and who will support us in having them. Sage Narada in his *Bhakti Sutras* said: "Keep good company." That is, keep the company of people, books, thoughts, and environments that support the achievement of your goals.

Knowing our purpose is essential both for planning and for setting goals. "What is my purpose for being?" is thus a great contemplation. We can rest assured that the answer already lies within. It is not something that has to be made up. As one's life unfolds, the understanding of one's purpose may also evolve; still, it was already there. Since one's purpose exists within, contemplation can bring it to conscious awareness. How?

Whenever we do not know what something is, it can be uncovered, discovered, by giving it a name. Next, we hold our awareness on the feeling and focal point that is evoked in our mind by saying that name mentally. The answer will eventually come to us — from within. This exercise is a form of contemplation.

How can something unknown be named? One effective way is to convert a question such as "what is my purpose?" into a phrase like "what-my-purpose-is." Or we could name it "my purpose in life." This phrase serves as a name of the answer even when the answer remains unknown. Repeating the phrase and focusing on the feeling that comes with it will evoke the answer. We do not know consciously what our purpose is, yet thinking either of these phrases will point our awareness right at it, and under that flashlight beam of attention our purposes will begin to reveal themselves in words, images, and feelings.

This is an effective form of contemplation. It does evoke an answer. If we are puzzling over an issue in our life, for example, and cannot even figure out what to call the issue, much less how to solve it, we can tag the undefined issue with the name "what-the-issue-is." Then, by holding this phrase in mind and letting our attention stay with the feeling evoked by the words "what-the-issue-is," we provoke it to emerge from our subconscious. It might be an hour later; we might even have given up contemplating and are doing something totally unrelated. Suddenly there is a gap in our activity, and the answer comes to mind. The words are simply there. Or the uncovering might take place in a dream the next morning, just before waking up.

Once I was contemplating "how I can stay in the state of equipoise." In this case, I knew the issue (staying in equipoise) but not the answer (how to). I believed that an answer specific to me was already in me; I just did not know what it was. So I mulled it over by giving that answer this name: "how-I-can-stay-in-equipoise." Then I repeated this phrase to myself several times and held my attention for a few moments on the unnamed feeling it evoked in my mind. The answer surprised me a few minutes later. It was a lecture from my inner wisdom: "Take the risk of staying with equipoise," it said. "You know what it is, and you know how to be there, but habit keeps you away. It's almost as though you think it is irresponsible not to get concerned and upset about things. If so, let people think that you don't care about the day's dramas, if that is how they want to interpret you. Do not ask circumstance to give you equipoise; give equipoise to circumstance."

This was a bracing lecture; it pointed me in a new direction. As the day passed, I continued contemplating this issue. I felt that the key to my staying in equipoise still remained unknown. So when I went to sleep that night, I prayed for the grace to learn the key to maintaining equipoise. In the early morning hours, I dreamt I was in the ashram at a big conference. At one point, as I was busily making my way through a crowd, my demeanor changed. I found myself walking calmly with my head held naturally high. I was alert and relaxed. Even in the dream, I recognized that the key to being in the state of equipoise had just happened. "What was it?" I asked as I began waking up, and I saw that I had become unafraid of myself. I was no longer trying to get away from myself, rushing along, grabbing on to events in an effort to hide. I was in equipoise.

Giving a name to your purpose or to your issue's answer not only evokes clarity about what the purpose or answer is, it puts you in direct touch with its power before you know it in words. Therefore, even when a person still does not know his or her purpose for being, he or she can benefit from a direct relationship with it, merely by giving it a name, for example "what-my-purpose-is."

Then, in any moment of self-awareness during the day when we wonder what to do next (or what we are doing now for that matter!), we can draw on the focusing power of our own purpose, on the direction-giving energy of our purpose, merely by remembering the name we have given it. Then its energy will feed into our actions and thoughts. Or we can simply remember that our purpose exists. Just being aware that we do have a purpose, without any further thinking about it, is enough to inform our actions, whatever they are, with the energy and focus of our soul's intention.

The same approach — of naming the unknown — works for solutions to specific events, too. We may be in the midst of a difficult situation, for which we do not consciously know the solution. Then we can name the solution, "what-the-best-solution-is," and let the responding energy that comes from within guide us intuitively through the next step in the situation, whatever that might be. The solution will be giving direction to our choices even though we do not yet consciously know what the solution is. Or we can simply have the faith that a solution exists, and hold the feeling of its existence in our mind as we go through the issue.

Faith — in one's purpose and in one's path — is essential. Baba Muktananda always said that doubt is one of the greatest enemies of a seeker. It undermines commitment and practice. After I met Baba and began meditating with his grace, I returned to my job. My lifestyle changed dramatically. I began to get up at 4:00 A.M. Before going to work each day, I would meditate and chant the *Guru Gita*. At noon, in the privacy of my office, I chanted *Om Namah Shivaya* for half an hour. Returning home in the late afternoon, I would perform and chant the *Arati*, prepare a simple meal, do some preparatory work, and then chant for forty-five minutes before going to bed at 9:00 P.M.

I had kept this schedule for a year without wavering. I had a whole new life, and I loved it. Then, suddenly, I was seized with a doubt: "Am I throwing my life away?" Although I was filled with *shakti* and my teaching was better than it had ever been, I was assailed with doubt about the monastic lifestyle I had embraced. In that moment, I decided to break out of my usual routine. So I pulled the television set out of the closet where it had been for a year. It was a Sunday afternoon. When I turned it on, the screen came alive with the National Figure Skating Championships. I was enthralled by the grace, skill, and power the skaters displayed, particularly one spectacular couple.

In the interview after the competition, they were asked to describe their lifestyle. They said they were full-time college students, and besides their studies, their lives consisted of working out routines and practicing skating — eight hours a day. "Wow!" I thought. "They live like me, and no one thinks they're throwing *their* lives away!" At that moment I realized that for anyone to attain anything great in this life, whether "worldly" or "spiritual," one has to give it time, energy, and attention. With relief and gratitude, I unplugged the television and rolled it into the closet.

A footnote to this incident: Almost ten years later, when I told this story during a Siddha Yoga Meditation Intensive, a participant spoke with me afterward, saying, "I was one of those figure skaters — and everyone *did* think we were throwing our lives away, but we stuck with it anyway!" Faith.

❀

WHERE DOES OUR FAITH COME from? Someone once asked Baba Muktananda, "How do you know when you have done the right thing?" He replied, "By the result." Faith comes from our *experience* on the path we have chosen.

Part of that experience can be the faith that the Guru has in us. When I first met Baba Muktananda, I saw myself as a person who could never stick with anything. I was always espousing this philosophy, then that path, then a different practice, and so on. Something would work for me for a while, and then I would come up to its ceiling and I would move on. I did not like my lack of follow-through. No "stick-to-it-iveness," no apparent purpose.

In the 1970s Baba would give Sanskrit names to people if they asked for one. People found that the name they received had great meaning for them and contained a contemplation. So one evening in darshan I asked Baba for a name. He spent what seemed like two minutes scanning pages of typed lists of names, flipping from one page to the next with great concentration. I became riveted to this process. So when he finally gave me the name, I was completely focused. "Nirantar," he said. The first thing I felt was how beautiful it is, and I was so grateful. Then he spoke to someone, who wrote it on a slip of paper for me. Filled with curiosity to find out what it meant, I went to the Sanskrit scholar who was there and showed her the paper. "Nirantar," she said. "It means 'constant' or 'constancy'."

In the days that followed, I contemplated that name. It didn't seem to be about me — one who never stuck with anything. Then one day, I finally saw my constancy: I had never given up the search for a path, for a way of living that would work for me. My moving from one thing to another was part of that constant search. Baba's perception of me gave me access to a new faith in myself.

Each of us has his or her own issues to deal with in sticking with a particular path or a course of action we have chosen for ourselves. Some of us cannot tolerate uncertainty. We want to know what is going to happen next and the meaning of what is happening now. Our stance toward new things is "why?" — expressed sometimes with petulance. Could we develop a willingness not to know right now? For the truth is, not knowing is an opportunity. Whenever we shut ourselves off from the feeling of not knowing, we rob ourselves. Life is full of mystery — of course. Allowing this, and letting ourselves be aware of the presence of the unknown, adds a dimension to daily experience that no additional information could ever provide.

Others of us have an issue about apparent fairness. If things do not seem fair, we get indignant and certain that something is wrong. Our faith wavers. But have we considered the possibility that what is wrong is our understanding? The word *consider* here does not mean "think about it out of polite cooperation for a few moments." It means opening ourselves to the experience that what we see before us really is fair at a deep level, and then letting this experience change our mind in whatever way it will. What is fairness? Is it that everyone is treated the same outwardly? Is it that everyone has the same inner spiritual experiences? That might be fairness if everyone were the same. But are we identical manufactured goods or human beings? Each one of us comes to the spiritual path with a unique history and a unique form of ignorance to overcome.

Other people may have strong ideas that spiritual life means living in an unheated, stone building and sleeping on straw. They have equated "spirituality" with outer austerity. However, the austerities that are called for in spiritual life are more subtle and demanding than physical discomfort. Spiritual life asks: Can you turn away from your personal attachments, your personal indignations, and your indulgence in infatuation, jealously, anger, greed, desire, and pride? And can you sacrifice these things moment by moment, again and again, for years? This is austerity.

What is it that gives us the strength to overcome these and other prejudices that we bring to spirituality? Grace, experience, and our sense of purpose. They give us a commitment to Truth and to love. And they give us the humility and strength to acknowledge that we do not know everything, that we are "works in progress" even while we are already "That."

Grace, as Baba Muktananda has said, is not withheld from anyone who gives his faith to grace, who values it and honors it as a precious gift. This can even be our stance unknowingly. In the early stages of my journey, I stumbled forward, searching for the way out of my own containment without even knowing what I was trying to accomplish. I only knew there had to be something different from the way I was experiencing life.

Faith, based on contemplation and experience, brings steadiness to the soul. This faith is rooted in the heart, not in the argumentative mind. It is generous and forgiving. It honors our own experience and lets others have theirs. This kind of faith does not need converts to shore it up. It does not argue who is right and who is wrong. It does not feel threatened by different points of view. It is relaxed and yet unshakable. Sage Narada, in his classic scripture the *Bhakti Sutras*, speaks of devotion as a path to God-realization. His seventy-fourth *sutra* affirms that the devotee should not waste his time or energies in arguments or controversy, because, says *sutra* seventy-five, the experience of God cannot be realized through argumentative reasoning. Such debate is pointless and counter-productive since it distracts one from the remembrance of God.

One of the chief enemies of faith is self-doubt. It is

ironic that our faith in God and a path often wobbles not because of God or the path but because of doubts about ourselves. When we do not trust our own heart, when we do not trust our own experience, when we do not trust our own relationship with God, we rob ourselves of the calm joy that comes with faith. Thus, a key element in sustaining faith is to have faith in one's faith.

Underpinning this faith in one's faith is faith in oneself. Part of the difficulty we have with faith in ourselves is that we don't recognize the faith we *do* have. If we have pursued any goal persistently for any length of time, we have at least a seedling of faith in ourselves, alive and well. If — as part of a determination to find happiness in life — we have chosen to examine our habits and the way we live, if we have committed ourselves to following a course of self-development or a spiritual path, we have faith in ourselves. And if we do not feel that faith, we can pray to recognize and experience it.

At different moments, I have experienced different break-throughs to faith in myself. One was when I recognized that the moment I am willing to pay the price for being true to myself in any situation, I am free in that situation. Another person can cause us to betray ourselves only when we're not willing to pay the price that being true to ourselves may exact. Being willing to pay the price does not mean that we will actually have to do so. Most "prices" are made up in the mind of our self-doubt anyway, and don't exist in actuality. Other prices do exist, but when we've become willing to pay them, they no longer matter. This understanding comes alive when we risk taking actions based on it.

Faith gives us the courage to trust that the present moment — lived consciously, with awareness of God — is enough. Letting go of identification with our thoughts and emotions, again and again, is an act of joyful courage, an act of faith. The world is mysterious and multidimensional when lived in in this way. The monopoly of familiar knowledge dissolves, revealing what is. As Gurumayi Chidvilasananda has said, "Whenever the haze that normally clouds your perception gives way and you see your own Self clearly, even for a moment, you experience the most exquisite peace rising up within you." And then she adds: "Peace is not as rare as you have been led to believe."

❧

SO WE CAN TRUST our soul's purpose even when we do not know in words what it is. It is an ancient and true guide. The fulfillment of that purpose is the reason each of us was born. The greatest expression of our selfhood will come through aligning ourselves to — and acting in accordance with — our soul's reason for being. So why wait until we think we have it figured out? Why not draw on its creative power and sustaining grace right now?

Remembering our purpose helps us at the moment of choice in the flow of the mind. We make choices aligned with our purpose instead of ones based on temporary desire. Whenever we become aware of ourselves once again after a train of thought, we have the choice "What's next?" Then, if we are in touch with our purpose, or if we merely remember that it exists, we feel immediately whether a thought or an action that we are engaged in supports our purpose or goes against it. Remembering our purpose for being gives direction to the moments of our life. Awareness of purpose is a rudder that keeps us from being tossed about by the winds and waves of circumstance: the phone rings for the tenth time, someone suggests we do this or that, the arrival of an interesting magazine just when we were settling down to study, a temptation to eat something more, and so on. We handle those things and stay on course.

When we have forgotten our purpose, we wander uncertainly. Days may be pleasant or a hassle, but the worst part is that neither the pleasure nor the hassle fits any larger picture. Hassles are quite tolerable when we experience them in the context of going for a greater goal. And pleasures have natural and happily accepted limits. But having forgotten our soul's purpose, we have no detachment from the ups and downs of life. Ultimately, even enjoyable things become tedious and boring. For example, you've achieved excellence in your career yet you don't know why you're doing it any more. The *Yoga Vasishtha* says very beautifully: "When the heart has no fixed purpose and is unsteady, its inner changes reflect the ups and downs of the outer world."

When we have forgotten our purpose, our lives are run by the senses, by momentary desires, by fears and worries, not by love and our will. The *Katha Upanishad* tells us: "The pleasant and the beneficial both present themselves to man, moment by moment. He who chooses the pleasant misses the goal. He who chooses the beneficial goes from greatness to greater greatness."

Will is the capacity to choose. It requires detachment and thrives with Witness-consciousness. Because desire, whose object is "the pleasant," is one of the choices available to will, will stands above desire. Yet this capacity to choose has to be exercised, since the default choice is to follow one's desires.

In this age and culture, living according to one's desires is so expected that it has become the standard of conduct. We even believe that when we want to do something, it is unhealthy not to. Therefore, we conclude, if we are not going to do something, first we have to get over wanting to do it. Not so. One can still want to do something and choose not to do it. A developed will has this freedom. It serves our greater purpose. It gives us the capacity to set aside short-term desires when pursuing them will interfere with our longer-term goals and best interests. As the Upanishad says, "He who chooses the beneficial goes from greatness to greater greatness." It is truly a liberation to realize that we do not have to be rid of a desire before choosing not to act on it.

None of this means that we should shun pleasure and lead austere lives of self-deprivation. It means we must develop the capacity to choose our own long-term best interests and happiness over short-term distractions and pleasures. Remembering our purpose helps us achieve this capacity.

Chanting the *Guru Gita* this morning, simply holding in awareness the fact that my purpose exists and then singing *to* that felt presence of purpose, I found my spirits uplifted, my mind steady and sure, and my heart filled with awe. For I saw that my soul's purpose and God's will for me are one. ❈

Epilogue

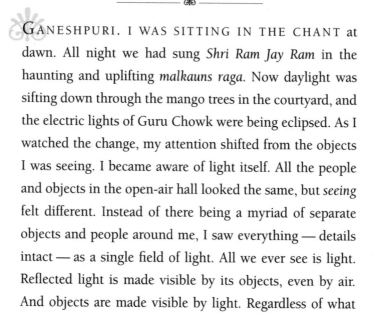

Begin to value your own Self. Know it. Remain aware of it. Then you will be your own best friend, and you will be able to cross the ocean of worldliness.

— Swami Muktananda

GANESHPURI. I WAS SITTING IN THE CHANT at dawn. All night we had sung *Shri Ram Jay Ram* in the haunting and uplifting *malkauns raga*. Now daylight was sifting down through the mango trees in the courtyard, and the electric lights of Guru Chowk were being eclipsed. As I watched the change, my attention shifted from the objects I was seeing. I became aware of light itself. All the people and objects in the open-air hall looked the same, but *seeing* felt different. Instead of there being a myriad of separate objects and people around me, I saw everything — details intact — as a single field of light. All we ever see is light. Reflected light is made visible by its objects, even by air. And objects are made visible by light. Regardless of what objects are in our field of vision — how many or how few, and what kind — what we see is not objects as such but the light they reflect.

In a country field or a city street, the trees, grass, clouds, cars, buildings, fire hydrants, or people walking are all reflection-forms taken by one light. There is nothing mysterious or esoteric here. It is the simple, physical truth: all one sees is reflecting light. Only when we look right at the sun do we see emanated light. There are a few other exceptions, like molten lava, lightning, candle flames, any fire, the light of a firefly, stars, a luminescent sea creature, and electric lights. But these are exceptions. Otherwise, during the day, each person, each blade of grass, each cloud, each building is a shape of reflected sunlight. And in any case, light and only light is what we see.

The forms are many and the light is one. Yet what are we primarily aware of: the many forms or the one light? The forms, of course. We focus almost completely on all the differences in shape, color, brightness, and texture that make up the items in our visual field. This habit is forgetfulness. With a small shift of attention, we can also remember the light itself — not some mystical notion of light, but physical light appearing as the shapes that comprise the visible world we constantly live in.

In this moment, if your attention is focused only on the different forms that light is taking — book, hands, desk, paper, curtain, clock — shift your awareness to light itself. You still see all the same things — the book, your hands, the table — but now it is with the understanding and feeling that they are different forms of one light. Let yourself *feel* the effect of this awareness.

Do you find yourself becoming more detached in the situation, yet no less aware of details? Do you find yourself becoming calmer and more centered? Whenever I practice this exercise, it is as though I have traded my scattered and wandering attention for a unified awareness which contains all individual things, including myself, in one larger whole.

When we are aware of the one light which is taking the form of the many things in our field of vision, our mind rests from its wandering. A benign detachment sets in. The field of our visual experience becomes unified. We integrate ourselves and our situation. This practice befriends the mind and lets it be calm.

Changing our habitual focus this way has unexpected practical consequences. How often do we come home mentally exhausted from a trip to a shopping mall or a great museum? How often does a walk through the city do the same thing? When we constantly focus on the individual items and people on Broadway, at the mall, or in a museum, we quickly wear out from the stimulus overload. What started with delight ends with "Get me outta here." It is impossible to take it all in and maintain freshness. We keep trying, but finally all we want to do is go home and recover. When we maintain whole-field awareness, however, and stay in touch with the Self, this exhaustion does not occur.

Furthermore, through this practice we also stay in touch with our reason for being there and don't get diverted from it by the pull of the senses. A mall, a museum, or a busy city street is not exhausting when we practice seeing it as *one* field of light, as a single event. This does not mean we don't see individual items. It means we see them without visually grasping them, right and left. We stay in touch with ourselves, with our own awareness, and in charge of which items we will pay attention to. Whole-field awareness, the act of staying aware of the one light while seeing its many forms, keeps us detached in just the right way.

During the chant, when I focused on the light, I became aware that the sight of my body was also a reflection of light. I had included myself in the picture. Then I became aware of the space behind my eyes, that full emptiness. It was not darkness; it was invisibility.

By what light was this invisibility visible? By what light was *it* known?

And by what light is physical darkness visible? For it is. In darkness there is no light. Yet we do see it. This perception made me aware of the light that illumines both light and darkness; it is the light that constitutes (or is) Consciousness, which is our own awareness. The *Shiva Sutras* say, "When the mind is united to the core of Consciousness, every observable phenomenon and even the void appear as a form of Consciousness." Consciousness is the light that makes all light and all darkness visible. When the body dies, the eyes are still good but they do not see. Consciousness makes physical light into *light*. "Without you," Baba Muktananda said, "your world does not exist."

After the chant, in the fresh morning, I walked around Dakshinkashi. The sky was delft china blue. The grass sparkled. Egrets stalked their prey, leaving dark green trails where their feet had shaken dew from the grass. Beyond the border trees, the nearest hill rose in its rainbow curve. Stacks of hills beyond displayed layers of blue haze, bespeaking distance. The world of meaning poured forth from my heart. Awareness was the sunlight of this lovely world. As it is with the objects of the world, so it is with the contents of the mind. Awareness illumines not only the world but also our thoughts, images, and feelings. We see them as reflections of its light. In the same way that our attention can be continually lost in the world of physical objects that present themselves to our sight, we can also spend a lifetime having our awareness pulled here and everywhere by the ceaseless play of our thoughts and emotions. Yet just as we can free our attention from being solely aware of physical forms by becoming conscious of the sunlight that illumines them, so, too, within the mind we can free our attention from slavish preoccupation with our thoughts and feelings by becoming aware of awareness itself. The light of awareness has the capacity to illumine itself. That is, in the midst of being aware of everything else that our consciousness illumines, we can also be aware that we are aware. Then we experience our true nature, which is independent happiness and ever-arising bliss. Remembering the Self, we are the Witness. We become our own best friend and cross the ocean of worldliness. ❋

Note on Sources

Most scriptural quotations were newly rendered, drawing from the following sources:

The Bhagavad Gita, translated by Winthrop Sargeant (Albany: State University of New York Press, 1984).

The Concise Yoga Vāsiṣṭha, translated and edited by Swami Venkatesananda (Albany: State University of New York Press, 1993).

The Philosophy of Love: Bhakti-Sūtras of Devarṣi Nārada, translated by Hanumanprasad Poddar (Rajganpur, India: Orissa Cement, Ltd., 1940).

The Upanishads: Breath of the Eternal, selected and translated by Swami Prabhavananda and Frederick Manchester (Hollywood: The Vedanta Society of Southern California, 1975).

Both verse and commentary were quoted from *Vijñānabhairava or Divine Consciousness*, translated by Jaideva Singh (Delhi: Motilal Banarsidass, 1979).

Guide to Sanskrit Pronunciation

Vowels

Sanskrit vowels are categorized as either long or short. In English transliteration, the long vowels are marked with a bar above the letter and are pronounced twice as long as the short vowels. The vowels *e* and *o* are always pronounced as long vowels.

Short:	Long:
a as in cup	*ā* as in calm
i as in give	*ī* as in seen
u as in full	*ū* as in school
e as in save	*ai* as in aisle
o as in phone	*au* as in cow
ṛ as in written	

Consonants

The main variations from the way consonants are pronounced in English are the aspirated consonants. These are pronounced with a definite *h* sound:

Aspirated Consonants:	Other Consonants:
th as in boathouse	*c* as in such
ṭh as in anthill	*ñ* as in canyon
ḍh as in roadhouse	*ṇ* as in none
dh as in adhere	*n* as in snake
bh as in clubhouse	*ś* as in bush
jh as in hedgehog	*ṣ* as in shine
ḥ is an aspiration that	*s* as in supreme
repeats the preceding	*kṣ* as in auction
vowel	*ṃ* is a strong nasal *m*

For a detailed pronunciation guide, see *The Nectar of Chanting*, published by SYDA Foundation.

Glossary

ARATI [*ārati*]
A ritual of worship during which a flame, symbolic of the individual soul, is waved before the form of a deity, sacred being, or image that exemplifies the divine light of Consciousness.

ASHRAM [*āśrama*]
(*lit.*, without fatigue) The abode of a Guru or saint; a monastic place of retreat where seekers engage in spiritual practices and study the sacred teachings of yoga.

BHAGAVAD GITA [*bhagavadgītā*]
(*lit.*, song of God) One of the world's great spiritual texts; an essential scripture of India, in which Lord Krishna instructs his disciple Arjuna on the nature of God, the universe, and the supreme Self, and on the different forms of yoga.

BHAKTI SUTRAS [*bhaktisūtra*]
India's classic scripture on devotion to God, composed by the sage Narada.

BRAHMAN [*brahman*]
The Absolute; the all-pervasive and supreme Principle of the universe. The nature of Brahman is described in the Upanishads and in Vedantic philosophy as: *sat* (Existence absolute), *chit* (Consciousness absolute), and *ananda* (Bliss absolute).

CHAITANYA [*caitanya*]
The fundamental Consciousness, which has perfect freedom of knowing (*jñana shakti*), willing (*iccha shakti*), and doing (*kriya shakti*). When used in reference to a mantra, *chaitanya* means that the mantra is enlivened with grace and thus has the capacity to draw one's mind spontaneously into meditative stillness.

CHIDVILASANANDA, SWAMI [*cidvilāsānanda svāmī*]
[*lit.*, the bliss of the play of Consciousness] The name given to

Gurumayi by Swami Muktananda when she took the vows of monkhood.

CONSCIOUSNESS
The intelligent, supremely independent, divine Energy that creates, pervades, supports, and is the entire universe. Known as the Witness of the mind, or expanded "I"-awareness. See also SHAKTI, WITNESS-CONSCIOUSNESS.

DAKSHINKASHI [Hindi: dakṣinkaśi]
(lit., south field) A beautiful twenty-five-acre field in Shree Gurudev Siddha Peeth, the Siddha Yoga Meditation ashram near Ganeshpuri, India. The field is ringed by a tree-lined path, which is used for walking contemplation.

DARSHAN [darśana]
(lit., to have sight of; viewing) A glimpse or vision of a saint; being in the presence of a holy being; seeing God or an image of God.

DHARANA [dhāraṇā]
1) In Kashmir Shaivism, a centering technique as described, for example, in the book of dharanas called Vijñana Bhairava. 2) Concentration; the sixth of the eight limbs of the path of raja yoga. In this practice, the mind becomes stabilized by being fixed on an object. See also PATANJALI; YOGA SUTRAS; VIJNANA BHAIRAVA.

GANESHPURI [gaṇeśapuri]
A village at the foot of Mandagni Mountain in Maharashtra, India. Bhagawan Nityananda settled in this region where yogis have performed spiritual practices for thousands of years. The ashram founded by Swami Muktananda at his Guru's command is built on this sacred land. See also GURUDEV SIDDHA PEETH.

GURU [guru]
(lit., gu, darkness; ru, light) A spiritual Master or teacher; one who has attained union with the Divine, is learned in the scriptures, and who has been empowered by his own Guru to initiate seekers and guide them on the path to liberation. See also SHAKTIPAT; SIDDHA.

GURU CHOWK
The open-air meditation and chanting hall adjoining the court-yard in Shree Gurudev Siddha Peeth, the Siddha Yoga Meditation ashram near Ganeshpuri, India.

GURU GITA [*gurugītā*]
(*lit.*, song of the Guru) A Sanskrit text; a garland of mantras that describe the nature of the Guru and the Guru-disciple relation-ship. In Siddha Yoga Meditation ashrams, the *Guru Gita* is chant-ed every morning.

GURUDEV SIDDHA PEETH [*gurudeva siddha pīṭha*]
(*lit.*, abode of the Siddhas) The main Siddha Yoga ashram and the site of the Samadhi Shrine of Swami Muktananda. It was founded in 1956 when Bhagawan Nityananda instructed Swami Muktananda to live in a simple three-room house near Ganesh-puri, India. The ashram is a world-renowned center for spiritu-al practice and study under the guidance of the living Master Swami Chidvilasananda. See also ASHRAM; GANESHPURI.

GURUMAYI [*Marathi: gurumāyi*]
A term of respect and endearment in the Marathi language often used in addressing Swami Chidvilasananda.

INTENSIVE
A program designed by Swami Muktananda to give direct initia-tion through the awakening of the *kundalini* energy. See also KUNDALINI; SHAKTIPAT.

KABIR [*Hindi: kabīr*]
(1440-1518) A great poet-saint and mystic who lived his life as a simple weaver in Benares, India. His followers included both Hindus and Muslims, and his influence was a powerful force in overcoming the fierce religious factionalism of the day. His poems describe the experience of the Self, the greatness of the Guru, and the nature of true spirituality.

KATHA UPANISHAD [*kaṭha upaniṣad*]
One of the principal Upanishads. It contains the story of the sage

Nachiketas, who, given a boon by Yama, the lord of death, asks for the supreme teaching of the knowledge of the Absolute. See also UPANISHAD(S).

KRISHNA [krṣṇa]
  (lit., the dark one; the one who attracts irresistibly) The eighth incarnation of Lord Vishnu. His life story is told in the *Shrimad Bhagavatam*; his spiritual teachings are contained in the *Bhagavad Gita*, which is a portion of the epic *Mahabharata*.

KSHEMARAJA [kṣemarāja]
  (Tenth century) A scholar and Guru from Kashmir, author of many commentaries on Shaivite scriptures.

KUNDALINI [kuṇḍalinī]
  (lit., coiled one) The supreme power, primordial *shakti*, or energy that lies coiled at the base of the spine in the *muladhara chakra* of every human being. Through the descent of grace (*shaktipat*), this extremely subtle force of Consciousness is awakened and begins to purify the whole system. See also INTENSIVE; SHAKTIPAT.

MAITRI UPANISHAD [maitri upaniṣad]
  One of the principal Upanishads, which recounts the teachings of the sage Maitri.

MANTRA [mantra]
  (lit., sacred invocation; that which protects) A name of God; sacred word or divine sound invested with the power to protect, purify, and transform the individual who repeats it.

MAYA [maya]
  (lit., to measure) The term used in Vedanta for the power that veils the true nature of the Self and creates the experiences of multiplicity and separation from God.

MUKTANANDA, SWAMI [muktānanda svāmī]
  (1908-1982) Swami Chidvilasananda's Guru, often referred to as Baba. This great Siddha brought the powerful and rare initiation

known as *shaktipat* to the West on the command of his own Guru, Bhagawan Nityananda. As the inheritor of a great lineage of spiritual Masters, Baba Muktananda introduced what he called "Siddha Yoga" to the modern world, making the scriptures come alive, teaching in words and actions, by example and by direct experience.

NARADA [*nārada*]
A divine *rishi*, or seer, who was a great devotee and servant of Lord Vishnu. He appears in many of the Puranas and is the author of the *Bhakti Sutras*, an authoritative text on devotion to God.

OM NAMAH SHIVAYA [*om namaḥ śivāya*]
(lit., *Om*, I bow to Shiva) The Sanskrit mantra of the Siddha Yoga lineage is known as "the great redeeming mantra" because of its power to grant both worldly fulfillment and spiritual realization. *Om* is the primordial sound; *Namah* means to honor; *Shivaya* denotes divine Consciousness, the Lord who dwells in every heart.

PATANJALI [*patañjali*]
(Fourth century) A sage and the author of the famous *Yoga Sutras*, which is an exposition of one of the six orthodox philosophies of India and is the authoritative text of the path of *raja yoga*. See also YOGA SUTRAS.

PRANAM [*praṇāma*]
To bow; to greet with respect; a form of greeting often made by folding one's hands in front of one's heart and bowing one's head.

RAGA [*raga*]
A melodic form used in classical Indian music. The *ragas* evoke particular moods in the listener and are often performed to resonate with a season or time of day. The *malkauns raga* (mentioned in the text) evokes the qualities of valor and courage on the spiritual path.

SADHANA [*sādhana*]
Spiritual discipline or path; practices, both physical and mental, meant to further one's spiritual development.

SAMA VEDA [*samaveda*]

One of the four Vedas, the *Sama Veda* is a liturgical collection of hymns sung to melodies of great beauty. The four Vedas are among the most ancient, revered, and sacred of the world's scriptures. They are regarded as divinely revealed, eternal wisdom.

SAMSKARA(S) [*saṃskāra*]

Impressions of past actions and thoughts that remain in the subtle body. They are the basis of physical, mental, and emotional habits, of reactions and judgments. By the action of the awakened *kundalini*, they are brought to the surface of one's awareness and then eliminated.

SANSKRIT [*saṃskṛta*]

(*lit.*, perfectly constructed speech) The scriptural and scholarly language of India; first found in its ancient form in the Vedas and Upanishads, dating from at least 1200 B.C.

SELF

The divine Consciousness residing in the individual, described as the Witness of the mind or the pure "I"-awareness. See also CONSCIOUSNESS.

SEVA [*sevā*]

[*lit.*, service] Selfless service; work offered to God or to the spiritual Master, performed with love and without concern for receiving the benefits of that work.

SHAKTI [*śakti*]

Force, energy; spiritual power; according to Shaivite philosophy, the divine or cosmic energy that manifests the universe; the dynamic aspect of supreme Shiva. See also KUNDALINI.

SHAKTIPAT [*śaktipāta*]

(*lit.*, descent of grace) The transmission of spiritual power, or *shakti*, from the Guru to the disciple; spiritual awakening by grace. See also GURU; KUNDALINI.

SHANKARACHARYA [*śaṅkarācārya*]

(788-820) One of the greatest philosophers and sages of India, he traveled throughout India expounding the philosophy of absolute nondualism (Advaita Vedanta). In addition to teaching and writing, he established ashrams in the four corners of India. The tradition of monks to which Swami Muktananda and Swami Chidvilasananda belong was created by Shankaracharya.

SHIVA DRISHTI [*śivadṛṣṭi*]

(*lit.*, the outlook of Shiva) 1) A text of Kashmir Shaivism written by the Shaivite Master Somananda in the tenth century. 2) The state of equipoise and equality-consciousness that is the outlook of the Lord.

SHIVA SUTRAS [*śivasūtra*]

A Sanskrit text revealed by Lord Shiva to the ninth-century sage Vasuguptacharya. It consists of seventy-seven *sutras* or aphorisms, which according to tradition were found inscribed on a rock in Kashmir. The *Shiva Sutras* are the fundamental scripture of the philosophical school known as Kashmir Shaivism.

SIDDHA(S) [*siddha*]

A perfected yogi; one who is in the state of unity-consciousness and who has achieved mastery over the senses and their objects; one whose experience of the supreme Self is uninterrupted and whose identification with the ego has been dissolved.

SIDDHA GURU *or* **SIDDHA MASTER** [*siddhaguru*]

One who has attained the state of enlightenment and who has the capacity to awaken the dormant spiritual energy of a disciple and guide him or her to the state of the Truth, the state of enlightenment.

SIDDHA YOGA [*siddhayoga*]

(*lit.*, the yoga of perfection) A method of uniting the individual with the Divine that begins with *shaktipat*, the inner awakening by the grace of a Siddha Guru, and proceeds through the specific spiritual practices outlined by Swami Muktananda and his spiritual heir,

Swami   Chidvilasananda.   See   also   GURU;   KUNDALINI;
SHAKTIPAT.

SIDDHA MEDITATION
A form of spontaneous meditation in which one's awareness is
naturally drawn within oneself after initiation by a Siddha Guru.
See also SIDDHA YOGA.

THAT
When capitalized, as in "Thou art That," it refers to the inner
Self or to the supreme Absolute.

TIRTH, RAM [*Hindi: ram tirth*]
(1873-1906) Born in the Punjab of a poor family, he became a
distinguished professor of mathematics. Out of his longing for
God, he withdrew to the Himalayas, where he attained enlightenment. Ram Tirth lectured on Vedanta in India, Japan, and the
United States (1902-1904). He wrote many beautiful poems in
the Urdu language.

UPANISHAD(S) [*upaniṣad*]
(*lit.*, sitting close to; secret teachings) The inspired teachings,
visions, and mystical experiences of the ancient sages, *rishis*, of
India. These scriptures, exceeding a hundred texts, constitute
"the end" or "final understanding" (*anta*) of the Vedas; hence the
term *vedanta*. With immense variety of form and style, all of
these texts give the same essential teaching: that the individual
soul and God are one.

VEDANTA [*vedānta*]
(*lit.*, end of the Vedas) One of the six orthodox schools of Indian
philosophy; usually identified with Advaita Vedanta, absolute
nondualism. See also UPANISHAD(S).

VIJNANA BHAIRAVA [*vijñānabhairava*]
An exposition of the path of yoga based on the principles of
Kashmir Shaivism. Originally composed in Sanskrit, probably in
the seventh century, it is a compilation of 112 *dharanas*, or centering exercises, which give the experience of union with God.

VIKALPA(S) [*vikalpa*]
Thoughts; imagination; mental oscillations; concepts.

WITNESS-CONSCIOUSNESS
The awareness that one has when observing one's body, thoughts, and emotions, not as one's identity but as objects of perception along with the rest of the sensory world. See also SELF; CONSCIOUSNESS.

YOGA [*yoga*]
(*lit.*, union) Union with God or the inner Self; a method or practice leading to that state.

YOGA SUTRAS [*yogasūtra*]
A collection of aphorisms, thought to have been written by the sage Patanjali in the fourth century and forming the basic scripture of the path of *raja yoga*. They expound different methods for the attainment of the state of yoga in which the movement of the mind ceases and the Witness of the mind rests in its own bliss. See also PATANJALI.

YOGA VASISHTHA [*yogavāsiṣṭha*]
A text in which Vasishtha, an ancient sage and the Guru of Lord Rama, answers Lord Rama's philosophical questions on life, death, and human suffering.

Swami Chidvilasananda

The Siddha Yoga Tradition

THE SPIRITUAL UNFOLDMENT that is inspired by the grace and guidance of an enlightened Master, known as a Siddha Guru, is the essence of the Siddha Yoga tradition.

A Siddha Guru is one who has the power and knowledge to give others the inner experience of God. Through the transmission of grace, known as *shaktipat* initiation, the Siddha Master awakens a seeker's inner spiritual energy. Having walked the spiritual path to its final goal, Siddha Gurus dedicate their lives to helping others complete the same journey.

Swami Chidvilasananda, widely known as Gurumayi, is a Siddha Guru. Since early childhood, she has been a disciple of the Siddha Master Swami Muktananda Paramahamsa (1908-1982). It was he who invested Swami Chidvilasananda with the knowledge, power, and authority of the ancient tradition of Siddhas.

During his lifetime Swami Muktananda became adept at many of the classical paths of yoga, yet he said his spiritual journey did not truly begin until Bhagawan Nityananda, one of the great saints of modern India, awakened him to the experience of the supreme Power within himself.

Bhagawan Nityananda chose Swami Muktananda as his successor and directed him to bring *shaktipat* initiation and the timeless practices of yoga to seekers everywhere. Gurumayi continues in her Guru's tradition, offering the teachings of the Siddhas and *shaktipat* initiation to seekers around the world.

Through the Siddha Yoga principal practices of meditation, chanting, contemplation, and selfless service, thousands of people from many different traditions and cultures have discovered within themselves the source of lasting happiness and peace: the awareness that we are not separate from God. ❀

Further Reading

SWAMI MUKTANANDA

Play of Consciousness
Bhagawan Nityananda of Ganeshpuri
From the Finite to the Infinite
Where Are You Going?
I Have Become Alive
The Perfect Relationship
Selected Essays
Reflections of the Self
I Am That
Ashram Dharma
Kundalini
Mystery of the Mind
Meditate

SWAMI CHIDVILASANANDA

The Yoga of Discipline
Kindle My Heart
Inner Treasures
My Lord Loves a Pure Heart
Ashes at My Guru's Feet

BOOKS OF CONTEMPLATIONS

Resonate with Stillness
Be Filled with Enthusiasm
Blaze the Trail of Equipoise
Everything Happens for the Best

You may learn more about the teachings and
practices of Siddha Yoga Meditation by contacting:

SYDA Foundation
371 Brickman Rd.
South Fallsburg, NY 12779-0600, USA

Tel: (914) 434-2000

or

Gurudev Siddha Peeth
P.O. Ganeshpuri
PIN 401 206
District Thana
Maharashtra, India

For further information about books in print by
Swami Muktananda and Swami Chidvilasananda,
and editions in translation, please contact:

Siddha Yoga Meditation Bookstore
371 Brickman Rd.
South Fallsburg, NY 12779-0600, USA

Tel: (914) 434-2000 ext. 1700

$19.95

Hazel Speer

July, 1988

THE
MYSTERIOUS
CAUSE OF ILLNESS

AND HOW TO
OVERCOME EVERY DISEASE
FROM
CONSTIPATION TO
CANCER

Eati

D0973827

THE
MYSTERIOUS
CAUSE OF ILLNESS

AND HOW TO
OVERCOME EVERY DISEASE
FROM
CONSTIPATION TO
CANCER

Eating Alive

Dr. Jonn Matsen N.D.

140 recipes by Jeanne Marie Martin
Illustrations by Nelson Dewey

Fischer Publishing Corporation
Canfield, Ohio 44406

This book is dedicated to Dr. Joe Boucher
whose strong shoulders and gentle heart helped
carry Naturopathy through some of its hardest years.

© 1987 by Jonn Matsen. All rights reserved.

Originally published in Canada by
Crompton Books under title
"EATING ALIVE" PREVENTION THRU GOOD DIGESTION

ISBN 0-915421-09-7
Printed in the United States of America

United States edition published under license by

FISCHER PUBLISHING CORPORATION
Canfield, Oh 44406

"The doctor of the future will give no medicine but will interest his patients in the care of the human frame, in proper diet, and in the cause and prevention of disease."

Thomas A. Edison

CONTENTS

PART II-EATING ALIVE

PART III - MENU PLANS AND RECIPES

"The physician who can cure one disease by a knowledge of its principles may by the same means cure all the diseases of the human body; for their causes are the same."

Benjamin Rush, Physician

Signer of the Declaration of Independence

INTRODUCTION

There is an incredible healing power within each of us that knows exactly what and where each of our ailments is and knows exactly what to do to correct them. That healing power is available to you at little cost and in unlimited quantities. It is, unfortunately, often stifled and dormant.

To activate this potential power all you need is to learn a little about how the body works and then follow through with a few simple steps.

Healing begins immediately. Within one week there is usually noticeable improvement. In three weeks many people feel better than they can ever remember. Deeper physical healing may take three months or more.

This book is intended for those who are healthy and want to stay that way, for those who are told they are healthy by conventional medical standards but who suspect otherwise, for those whose allergies haven't responded to shots, whose weight still hasn't come off, whose skin is still poor in spite of all the creams and ointments and lotions, and for those whose energy is so low that it seems they must be stuck in first gear.

It is for those whose menstrual cycles are full of cramps and bloating and wild mood swings which they still think are normal, for those whose digestion sputters and coughs like a car in need of a tune-up, for those who haven't become better from all the other diets, for those who've actually gotten worse from other diets, and most importantly for those who will one day have children, because a few months spent in improving health now will pay dividends for generations to come.

We've all known apparently innocent people who've been "struck down" by disease in the prime of life. Perhaps they were spiritually minded, athletic, have "eaten well" for years, never drank or smoked, loved and were loved by their families and enjoyed their jobs, yet still fell victim to an insidious disease. Disease looms as a deep dark ugly mystery in the face of this seeming injustice. Why should they, of all people, fall victim to disease? By the end of this book there will be little mystery left to disease. You will understand

what disease is and how to activate your body's suppressed desire to NOT have disease. Disease is truly weakened by the light of applied understanding.

It is so simple to prevent or even reverse most of those little nagging health problems that you will be amazed that a multi-billion dollar health care system has been built up that often is powerless to help and in some cases makes problems worse.

The examples of the healing process in action as shown later in letters from patients are true. The material in the book will not be "true" per se, however. The reason is that the explanations given are in terms of physiology. Human physiology is an inexact science and future insights into health and disease will prove some of the explanations to be incomplete. This will make little difference to the success of the program as the unpatentable healing medicine within us will not change even as future insights expand the knowledge of the human body.

This book is literally the best "story" that could be put together at this time to explain the improvements in health seen every day in my practise. It could be explained in a great deal more biochemical detail but I decided to emphasis concept rather than data. For those with a scientific mind and the need to know every little biochemical nuance I would suggest they subscribe to "A Textbook of Natural Medicine". This is an major ongoing project by the John Bastyr College of Naturopathic Medicine in Seattle to document in minute detail the biochemistry of Naturopathic Medicine.

While some of these testimonials are more dramatic than for the average patient, they are nonetheless typical. They are dramatic because the problems were considered irreversible and the agony of no hope can be more excruciating than the physical complaints. They are typical in that in spite of the wide variety of disease signs and symptoms, little or nothing was done for their specific complaints. Nothing was applied to the skin of the eczema patient, nothing was done for the hair of the girl with alopcia totalis, nothing was done for the thyroid of the lady with Hashimoto's. The testimonials could easily be expanded to include asthma, arthritis, acne, weak immunity, phobias, hypoglycemia, allergies, sinusitis, chronic indigestion, PMS, irregular menses, headaches, psoriasis, colitis etc.

All of these problems and more I have seen reversed without doing anything for the specific complaint. This doesn't mean that naturopathic medicine doesn't have local treatments or that local treatment should not be given. Neither is the case. It's just that when you activate the internal healing power the results can sometimes be so quick that the problem is healed from within before local treatment would be of any benefit.

Some patients have such weakened vitality that a doctor's skill will be tested to the limit and perhaps beyond. In these cases cooperation between the different health professions is important, to maximize the chances for return to health.

Some patients with major chronic problems may not experience improvement. It is imperative that anyone with a major problem be guided by a knowledgeable physician, as numerous hurdles to cure can present themselves.

Eating Alive will not solve all of your life problems, but if it leaves you with a little more understanding of the majesty of your body and a little less fear of disease, then it will have fullfilled its purpose.

If you use the information within wisely, you will enhance the innate desire of your body to prevent disease or possibly even to reverse it. Drugs and surgery are important and sometimes irreplaceable components of the conventional arsenal in the battle against disease. However, you will soon learn how to activate the more subtle but sometimes more effective healing force within you.

Dr. Jonn Matsen
North Vancouver, B.C.

PATIENTS' LETTERS

Hi, I'm a registered nurse. I was diagnosed as having mild osteo-arthritis of the left hip in the mid 1970's. The pain radiated from my lower back and hip up my whole spine. I was told that stress and coffee were causing this pain so I tried to overcome both these "causes".

I continued to get worse and was finally diagnosed as having ankylosing spondylitis which, if untreated, can become a crippling, deforming arthritis of the spine. In spite of therapy, I continued to need stronger anti-inflammatory drugs, to which I was allergic.

I did not wish to continue being dependent on medication so be-gan trying natural forms of treatment. I stopped all the medication and tried to live with the pain and discomfort. The pain would be-come so severe that I would be forced to resort to medication for relief.

As I continued to seek natural source relief, I was introduced to Dr. Jonn Matsen, who tested me for food sensitivities, guided me through a cleansing period, hydrotherapy, food elimination and proper food combining. This was followed by an anti-fungus product containing caprylic acid.

Within the first two to three weeks of this program, I began to feel better physically and mentally, and became pain-free. An added bonus was the loss of weight. I have not resorted to medication since then.

Jean M. Empey R.N.
Vancouver, B.C.

I have scoliosis which resulted in muscle spasms in my back and neck and headaches. My chiropractor recommended that in conjunction with his treatments I consult Dr. Matsen regarding my nutritional status.

I would have thought of myself as already in good health as I am a registered nurse and run five miles a day, but I followed his instructions. There is much to be said for the success of this regime. I feel good! My energy level is much greater and my thought processes are much clearer. My back and neck tension is much less and I rarely have headaches.

Muriel Shaw R.N.

PART I

EATING TO DEATH:

Aspects of Anatomy, Physiology and Pathology in a NutShell

An Adventurous Journey Through Our Digestive System to Explore
the Mysterious Causes of Disease

"All the rules of prudence or gifts of experience
that life can accumulate will never do as much for
human comfort and welfare as would be done by a stricter
attention and a wiser science directed to the digestive
system."
Thomas DeQuincy 1785-1876

CHAPTER 1

The Stomach

Our poor digestive systems! From morning till night, from childhood to death, we put into our mouths more or less whatever we feel like having, whenever we feel like it. Whatever is within arm's reach may be consumed: Foods, liquids, stimulants, relaxants, chemicals, drugs. Anything and everything goes down the old hatch at some point in our lives.

We expect our system to somehow magically grind it all up, sort it out, use the good, eliminate the bad, all without any noise or complaint, and still leave us lots of energy. That the human system can withstand the abuse it does has to be one of the miracles of life. In fact, treating the digestive system like a garburetor may be harmful to your health.

The apparent stamina of the digestive system is illusory. From one to two years of age virtually everyone's stomach is in a state of "shock". Of over five thousand patients whom I've seen, only four people's stomachs showed adequate vitality. When the situation gets worse, it is called a hiatus hernia. Some doctors believe that over fifty per cent of the population over fifty has some degree of hiatus hernia. I would say that over 90% of the population has an early stage hiatus hernia starting by age three, though it may not show on an X-ray for many decades.

To get an idea of how we treat our stomach let's sit down and write a list of everything that we've put into our stomach in our life. Good Luck.

To begin digestion we first chew up food into swallowable portions. If we chew carbohydrates long enough, some will be completely digested by the alkaline digestive juices right in the mouth.

On swallowing, the food passes through a long tube called the esophagus (which penetrates a flat breathing muscle called the diaphragm) into the stomach. A fold of tissue functions as a valve to prevent the food and digestive juice from going back up the esophagus. The stomach has many layers of heavy muscle which make the stomach "churn" like a washing machine. As the stomach churns, it begins making acid digestive juices that digest protein, and mucous which protects the stomach from its own acid.

When the stomach is shown on an X-ray to have pulled up through the diaphragm so that part of it is now in the chest cavity, the patient has a hiatus hernia. It is a mystery to some doctors as to why this should be so common. Some blame a genetically short esophagus, but it's hard to imagine 50% of the population having a genetic problem. Obviously the diaphragm had a weakness that allowed the stomach to pull up through it.

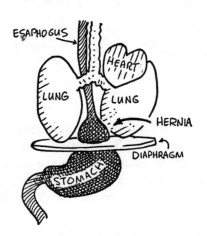

When the stomach is in a state of shock, this may slowly develop into an actual spasm of the stomach muscles. Spasm results in shortening of the muscle. In the more severe states even the muscles of the esophagus can spasm, causing it to shorten. Combine this shortened esophagus with a weakened diaphragm and you have a hiatus hernia. The irritation of the stomach begins early in childhood, even though the physical signs may not show on an X-ray till years later.

STOMACH TROUBLE IS THE BEGINNING OF DISEASE

Those little tummy aches as a child were the first signs of what might result in a chronic malfunction of the entire digestion system. The malfunctioning digestive system may result in almost every disease known to mankind.

Watch a baby. If there is something that doesn't agree with its stomach, the stomach quickly contracts, squeezing the irritant out one end or the other. Vomiting and diarrhea are two of the body's acute reactions to get rid of unwanted substances, to maintain homeostasis.

If the stomach which is continually exposed to irritation were to keep vomiting and having diarrhea, the health of the whole body would be put into jeopardy, so the stomach becomes "hardened". It still reacts to abuse by going into a state of shock, but no longer follows through with complete contraction to the point of actual vomiting and diarrhea. When that is the case we have established one-way communication with the stomach. We eat something and tell the stomach to take it and shut up, so the stomach stops telling us what it feels. This is the way we have gone through life. Thus is the soil readied for many a disease to germinate in.

The stomach is a pretty conscientious character. If we push it past its "hardened" state it will react. Nausea, vomiting, diarrhea, heart burn, indigestion, belching, gas, bloating, appetite disorders, and

ulcers are some of the signals that the stomach is having trouble. Rather than stop irritating the stomach so that it will go back to working properly, we often shut the stomach up even more. The biggest-selling drug in the world is Tagamet (cimetadine), which blocks histamine production by the stomach. Histamine is a chemical produced by tissue to aid inflammation, which is the body's natural reaction to irritation. Thus Tagamet effectively blocks the stomach's natural reaction to irritation. But does it stop the irritation?

The quantities of antacids, digestive aids and laxatives sold by pharmacies, health food stores and pyramid systems staggers the imagination. Everything from powerful drugs to foul-tasting herbal concoctions is sold. You would think that there wasn't a stomach left that worked properly. And you would be closer to the truth than you might suspect.

Some people get very severe and dramatic digestive symptoms when they eat, and it's not hard to convince them that abuse of the stomach is the cause of their problems. There are other patients, who eat with abandon and believe that their digestive systems are like garbage cans. "I can eat anything and everything," they say. If they have arthritis, heart attacks, skin problems, allergies, men-

strual problems, impotency or cancer, they don't correlate those problems with their diet or digestion, because they don't have the obvious digestive symptoms. They do have shocked stomachs however. Stomach malfunction is the cause of the other symptoms as well, even though they may appear to be unrelated.

ASSIMILATING MINERALS AND PROTEIN

There are several ways that stomach malfunction can cause problems far distant. If the stomach doesn't churn properly then a person won't make enough digestive juice. If there's not enough digestive juice, the nutrients won't be absorbed as well as they should. Stomach acid is important for the absorbtion of minerals and amino acids.

Calcium and iron have a positive charge and so does the lining of the intestinal tract. Like repels like, so the minerals tend to pass through the digestive system without being absorbed. If the stomach makes enough acid, the minerals pick up an extra positive charge from the acid, which then allows the mineral to bind with a protein. This protein is readily absorbed and it drags the mineral through with it. This is called chelation.

Mineral deficiencies are common in patients. Lack of stomach acid is one of the main causes of poor absorption of minerals. Though minerals are often not found in adequate amounts in processed-food diets, improving the diet will be of little benefit if the stomach doesn't also improve in function.

Proteins are long chains of amino acids coupled together like freight trains. There are more than twenty different types of amino acids, and the different sequences that they're arranged in determines what type of protein will be made. These protein "trains" have to be uncoupled so that the individual amino acid "cars" can be absorbed properly. It's the stomach acid that begins the breaking down of the proteins, so obviously poor stomach function could lead to amino acid deficiency, though this is relatively rare.

Poor protein digestion can also lead to "chunks" of amino acids still coupled together getting absorbed farther down in the intestinal tract. This can be an important factor in allergies.

Stomach acid is one of the natural antibiotics. Stomach acidity should be strong enough to kill most organisms in food.

Undersecretion of stomach juices can actually cause ulcers. If the stomach doesn't make enough mucous to protect itself from acid, even the slightest amount of acid can result in acid irritation, which can cause ulceration.

Stomach juice is also the "spark" that ignites the action of the intestine. The rhythmic contraction that is set into motion by stomach acid is called peristalsis. Poor stomach function can be one of the causes of constipation, as lack of acid stimulation can result in decreased peristalsis. You know that a car with fouled-up spark plugs can't run smoothly, and neither can the intestine with a fouled stomach.

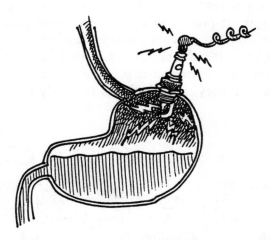

So we can see that the stomach is extremely important for absorption of nutrients, especially of the building materials: amino acids and minerals. The stomach is also an important defense organ and provides the spark for the rest of the digestive system. It's no wonder that the stomach is found in the center of the body or solar plexus, as it is truly the center of our physical universe.

Yet we've already talked about the stomach as malfunctioning in virtually everyone since early childhood. How could people continue to live in apparent health? Wouldn't medical doctors have discovered this?

The following is a quote from a book on the digestive system written by Eugene S. Jacobson, M.D.:

"The stomach is important to our lives in three main ways: first, it stores food and fluids temporarily, allowing us to eat large meals; second, it secretes the intrinsic factor without which a fatal pernicious anemia may develop; and third, the organ is involved in peptic ulcers, gastric carcinoma and gastritis, bleeding and indigestion. Because of the frequency of these latter disorders, the subject of gastric secretion is of enormous interest. Gastric secretions are also involved in the digestion of food and in bacteriostasis, but such actions of the stomach are not as critical contributions to the body."

This paragraph pretty much sums up the neglect that medicine has given to our poor abused stomach. We might just as well remove this sickly thing surgically and replace it with a garbage bag.

PANCREAS TO THE RESCUE

After the stomach has hopefully churned away and its digestive juices have worked over the mass of food, the food finally passes through the pyloric valve and into the duodenum, which is the beginning of the intestinal tract. The duodenum is about ten inches long. A small duct enters it just below the stomach. This duct brings alkaline bile from the liver and gallbladder to help emulsify fats and lubricate the intestine, and also large quantities of alkaline enzymes from the pancreas. These digestive enzymes from the pancreas can digest carbohydrates, proteins and fats.

The pancreas is thus the cleanup hitter of the digestive system. What the mouth and the stomach have failed to digest, the pancreatic enzymes will readily finish. It is this group of digestive enzymes that most of us are relying on for the bulk of our digestion, as the stomach is not contributing as much as it should. Not chewing carbohydrates thoroughly puts even greater stress on the pancreas.

Digestion can, then, go on reasonably well without proper stomach function, due to the pancreas doing most of the work. However, to stimulate the pancreas and gallbladder to work properly, the stomach juice and stomach activity are important.

Does it matter if the pancreas does the digestion rather than the mouth and stomach? What difference does it make if protein is digested by the alkaline pancreatic juices or the stomach acid?

There are two important differences. There is slower digestion because the food gets bogged down in the stomach, and there is less complete digestion. These two factors are the root causes of the smothering of the healing process, and thus the beginning of disease. When the digestion is quickened and made more complete, the body immediately reactivates its healing powers.

PATIENTS' LETTERS

My daughter Heather, age 11, first had unexplained illnesses when she was 9. The stomach aches and migraine headaches kept her home from school often in October of 1985. Then she got the chicken pox in November. That went away, but she still had the stomach aches and migraines, and then also neck and shoulder pain. In January, she began to have ringing and pain in her ear, as well as hearing loss. Up to this point the doctors had her in for X-rays, Ultra Sound and blood tests, and she was on Tylenol Extra Strength, Tylenol 3, and Ergomar (to constrict cranial blood vessels). The Ear, Nose and Throat doctor ordered a Catscan, thinking she could have a cyst on the nerve to the eardrum. All tests showed that there was nothing wrong with her, but she felt worse than ever. Our G.P. started her on massage therapy for "stress". That did nothing for her. A physiotherapist said that the chicken pox virus had never left, and her treatments relieved much of the pain.

In February, Heather got strep throat, for which another antibiotic was prescribed. Four days later she could not see out of her left eye. Our doctor's office was tired of seeing us by now and very rudely told us the doctor was too busy to see Heather. She then had an allergic reaction to the antibiotic. We then insisted that our G.P. send her to an allergist. The stomach aches and migraines continued until the allergist sorted out her problems with mold, mildew, dust, and the sun. Sudden changes of temperature, such as being hot and diving into the pool, were found to trigger the migraine headaches.

Up to this point Heather had been to three G.P.'s, one allergist, two pediatricians, two Ear, Nose and Throat specialists, one physiotherapist, one massage therapist and two chiropractors. She had the above-mentioned tests and many prescription drugs. Over the sum-

mer she had to quit the swim club because of the migraines and now, breathing problems when swimming. Last fall our new family doctor took her off milk. She was better but not great. In January this year she only made it to school four days. First there was an ear infection (two antibiotics), then the flu, then tonsillitis (another antibiotic).

In February, I decided to take a different route. I had no idea what a Naturopath did, but a friend recommended Dr. Jonn Matsen. Heather started to improve about two weeks after her first visit to him. She looks so healthy now and feels fantastic. She said a few weeks ago that she had no idea that people could feel as well as she does now. She thought that everyone had aches and pains all the time but that they just didn't say anything. She thought it was normal to feel a pain in her head or her stomach and feel generally not well. She only complained when she really felt awful. We are all delighted to have Heather smiling and happy now. No more doctors, antibiotics, or endless days in bed for her. Her allergies have nearly all disappeared and she is back at swim club. She is now enjoying life without drugs and is very happy. Thank you, Dr. Matsen.

> Elaine Reid
> North Vancouver, B.C.

For almost three years I had no health. I was tired, helpless with extreme digestive spasm, unbearable migraine headaches, sleeplessness, and no strength. My doctor sent me to nerve specialists and others but after many tests they could find nothing wrong with me.

I was told by someone to see the Naturopath who is Dr. Matsen. I came to see him and was told to go on a certain diet and some herbs and some hydrotherapy treatments.

I started his treatments but my pain was still so severe and spread to my chest so that I was afraid that I was having a heart attack. I went back to my Medical Doctor and he sent me to a heart specialist and after tests he said there was nothing wrong with me. My doctor finally said that I shouldn't see him so often as the Medical Plan had spent over fifteen thousand dollars on specialists and diagnostic test *and they thought I was abusing the system. Yet nothing at all had been done for me. I was just as sick and miserable.*

I went back to see Dr. Matsen and after an exam he told me my new chest pain was not from my heart but from a rib that was out of place and sent me to a chiropractor, Dr. Robson, whom I also began to see.

Dr. Matsen did something to my stomach with an instrument he has and after the first hydrotherapy there was not much improvement. The second day he said "tonight you will sleep." Well, before this I had been awake continuously for months with unbearable migraines but that night I slept and have slept well since. And the headaches have gone from the diet and and the chest pain is gone from the chiropractor and I have my strength back and have lost weight and have nearly completely recovered my health so I am thanking these two doctors Dr. Matsen, the Naturopath, and Dr. Robson the Chiropractor.

May God bless their hands always as they are now.

S.P.
North Vancouver, B.C.

CHAPTER 2

The Intestines

The food moves down the duodenum into the rest of the small intestine, which is twenty feet long and lies in the middle of the abdomen in coils. The walls of the small intestine secrete further alkaline digestive enzymes which continue the breaking down of

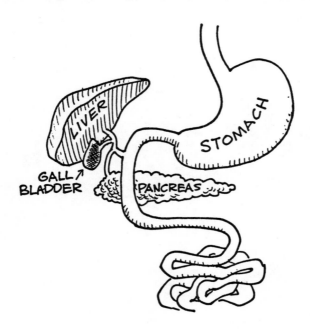

proteins into amino acids, of the long fatty chains into fatty acids, and of the starches and complex sugars into glucose.

The inner surface of the small intestine is covered with millions of tiny villi which dramatically increase the surface area of the small intestine. Like palm trees waving in the breeze, they are constantly moving, "sucking" up the small digested food particles. Each villus

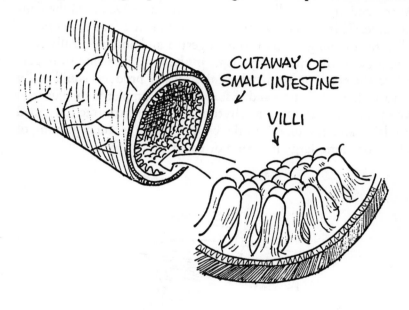

CUTAWAY OF SMALL INTESTINE

VILLI

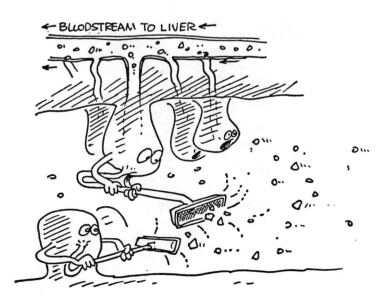

← BLOODSTREAM TO LIVER ←

has lymph vessels which pick up fat, and veins which pick up the other digested nutrients. The veins gradually join together until they form one large vein called the portal vein, which goes directly to the liver. The fat is picked up by the lymph system instead of by the portal vein, because too much fat interferes with both liver and red blood cell function.

At the end of the small intestine is a circular valve called the ileocecal valve. This is usually kept closed so that the food stays in the small intestine long enough to be digested and absorbed fully, and also to prevent the micro-organisms in the large intestine from getting into the small intestine where their waste products could easily be absorbed. As digestion and absorption are completed the ileocecal valve opens and the smooth, rhythmic waves of contraction called peristalsis move the food into the cecum, which is the beginning of the five-foot-long large intestine or colon.

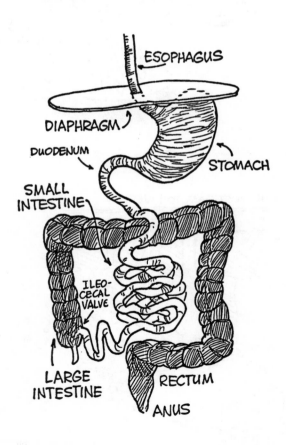

INTESTINAL FLORA

The large intestine isn't a sterile place. There are over four hundred different types of micro-organisms found there which together are called the intestinal flora. Most of them are our little friends, important aids to the digestive process. They make B-vitamins for us. They make lactic acid, which improves digestion of foods and increases absorption, as well as aiding peristalsis of the intestine. They make vitamin K, which aids in blood clotting. They make chemicals which are healing to the large intestine, and their secretions hinder the "bad guys". After they die they still help us because their bodies provide much of the bulk of a stool. There is much more to be learned about the benefits of our "little buddies".

Since it has billions of micro-organisms in residence whose waste products might inadvertently get absorbed into the portal vein, the large intestine doesn't absorb as actively as the small intestine.

When the food enters the cecum it is liquid. It gets squeezed up and down the ascending colon by peristalsis a few times, and as it moves along the transverse colon liquid is extracted. By the time it is in the descending colon, it is beginning to get the harder consistency of a stool.

"Patients with hypochlorhydria (low stomach acid) have higher bacterial counts and anaerobes(bacteriodes) and coliforms not usually found in the normal stomach." (Human Intestinal Microflora in

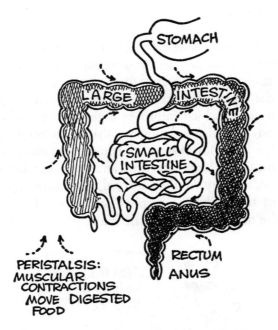

PERISTALSIS:
MUSCULAR
CONTRACTIONS
MOVE DIGESTED
FOOD

Health and Disease, 1983). So we see that if the stomach doesn't work properly, there will be micro-organisms from the large intestine getting into the stomach and small intestine, rather than just in the large intestine where they belong.

While poor digestion leads to the spread of flora, other influences can lead to imbalances of the types of intestinal flora. Quoting further from the same source:

"There is convincing evidence that the indigenous intestinal flora provide natural protection against infection by a number of pathogenic bacteria. The protective mechanism is impaired, however, when antimicrobial agents are administered. Antibiotics frequently produce profound changes in the composition of the human intestinal microflora, permitting overgrowth of resistant endogenous bacteria or colonization by exogenous organisms acquired from the environment. Once resistance is reduced by antibiotic administration, even a small number of pathogenic organisms can produce serious infections in the host. Clearly, the integrity of the intestinal flora is important to the well-being of the host, and antibiotics, which upset it, should be used with extreme caution".

Chlorine is added to drinking water to kill bacteria. Does it also affect the intestinal flora? What about the thousands of other chemcals that have found their way into the food chain? Someday we will know their effect on humans, but right now we're guinea pigs. It may turn out that our long-range ability to resist these chemicals will be in direct proportion to the resistance of our intestinal bacteria.

YEASTIES AND OTHER BEASTIES

Controversy has raged within conventional medicine over Candida yeast. One school of thought says that conventional medical treatment involving medications and ignoring lifestyle has resulted in Candida yeast overgrowths in the great majority of the population. Yeast toxins can cause virtually any disease anywhere in the body. This view has been met with contempt by most of the mainstream practitioners, who ignore the volumes of evidence (see the books The Yeast Connection, Back to Health and The Yeast Syndrome) and who keep practising the same way they learned in medical school.

My clinical experience verifies that of the yeast-oriented school of thought, and perhaps the extent of the problem is even under estimated. Virtually every patient I've had has benefited to some degree from using yeast killers. This would indicate clearly to me that every one of us has an overgrowth of yeast, whether or not it is active enough to cause symptoms or to show on conventional tests.

While drugs and refined modern foods are now blamed as the major causes of the yeast problem, I find that that isn't so. Drugs and refined foods have greatly contributed to the problem, but they are of recent origin. The underlying problem goes back thousands of years. Faulty digestion is the true cause. If you don't digest your food quickly some micro-organism will digest it for you, making toxins. Antibiotics and refined foods have just recently given yeast an advantage over many of the other toxin-producing micro-organisms.

However, while yeast is presently in the limelight, it is important to remember that it isn't alone. There are hundreds of other critters with them that can make toxins, and even "good" bacteria can make toxins under certain conditions. The purpose of this book is to help you avoid these conditions. With a little understanding of how digestion works, digestion can be quickly improved and then the yeast can readily be gotten rid of permanently.

When you put slow digestion together with hungry critters you've got problems. Would you leave food lying around in a dark, damp, warm germ-infested tube for a day or more? Not if you're smart. The nasty little guys would gladly digest anything that you're slow to digest. To add insult to injury, they spew their excretions out into your intestine. They make at least seventy-eight different types of toxins. Skatols, indols, phenols, alcohol, ammonia, acetaldehyde, even formaldehyde are a few of them.

These toxins can prevent good bacteria from returning, and can provide a comfortably toxic environment that invites any other bad

guys to come on down and make themselves at home. That's another reason why we're so vulnerable when we go to the tropics. Not only do we not have the stomach juices to kill off the organisms in food, but when the organisms get into the intestine they are met with welcoming arms by our already-well-established co-hosts, the toxin-producing flora.

Many people have accumulated an assortment of intestinal critters that would make the bar scene in Star Wars look tame in comparison. Bad bacteria abound and yeast has risen high in the popularity charts. Giardia, Campylobacter, Amoebas and Yersinia are not members of the Mafia but they are members of the intestinal mob that can disrupt the peace in your intestine. Some people even pick up larger organisms such as worms, or have provided such a comfortable environment for the yeast that they can become extremely noxious fungi. You seldom find just one type of bad guy, as they provide co-operative housing for the whole nasty family. It's not that hard to get rid of them, if you get the stomach working first. If you don't, they just keep coming back again and again virtually as fast as you can kill them off.

Often associated with fermentation and putrefaction toxins are large quantities of gas. Bloating, burping, belching and flatulence are familiar signs that the little guys are blowing bubbles. For some people the formation of toxins is a quieter process, with few of the bubbly risings.

Still, as long as there are nasty hitchhikers within us, and as long as they are well-fed, the formation of toxins goes on. If the mem-

brane of the intestine gets irritated, it may secrete more mucous as
protection against the irritants. This can eventually create a thick
coat on the membrane, which will reduce the absorption of toxins.
Of course the absorption of nutrients will be reduced as well.

If the intestine gets even more irritated, inflammation will ensue.
Inflammation is one of the body's standard reactions to irritation. It
basically consists of sending more blood to the area, to flush away
the irritants and to increase the supply of nutrients and white blood
cells to speed healing. If the irritants are being produced faster than
the blood can remove them, the inflammation can become chronic.

Diseases of inflammation are usually named with the suffix-itis.
So inflammation of the colon is called colitis. If the inflammation is
in the sinuses it's called sinusitis; if it's in the bronchials it's called
bronchitis; and if it's in the joints it's called arthritis. However,
since the irritants are in the blood, the whole body is being subjected
to irritation. It is just the weaker links that are manifesting symptoms.

During inflammation, the "pores" of the intestine can become enlarged. This is called porous bowel syndrome. The enlarged pores allow the large incompletely-digested protein chunks we talked about
previously to be absorbed into the blood. This can be a major factor
in the triggering of allergies.

The standard treatments for inflammation are antibiotics if there is a bacterial infection behind them, or anti-inflammatory drugs if the irritant cause is of more mysterious origin. The strongest anti-inflammatory drug is cortisone. Cortisone often stops inflammation, but remember that inflammation is the body's natural reaction to irritation. So once you've stopped the body's natural reaction to irritation, have you stopped the irritants? Not usually. Going off the anti-inflammatories usually results in a return of the inflammation.

As we have have recently learned, antibiotics and cortisone are now believed to suppress the proper intestinal flora, so it looks like the medical profession is creating its own business by turning short-term suppression of inflammation into chronic disease. Obviously, antibiotics and anti-inflammatories belong in Emergency Medicine rather than General Practise.

Since antibiotics and anti-inflammatories are among the keystones of medicine, how can one even consider doing without them? Well, how about enabling the body's own immune system to work better, and how about stopping the cause of the inflammation?

An irritated intestine will often develop diarrhea as an attempt to flush out the irritants. Constipation is a common result of poor diet, digestion and intestine function. Treating only one of these factors usually gives only a partial improvement. Of course, the more constipated a person is, the more time for the "bad guys down-stairs" to do their nasty work, and the more time for their toxins to be absorbed into the bloodstream.

While the intestinal flora are confined to the intestine in a healthy person, "Debilitated patients ... are especially prone to infections caused by bacteria of their own indigenous flora. Immunosuppressive chemotherapy and oral antibiotic treatment synergistically promote the translocation of certain indigenous bacteria from the G.I. tract." This quote from Human Microflora in Health and Disease tells us that even the good little guys can become the bad guys if things get really tough down in the digestive tract.

I find not only that nearly everyone's stomach is underfunctioning due to chronic dietary irritation, but also that nearly everyone's
intestinal flora are imbalanced, overgrown with "the bad guys".

These critters of malcontent have sometimes spread from the
large intestine into the small intestine, and even into the stomach.
In more severe cases they may actually get out of the intestinal tract
and affect any part of the body. They throw what amounts to "a
great party", and you're their host and benefactor.

Virtually everyone has an overstressed, underfunctioning digestive system, imbalanced intestinal flora, and a steady load of intestinal toxins seeping into the bloodstream. So what's the difference between someone who has actual "disease" symptoms and
someone who can still eat anything without noticeable ill effects?
The difference has a lot to do with the liver and gallbladder.

PATIENTS' LETTERS

*I had had over a year of pain, diarrhea and blood in my stool
which my G.P. (an M.D.) did not succeed in diagnosing. She re-*

ferred me for a G.I. examination, and this, too, revealed nothing of value. Next, I went to a prevention oriented medical doctor who had my stool cultured for infection, and Yersinia was discovered. He told me that there were no reliably successful drugs to treat this condition.

I went to Dr. Matsen with the encouragement of my Medical Doctor. After an intensive naturopathic regime of dietary changes, naturopathic medications, self-applied acupressure and a course of hydrotherapy treatments, I was completely free of symptoms and there was no blood in my stool. My Medical Doctor was as delighted as I when, after a later follow-up stool culture, I remained free of this infection.

> *Sue Tauber*
> *Vancouver, B.C.*

In the spring of '84, being averse to suggested diagnosis and treatment of the allopathic method for a suspected colonic polyp, I went to see Dr. Matsen.

After one month of his dietary system my painful abdominal gas had almost disappeared. Within six months my blood pressure was normal and the "bulge" I'd battled hopelessly for fifty years was disappearing. All this and I was eating more of the foods I had been avoiding because they were considered fattening. The diet and supplements have given me two and a half great years and I look forward to many more.

> *Gratefully-*
> *A. M. Fraser*
> *Vancouver, B.C.*

The Liver, Gallbladder and Kidneys

T he blood from the intestinal tract, with its rich and varied load of nutrients, toxins, chunks and possibly good/bad flora goes directly to the liver, via the funneled-down blood supply called the portal vein.

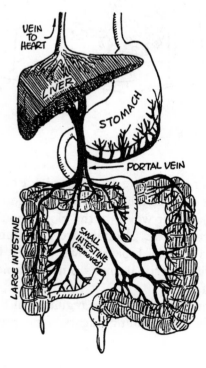

The liver is firstly a massive filter, the major filter of the blood stream. It screens everything in the blood entering it. Most toxins are immediately set upon by liver cells in order to de-activate them. The difference between a person with symptoms and one without is often related to whether the liver can handle intestinal toxins and still have enough capacity left to do its other jobs.

The liver is not only the detoxifier of poisons of intestinal origin. Heavy metals such as aluminum, copper, lead, mercury, and cadmium that find their way into the blood should be de-activated by the liver. Coffee toxins, alcohol, nicotine, drugs, pesticides, and additives should also be broken down quickly by the liver. A liver overloaded with intestinal toxins is more vulnerable to the cumulative effects of these.

In effect the liver is the main regulator of the blood. It regulates contents of blood including sugars, fats, protein and hormones,

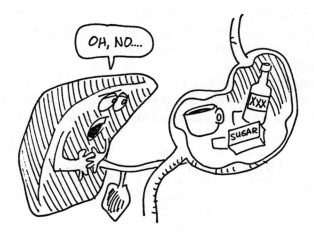

which are messengers from other parts of the body. Many of the symptoms of disease are a result of the liver being unable to regulate properly due to an overload of toxins, many of which come from fermentation or putrefaction in the intestines.

The liver regulates the blood sugar level, along with the pancreas and the adrenal glands. Glucose sugar in the blood is the common fuel for all the cells. While some parts of the body can turn proteins or fats into glucose, the brain's only fuel is from the blood glucose, so it is especially important for the brain to have the proper amount of blood glucose. If there is too little sugar in the blood, and the brain doesn't get enough nutrition, symptoms of lightheadness, anxiety, panic, weakness, dizziness, even fainting can occur. This is called hypoglycemia. Fainting is the body's way of laying the body horizontal so blood can flow into the brain without fighting against gravity, thus taking more sugar and/or oxygen to the brain.

If the sugar level gets too low, the adrenal glands secrete hormones, which stimulate the liver to release glycogen (dried glucose) from storage (add water and stir), releasing glucose into the blood. Since too much sugar in the blood can cause numerous problems (diabetes), the pancreas secretes insulin to tell the liver to remove glucose from the blood (wring the water out) and to store it as glycogen.

The regulation of the blood sugar level should be so smooth that we can go several days without eating and still not experience any major symptoms of high or low blood sugar levels. However, the brain tends to function a little better at a higher blood sugar level. We feel a little better when the glucose level is at a high level. Our

"high society" has found a number of favourite ways of forcing up the blood sugar levels.

Refined sugar, coffee, tobacco, tea, chocolate, alcohol, drugs, and emotional excitement can raise the blood-sugar levels and help us to feel good. The problem is that the pancreas and liver will immediately try to decrease the sugar to a safer level. The resultant drop in blood sugar results in a craving for more sweets, coffee, alcohol, cigarettes, drugs or emotional tirades.

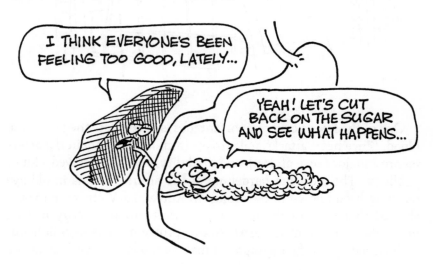

An interesting example of the relationship between these is seen at some Alcoholics Anonymous meetings, where the deleterious effects of alcohol may have been replaced with tremendous use of other stimulants such as coffee, sugar and tobacco, which may not have as bad an effect on the emotions but can be equally destructive physically.

This roller-coaster effect puts an incredible stress on the triad of pancreas, liver and adrenals, and eventually they can break down under the strain. In addition, if the liver is bogged down with an overload of intestinal toxins, its ability to regulate blood sugar can be greatly affected.

One of the liver's other important jobs is to regulate the fats in the blood. Since heart attacks and strokes from fat build-up in the arteries are a major cause of death and disability, this has received a lot of publicity. The idea that hardening of the arteries begins in old age has long been known to be wrong. In Korea and Vietnam autopsies showed that most of the teenage American troops already had fat lining the arteries to the heart, so this problem starts in childhood. Unfortunately the first symptoms may be too late a warning, as the problem usually isn't detectable until the arteries are considerably blocked.

While fats in the diet have received a lot of bad press, the major overlooked cause of fat problems is actually inadequate liver and gallbladder function. The liver and gallbladder regulate blood fat levels. When these organs are rendered sluggish by intestinal toxins, they don't regulate adequately. This is the single most important cause of high blood fat levels.

An unexpected clinical finding is that some vegetarians have actually developed chronic infections from a deficiency of cholesterol. A certain amount of cholesterol appears necessary to manufacture hormones that are essential for regulation of homeostasis.

Another of the liver's jobs is the regulation of blood-protein levels. If the protein levels are too low, the liver assembles protein "trains" from the various amino acid "cars" and dumps them into the main blood stream for distribution throughout the body. If the liver doesn't make protein properly, wasting of muscle is the most obvious sign.

The last of the main substances that the liver regulates is hormones. Hormones are messengers secreted by glands which travel through the blood to tell cells what they should be doing, to help maintain smooth functioning of all the cells together. Thus hor-

mones are important to help coordinate body homeostasis. If the hormones were allowed to keep circulating indefinitely, their messages would become out-of-date. Therefore, the hormones have to be broken down regularly. Since the liver filters all the blood in the body, it is the appropriate organ to break down most of these messengers. Poor liver function can result in sluggish hormone breakdown. Since the hormones then circulate through the blood system an extra time or two, they stimulate the cells longer than they should, disturbing homeostasis.

An obvious example of this is seen in men whose livers were damaged by drugs and who then developed breasts. It is also seen commonly in pubescent boys whose livers may not be damaged, but whose liver function is affected enough that the increase in hormones causes breast enlargement. The signs of hormonal imbalance are seen especially in women. The bloating, breast tenderness and mood changes of premenstrual syndrome (PMS) are symptoms that usually vanish quickly with improved liver function. Irregular menstrual cycles and menstrual cramps can sometimes be eliminated if proper liver function can be attained.

THE LIVER AS METABOLIC DIRECTOR

"Doctor, I'm so tired." That is the complaint a naturopathic physician hears most frequently. Fatigue is very common.

If we look at the liver as being a powerhouse, we will realize that we can only throw sand in it for only so long before the energy output decreases. While there are many causes of fatigue, the factor that leads to improved energy the quickest and most reliably is improved liver function. Decreasing the intestinal-toxin load on the liver usually allows it to quickly spring back to life, with a resultant increase in energy.

The metabolic rate has long been known to be regulated by the hormones from the thyroid gland, and synthetic thyroid hormone is commonly used to replace that not produced by a sluggish thyroid. Some popular books would have you believe that half the population

MY COMPLIMENTS TO YOUR LIVER AND GALL BLADDER!

have a genetically weak thyroid that requires us to take synthetic thyroid hormone the rest of our lives. However, since the liver is the main regulator of the blood, it is the true key to proper metabolic rate. A sluggish thyroid is often secondary to a long-term sluggish liver. The trick to improving the thyroid permanently is to first improve the liver. To do that, improve digestion.

In the same way that the body knows what temperature it should maintain and the millions of minute steps which must be taken to keep the temperature at that point, the body also knows exactly what weight it should be and how to get there. There is no need to waste your precious brain cells and their low-voltage currents on trying to force your body into your own fashion-forged image of what you should look like. Get the liver and gallbladder working, and exercise regularly and the body will magically mold itself into shapes and forms beyond the limits of your imagination, without mental contortions and wasted effort. You may not look as anorexic as fashion temporarily would like, but your increased vitality will shine through no matter what genetic frame you have. Aim for health, and true beauty and weight control will eventually follow.

MOODINESS

In the same way that the liver regulates physical substances, it also regulates moods. The natural demeanour of a human being is positive, cheerful and stable. When the liver gets fouled up, anything can happen. Depression, pessimism, irritability, and rapid mood fluctuations are keynotes to problems of the liver. Improvement in digestion may relieve the liver of this burden, and the

brightening of personality will follow, especially in children, since they haven't had time to become accustomed to the role of the old grump as so many adults have.

In the same way that the intestinal blood flows to the liver, so does the blood in the veins. If the liver is overloaded, then the blood in the veins tends to back up, causing increased pressure on the walls of the veins. If this increased pressure is combined with weakened vein walls due to poor mineral and/or vitamin absorption, the walls may dilate. Thus liver overload can be expected when vein signs appear, such as varicose veins, hemorrhoids and dark blue bags under the eyes.

Altogether the liver has some five hundred known physical functions.

Though the liver is programmed to perform its multitude of jobs flawlessly, many people have an overloaded, malfunctioning liver. Many of my patients have a number of symptoms, but have just come from routine physical exams, blood tests, ultra sound tests and CAT scans and since nothing has been found they have been told that nothing is wrong with them. They know better, as verified by the more subtle types of energy examination. Most people with a medical symptom are found to have an overloaded liver, and/or gallbladder. Many people without symptoms do as well. The best proof of this is the sometimes dramatic improvement of symptoms as therapy improves liver function, as you will see in Part II.

LIVER TESTS

How could high-tech western medicine have overlooked such a common problem as an overloaded liver? Diagnosis in western medicine is based primarily on tissue conditions. If tissue shows no sign of damage, it's considered to not have a problem. Therefore lab work, X-rays, CAT scans, etc. have been developed to pick up these damaged states. In China, however, for over three thousand years physicians cared little about tissue. Chinese physicians were aware that the energy of an organ would be imbalanced long before the organ itself would show any physical signs of malfunction. They would attempt to maintain energy balances, to prevent damage to the organs. It was considered to be a poor physican who would allow his patient to degenerate to the point that he would develop physical pathology.

The standard screening test for liver problems in western medicine is a blood test that looks for liver enzymes in the blood. Since the enzymes are normally contained within the liver cells, this test will only spot liver trouble after the liver cells have been ruptured, spilling their enzymes into the bloodstream. This is a wonderful test to pick up liver damage, but worthless to pick up early-stage liver overload. Unfortunately for the patient with early-stage functional problems, most doctors ignore their complaints if nothing shows on the standard lab tests.

PATIENTS' LETTERS

I have suffered with high blood pressure for more years than I can remember. I have spent a small fortune on drugs or so-called medications which never seemed to do any good. What I went through would take too long to repeat, so I will just start in January of 1987 when I had another of many severe dizzy spells I have had over the years. As usual I was bed-ridden for two weeks. If I tried to stand I fell and felt as though I was spinning around. After two weeks the dizziness stopped so I started trying to move around and get my strength back. It took me two months before I could take a short walk. My blood pressure was getting higher and higher, so I finally decided enough is enough, no more drugs that did nothing but give me a lot of side effects. I quite honestly thought that this time I was not going to get better.

In desperation or maybe fate, I looked in the "Yellow Pages" under Naturopaths and saw Dr. Matsen's name. I phoned and made an appointment. It was the best thing I have ever done.

I had a blood test, muscle testing, food sensitivity testing and a long talk with the doctor, who explained everything that was happening in my body in a simple way that I could understand. He told me which foods I shouldn't eat, and gave me some botanical remedies and a course of hydrotherapy.

After three days I began to feel better. After one month I felt like a different person. The chronic headaches I had had for years disappeared, along with blurred vision, pains in my legs, back and neck, etc.

My own M.D. couldn't believe it and was horrified at what I was doing, but after the first month of rapidly-decreased blood pressure he wished me well.

I will never be able to thank Dr. Matsen enough for what he has done for me.

I think each and every one of us should be able to choose which type of doctor is best for us and be covered for all treatments by medical insurance.

Alma Crighton
North Vancouver, B.C.

Before I came to see Dr. Jonn Matsen, I had trouble with my legs, especially my left side. Intermittently, they became stiff and weak. I gradually could not walk very far. At one stage, it was so bad that I could hardly make a 100-yard distance. My orthodox doctor could not pinpoint the cause of my complaint, but suspected that I had hardening of the arteries. This diagnosis could not be established until I was willing to go through an angiogram test. To avoid the ordeal of such a process, I decided to consult a naturopathic doctor.

I was strongly recommended by some of my friends to see Dr. Matsen. So I made an appointment on 20 May, 1986 to be at his clinic. On examining me, Dr. Matsen found that I had too much *toxin in my blood and fat from a sluggish liver. I went through a food sensitivity test which revealed sensitivities to certain foods like peanuts, tea, yeast and mushrooms.*

Based on the results of all these tests, he started to treat me stage by stage. First of all, a list of proper food combinations was given to me. I was advised to follow according to the instructions printed therein. At the same time, I underwent a hydrotherapy period. My blood was tested several times as my treament progressed. Dr. Matsen then gave me a course of caprylic acid to be taken for 16 days. This was to get rid of the yeast in my system. On my 11th visit during the first week of July, I was happy to know from the blood test that my system was cleansed of the toxin by 75%.

Ever since I was under Dr. Matsen's care, I have found that my health has improved tremendously. I can walk the normal distance as I used to do before, in fact much better than I expected. Here is an instance that has shown a marked improvement in me. Recently, I resumed my golf game. To my utter astonishment, I could complete a round of 18-hole golf without feeling tired. My legs gave me no trouble at all. Normally, I felt rather exhausted by the time I approached the 8th hole and I had to stop playing after a 9-hole round.

Another very heartening discovery is that my angina pains have more or less disappeared. I used to suffer from chest pains after a meal and also when I climbed long flights of steps. Now it looks that such complaints are something of the past.

With the new life-style which I have adopted through Dr. Matsen's guidance, I am now enjoying a newfound vibrant energy.

> *Diana Ng*
> *North Vancouver, B.C.*

THE GALLBLADDER

The liver filters and neutralizes the toxins, before concentrating them into bile. If bile is needed immediately in the small intestine to help emulsify fat, it is secreted from the liver through the bile ducts into the duodenum, just below the stomach. Bile also helps lubricate the intestine and gives the stool a golden color. Lack of bile gives the stool a light or clay color. If surplus bile is made it is shunted into the gallbladder, where storage turns it a darker color.

The conventional surgical viewpoint is that the gallbladder is as disposable as the tonsils and appendix were once thought to be. That is simply not so. My observations, based on clinical experience, tell me that good quality bile from the liver and gallbladder is of extreme importance to health.

However, to show that research is finally catching up with common sense I include the following quote:

"The yellow pigment in bile that causes the characteristic yellowing of jaundice sufferers may not be simply a body waste after all, scientists say. Bilirubin, long thought to have no value, may be beneficial in thwarting cancer, aging, inflammation and other health problems, researchers from the Berkeley and San Francisco campuses of the University of California have found. The researchers say bilirubin appears to be a powerful antagonist of oxygen compounds that play a role in numerous diseases and conditions. Roland Stocker, the lead investigator in the study, said the results indicate scientists should examine other wastes from chemical processes in the body to see if they also have other functions. Reporting in the most recent issue of Science, Stocker and his associates said in test-tube studies, bilirubin acted much like ant-oxidants vitamin C and E, neutralizing so-called oxygen radical compounds that destroy beneficial vitamin A and linoleic acid, a common fatty acid that is a major component of cell membranes. 'Instead of spending 95% of our time developing means to get rid of bilirubin, we should spend time on possible beneficial roles of bilirubin,' Stocker said." (Vancouver Sun, March 7, 1987). "Human Intestinal Flora in Health and Disease," speculates, "Secondary bile acids may very well be responsible for protection against a variety of enteric (intestinal) infections."

The two most important things to remember from this article are the effects of bilirubin on free radical oxygen compounds and on fatty acids. For decades western medicine has overlooked the obvious connection between lifestyle and disease, in the same way that primitive tribes couldn't see the connection between sex and babies. They seemed too remote and separated to be connected. However, the two most important missing links between diet and disease have been found recently. They are free radicals and prostaglandins.

Gallbladder problems start when the liver is so overloaded with intestinal toxins that they get dumped into the duodenum or gallbladder before they are fully neutralized. These toxins, if left simmering in the gallbladder, can cause so much irritation that the gallbladder begins to malfunction. If the gallbladder doesn't secrete bile properly, the fats and minerals in the bile can become stones. The most common symptom associated with gallbladder trouble is feeling worse after eating fatty foods.

If toxic bile is secreted from either the liver or gallbladder into the intestine, it can cause aggravation throughout the gastro-intestinal tract. The already "shocked" stomach can get even more aggravated. Many people who think they have stomach problems or duodenal ulcers may actually get these symptoms from toxic bile, which creates "hot" spots.

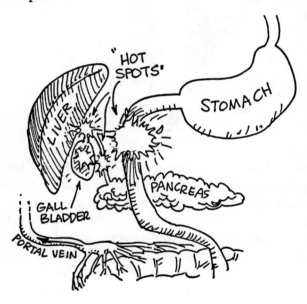

The majority of heart problems are caused by gallbladder trouble. Low-cholesterol diets have missed the boat as the body can make cholesterol even faster than it can extract it from food. When the liver and gallbladder are improved they can control the blood fat levels as they were designed to do. The best way to regain liver and gallbladder function is to stop overloading them with toxins.

Reference to an acupuncture clock shows that it is the gallbladder meridan that controls the heart meridan. It also plays an important role in immunity, by its impact on fat absorption and resultant effect on membrane strength, which is important for cell defense.

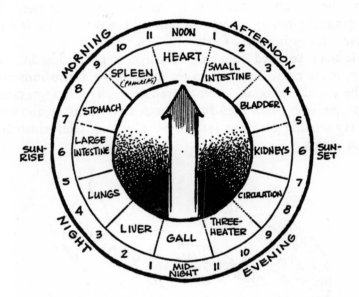

When you understand the acupuncture meridians you realize that the toxic gallbladder is often the cause of migraines, chronic neck problems, some knee problems and most skin problems.

The liver can be overloaded whether or not there are symptoms. Once the liver's capacity to detoxify is overwhelmed, toxins can spill past the liver into the main bloodstream. There are even some intestinal toxins that the liver is incapable of filtering, which get into the main bloodstream regardless of the function of the liver.

Once the toxins are in the main bloodstream the kidneys are the only filters left that can de-activate them. The kidneys, however, aren't well-suited to this task. Irritation throughout the kidneys, bladder and urethra may occur. This irritation can make the urinary tract more prone to infection. Also, interference with the kidney's normal functions such as regulation of fluids and minerals may occur, resulting in fluid retention and/or mineral deficiencies, or crystalization of minerals into stones.

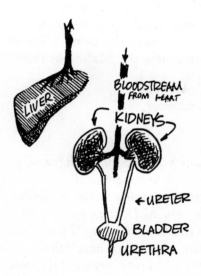

PATIENTS' LETTERS

My difficulties started in 1970. They began with inability to hold urine, which resulted in excruciating restlessness and anxiety. This caused such insomnia that I became a dopey wreck.

Urine tests showed nothing. I went back to England. Seven times they stretched my bladder. I was admitted to the emergency room for catheterization. They took kidney X-rays and repeatedly gave me antibiotics for bladder infections. I became a nervous, irrational wreck. The best doctors in Toronto, Crewe and Chester, could do nothing except recommend I take a two-year vacation. I was put on Valium, to no avail.

I remember lying in my bed looking out my window thinking that I have been ill for fifteen years. I coped, I existed but I couldn't carry on like this for another fifteen years.

When I visited Dr. Matsen, he checked me over and gave me a diet sheet indicating things I was to avoid. He also gave me some supplements which really stirred my system up. I felt rotten but not pathetic and indeed didn't get out of bed for five days. When I returned to him he gave me a homeopathic medicine which helped right away. After six months on his diet and some herbs and supplements, I sleep like a log and wake up a new person every morning.

My bladder is only a problem if I go too far off my diet. I have lost thirty-five pounds and I look good and feel wonderful.

Tell me, what are all the people in this world today who suffer the way I did, going to do without a Dr. Matsen of their own?

Hilary C. Venecek
North Vancouver, B.C.

I want to write and thank you so very much for all you have done to help me find the way back to good health.

In May I suddenly started retaining fluids and within two weeks I put on thirty-six pounds. My M.D. who put me on several water pills, which did not help the fluid build-up. I was finally diagnosed as having nephrotic syndrome and was hospitalized. After a kidney biopsy, a specialist told me I had focal segmental glomerulosclerosis and that nothing could be done but that he would monitor the protein loss in the urine and check for further deterioration.

Another person you helped recommended that I see you. After your testing, diet, supplements and hydrotherapy treatments I very soon began to feel better. The protein loss went from very high to minimal within three weeks. I was no longer retaining fluids.

I am now even slightly below my normal weight and I feel just great, full of energy again and living a very normal life.

Christian J. Resch
Surrey, B.C.

CHAPTER 4

Blood and Lymph

Once past the kidneys, there is little to prevent the toxins from circulating through the entire bloodstream, irritating the membranes of every single cell in the body. These toxins act upon the whole body, but manifest as disease wherever a person has his or her weakest link. The weakness may be caused by genetic make-up, accident or injury, nutritional deficiencies, physical or emotional stress, or psychological troubles. A person with a minor genetic weakness may develop noticeable symptons only after years of toxins aggravating that weak area.

A person with mineral deficiencies may get degeneration of the intervertebral discs, as the discs are softer and therefore more prone to erosion when deficient in manganese, cobalt, calcium and other minerals. The discs under the most physical wear and tear will likely be affected first. If there was a whiplash, that area might be the most susceptible to degeneration.

A person who is vulnerable to skin trouble due to poor fat absorption may develop eczema, as the toxins "eat their way" through the weakened skin from the bloodstream. Exposure to detegents may be blamed as the cause, but this is simply something that further weakens the skin so that the toxins "leak out". The main problem is with the blood, not with the external agent.

Another person, after years of heavy physical labour, may develope osteoarthritis as the toxins make the wear-worn joints more vulnerable to erosion.

A person with a stressed nervous system may develop a nervous disease.

A person with high blood fat and hormonal imbalance due to sluggish liver and gallbladder may develop acne.

Membranes secrete extra mucous to protect themselves from the constant irritation. If this mucous isn't drained off quickly, it can cause congestion and further aggravate poor circulation in the effected area.

Any area with decreased circulation of blood and the nutrients it should be carrying is prone to developing problems, especially if the waste removal from the area is also sluggish.

Chronic irritation makes an area hypersensitive, causing it to

react against things that normally shouldn't bother it, such as pollen, dust, feathers, furs, and certain foods. The hypersensitive area may be the nose, the lungs, or the sinuses.

In any sensitive-membrane disease, the membrane of the large intestine was irritated long before the problem manifested elsewhere. It is difficult or impossible to truly heal such problems without first correcting the intestinal problems. If digestion is improved, detoxification leads to desensitization.

Since the stomach itself is aggravated by these toxins in the blood, it too can become hypersensitive. We found earlier that the stomach is in "shock" from dietary abuse beginning in early childhood.

We also found that the stomach can be aggravated by toxic bile. Now, as the stomach becomes even more sensitive, it can react to a large number of things. Even foods that would never be suspected of being harmful to a person can aggravate the already weak digestion. The result is slower digestion, increased growth of the intestinal bad guys, more fermentation and putrefaction toxins, more liver overload and increased sensitivity. The problem becomes a vicious cycle, which can get even worse.

In my practise I use a simple blood test called the HLB test. A few drops of blood are taken on a slide so that they are one cell-layer thick. As the blood dries, the fibrin forms a net-like pattern. If there are substantial quantities of free radicals in the blood, they will tear holes in the fibrin net as the blood dries. Under microscopic magnification (200 magnification) these holes can be readily observed. Since these free-radicals are in the main blood stream, they subject every cell in the body to the same irritation that the fibrin net is receiving. This test can thus be used as a general indicator of systemic free-radical activity, though it cannot be used to diagnose any particular disease or a problem that is localized to one area and therefore not affecting the entire blood stream.

An interesting new technological addition to this test was demonstrated recently. Instead of the 200 magnification, new equipment boosted the magnification up to 6800 power. What is seen then in the blood is that the little critters that we once thought were only in the intestine are also in the bloodstream. Small "buds" of yeast are seen in almost everyone. Many people also have L-form bacteria, fungi and mycoforms. One lady, apparently in good health, actually had worms in her blood. The white blood-cell activity can also be seen and of course the more active this is, the less numerous the critters.

We truly are living in a sea of micro-organisms. A balance is in play between our immune system and these organisms, and a person with an active immune system has little to fear from these little guys. Infection is a word that must be used cautiously because many of these organisms are already found within us. An overgrowth is more of an indication of our own weakened state than a sign that these small creatures have any great powers of destruction. Many of these guys are nature's recyclers. When we are done with our bodies they convert us to plant food so that the cycle of life can continue. Unfortunately, by weakening our vitality with poor diet and faulty digestion and absorption of toxins, we weaken our immune system so the critters think we're finished with our bodies and begin the composting process before we think we're done.

Improved diet, digestion and absorption usually result in quick improvement in the blood pictures. As free-radical levels decrease, consequent improvement in disease signs and symptoms usually soon follows.

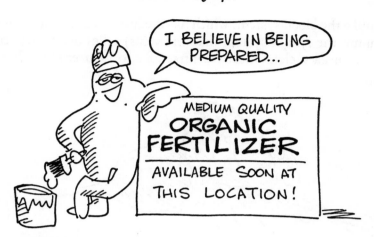

THE LYMPH SYSTEM

Much of the toxicity gets drained away through the lymphatic system. Waste drainage is so important to cell health that the lymph system is three or four times larger than the blood system. Unfortunately, it is designed to handle only cell wastes. When the blood is also dumping toxins from the intestinal tract into the lymph system via the overloaded liver, the lymph system can get overloaded too.

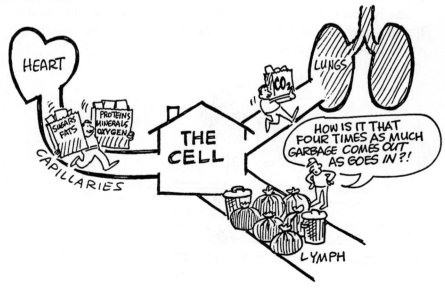

Unlike the blood system, which has the heart as a consistent built-in pump, the lymph system (like the veins) relies on the less consistently used skeletal muscle contractions to "squeeze" the lymph along.

Lack of exercise can greatly aggravate lymph overload. This sluggish lymph drainage is most commonly felt in the throat area because the lymph is closest to the surface there, but it is actually most overwhelmed in the large intestine area. Of course this is because the large intestine is where the critters are having the main party, and their "spilled drinks" are overwhelming the drain.

The lymph system is also the home turf of the immune system. Tonsils, adenoids and lymph nodes are fortresses in the lymph where the immune system attacks any invaders.

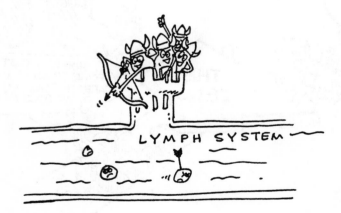

Large chunks of poorly-digested protein can be mistaken by the immune system invaders. This false alarm can result in an overly-reactive immune system which may cause allergic reactions. Overloading these lymph glands results in swelling. Enlargement of the lymph glands in the throat can block the drainage from the middle ear via the eustachian tube, since this tube enters the throat near the tonsils. The resulting congestion of the ear can lead to decreased hearing, ruptured ear membranes or ear infections.

Most people are afraid of infections, whether viral, bacterial, yeast or fungal. If the truth is known, very few of these organisms could be called contagious. Even in an epidemic it's usually only a small portion of the population that gets the disease, and an even smaller portion that succumbs to it. Most of the victims also suffer from obvious sanitation or nutritional problems, or weakened immunity due to old age, drug use, severe emotional stress or severe disease already existing. Many of the germs that people fear most have such delicate life cycles that it is only with the greatest difficulty that they can even be grown.

MEET YOUR DEFENDERS: THE WHITE BLOOD CELLS

There are monsters found in the body far more hideous and destructive than any known virus or bacteria. They lumber through the blood-stream engulfing and eating anything they don't like. They shoot bullets containing powerful toxins that can rip apart the membranes of anything that dares get in their way. They send powerful signals that invite their cronies to come scurrying to join the feast. They multiply in a day from a few to tens of thousands. They actually change shape to slip through gaps between cells so that they can attack from all sides. They have little mercy for their enemies.

Fortunately, they're on your side. They are the White Blood Cells, your defenders. They have such an amazing bag of tricks, and such overwhelming tenacity that no germ can withstand a pitched battle with these phagocytes, B-cells and T-cells, when they are in prime fighting condition.

There are trillions of these little heroes, the White Blood Cells, in your body. They have the ability to recognize what is you and what isn't and they attack with incredible ferocity.

The first on the scene is usually the macrophage, which resembles a bouncer at a late-night club: big and tough and afraid of nothing. Bacteria are eliminated as easily as you would step on an ant. Macrophages easily gulp down micro-organisms unfortunate enough to fall within their long grasp and are digested by strong enzymes. Macrophages "scalp" their victims and display this "germ skin" like a medal. This excites the Helper T-cells who run around excitedly like Olive Oyle: "Help, somebody help me".

This stimulates the B-cells and Killer T-cells to multiply and come to the assistance. With these other cells, macrophages can readily destroy many types of cancer cells.

The most numerous of your defenders are the Neutrophils. These are smaller, more nimble versions of the macrophages that specialize in tracking down and devouring bacteria.

The excited cries of the Helpers stimulate the B-cells to unleash thousands of chemical compounds per second called antibodies that work like packs of angry Pit Bulls. Though small, they're fierce; they bite hard and hang on for dear life.

This weakens the invader and also further marks it as an enemy. The antibodies pick up a series of chemicals from the blood, that can detonate, blowing a large hole in the membrane of the would-be invader.

Enter the Killer T-cells. A hush falls as they enter the duel. At first the intruders laugh because "Killer" cells look like harmless cotton balls, but behind that soft exterior is a hair-trigger hired gun.

Quick on the draw. Shoot first, ask questions never. There's a mean glint behind those eyes. Ruthless. Fortunately they're on our side. Usually. They'd be behind bars if it weren't that we needed

"REFEREE"

them at times. The bullets that the Killers fire contain chemicals that rip holes in membranes. The membranes that are attacked are yours, or at least once were, because Killer cells primarily attack cells that have been taken over by viruses or become cancer. Thus in effect the Killers are hired assassins brought in to eliminate weaklings and traitors: a dirty job, but one that has to be done. A job they do very well.

Our immune system consists of so many monsters that are so powerful and relentless that disposing of the endless array of creatures within and around us is seldom a long-term problem. Bacteria, viruses, yeast, fungi, parasites and cancer are all readily controlled by an active, alert immune system. There is even a type of cell called the Suppressor cell that goes around to simmer down an overly-exuberant immune system so that it doesn't destroy the whole body.

The body also makes Memory cells that remember particular invaders so that if they return the defenses can be activated more quickly.

THE THYMUS GLAND AND THE SPLEEN

The thymus gland and the spleen are the conductors of the "immune wars symphony".

The thymus gland is known by medicine to be responsible in early childhood for programming the T-cells to recognize foreigners, but after puberty is thought to be of little value and is still removed with little thought for consequences. A large number of children had their thymus glands treated with radiation in the fifties and sixties, and their much higher incidence of cancer shows the thymus gland's importance. The thymus gland secretes a hormone called thymosin which regulates the function of the white blood cells. The spleen is the wrecking yard of the body and should be breaking down old and damaged blood cells. Serious trouble can occur when the lymph drainage of these glands gets overloaded to the point that they malfunction and thus lose control over the T-cells. One of two things can happen.

The T-cells can become underactive. Since they protect primarily against viruses, yeast, fungi, parasites such as worms, and cancer, a person with weakened T-cell function is vulnerable to these.

The simpler types of infections, such as warts, coldsores, chronic colds and flus, yeast and fungal overgrowths such as vaginal yeast problems and athlete's foot, may be the first indications of a weakened immune system. Using energy-testing techniques, it might be estimated that about a fifth of the general population has a weakened thymus gland, often without symptoms.

In the male gay population it is probably double that number, even before exposure to the Aids virus. The higher exposure to venereal disease and the resultant increased exposure to antibiotics causes greater intestinal overgrowth, and liver and thymus overload. This in turn increases susceptibility to infections, leading to greater dependence on medications. The resulting downward spiral in health can be reversed in the earlier stages with perseverance.

A great hazard to health is when the immune system is so inactive that cancer can develop. This is the body run amok within itself, and is the most difficult of the physical problems to overcome if it affects the important organs. Underlying most cancer is long-term underfunctioning of the stomach, intestinal toxicity, liver overload and a plugged lymphatic system.

However, I have seen several patients with cancer who only had a malfunctioning ileocecal valve and resultant gallbladder problems. Their weakened immunity was probably because the weakened fat absorption decreased the membrane strength of the cells so that they were less resistant in general. Unfortunately, cancer itself often generates even more toxins, which aggravate an already serious situation.

Treatment of cancer ideally should be done by those who specialize in it, whether conventionally or alternatively. Treatment of early-stage and simpler cancers by conventional treatment can often buy time to detoxify and reactivate the person's own immune system. However, most naturopaths could also give examples of patients who have had cancer reversed by activating the patient's own immune system. It takes little knowledge of how the immune system works to realize it is far easier to prevent cancer than to cure it in its advanced stages.

The other thing that can happen to the immune system is that the T-cells can become overactive. This is especially to be seen when the spleen is malfunctioning.

The white blood cells can now turn and attack the body itself. This is called auto-immune disease. It is believed there are hundreds of diseases that involve attack by the person's own defense system. Most of the diseases that have actual tissue destruction will turn out to be autoimmune disease. The ruthlessness of the Killers can be dramatic.

The classic example of autoimmunity is rheumatoid arthritis. The person's own white blood cells attack joints, resulting in inflammation. My first reversal of chronic disease by natural therapy was a case of rheumatoid arthritis. That was eleven years ago and the patient is still doing well.

While western medicine considers autoimmune diseases to be among the most serious, dramatic reversals may occur if the lymph glands can regain function, controlling the T-cells. Making changes before major damage is done, and before dependence on medication occurs, is of the utmost importance for complete reversal to be certain.

The only opponent of white blood cells that has a chance of stopping them is you. Their home base is the lymph system, but the lymph system is also the waste drainage system of the body. Obviously if the lymph system is overloaded with metabolic debris, the immune system is going to be less active. There are also specific nutrients that you have to provide for them to function properly, such as vitamins C and A and minerals such as zinc.

Studies have shown that eating white sugar and other sweets can in effect "paralyze" the white blood cells for half an hour or more. Any interference with the white blood cells' work can result in an infection or overgrowth of normal micro-organisms. The toxins produced by the infecting organism can further strain an already overloaded lymph system and make the immune system even weaker. This has been documented in "Human Intestinal Microflora in Health and Disease." (1983):

> "The presence of indigenous intestinal bacteria can reduce the host immune response to certain antigens (toxins) by . . . stimulating the production of suppressor cells, indigenous intestinal bacteria can also increase the host immune responsiveness . . . by stimulating . . . Helper T-cell functions."

Antibiotics are often used at this point. They can result in remarkable improvement by killing off invading bacteria, but they have no effect on viral infections. They may also produce long-range side effects.

The good intestinal bacteria are killed off along with the bad ones when antibiotics are used. This allows yeast to multiply unchecked. The toxins that the yeast makes protect its newly-claimed territory by inhibiting the good bacteria from returning and further overloading the liver and lymphatic system. This toxic irritation causes greater hypersensitization of the body.

This vicious cycle of infection to antibiotics to hypersensitization, to more infections to more antibiotics, is especially evident in the large numbers of allergic children in North America. According to the World Health Association, sixty per cent of doctors today prescribe antibiotics for the common cold, even though they know that antibiotics do not protect against viral infections. In addition, millions of pounds of antibiotics enter our system through the food chain.

To complicate things even more, it is unlikely that a child's health would be better than its mother's.

Most young mothers breastfeed these days, but in reality they are "shooting blanks". Some of the intestinal bacteria (lactobacillus bifidus) thrive on the mother's milk and help to prepare the way for the other intestinal bacteria to be established later in life (lactobacillus acidophilus). If the mother doesn't have the proper intestinal flora (which is likely in a majority of cases) the baby is off to a poor start, and the first few rounds of antibiotics could have a deleterious effect on the child.

Evidence is also appearing that vaccinations may be causing long term immune disorders. "There are reasons for believing that immunological challenge in the form of mass vaccination programs may now be precipitating aberrant immunological effects... in individuals who have suffered exaggerated effects from these injections of foreign disease agents". "The real danger from mass vaccines... appears to be an indirect impairment of the immune system... since this effect is often delayed, indirect, and masked, its true nature, is seldom recognized. (Text book of Natural Medicine. IV: Vacc Im-1-8).

PATIENTS' LETTERS

I've always been a very healthy, active person. At the age of 37 years, I began to experience periods of extreme exhaustion, anxiety, memory loss, terrible nightmares and my hair was falling out by the handful. I was unable to cope with the smallest of tasks.

After the blood tests and two very uncomfortable needles put into the thyroid gland, it was decided that I had Hashimoto's disease. For some reason my thyroid was being attacked by my own white blood cells.

I decided to find the natural way to solve this problem. Under Dr. Matsen's care a blood picture was taken which showed large amounts of fat and toxins in the blood. Food testing was done to identify foods that proved irritating to my body. I then went on a food combining diet following advice from the book Fit For Life, and had nine hydrotherapy treatments.

Within the week I began to notice improvements in energy. Weight loss came without trying.

After 5 weeks another blood picture was taken which showed great improvement. I didn't need to see this to know that I had improved because I was feeling so much better. The symptoms described above were gone.

After this I noticed a dramatic change in personality. I was so

much more positive about life. I am enjoying a deep feeling of inner
happiness which I haven't had for years. It's great to be alive again.
All I had to do was eat properly.

Darlene Rusin
Surrey, B.C.

Lesley Colleen Worbets was born on Nov. 29, 1977, three weeks
prematurely. Her birth was uneventful but she had a high level of
jaundice and spent a lot of time under the "light". Blood tests continued for a week after coming home until signs of the jaundice disappeared.

Lesley was a contented baby but was very hyperactive. At 11/2
years she was very independent. In Oct. 1979 a small bald patch became noticeable on her frontal crown. This quickly spread and
within fourteen days she had lost all her hair except a few wisps.

By Dec 1979 she had also lost her eyelashes and eyebrows. Numerous visits to doctors and specialists only confirmed the diagnosis
of "alopecia totalis". Lesley's hair was being attacked by her own
white blood cells. The prognosis was bleak-she would probably
never regrow her hair. We were told to go out and buy her a wig.

Beside being bald, her hyperactivity was increasingly disruptive
of the family routine. Her diet was carefully watched-sugars were
eliminated as were foods containing red dye. This helped a bit.

In May 1980, a friend who was a layman natural healer saw Lesley and asked if she could help. Having nothing to lose, we said yes.
Lesley was given "Bioplasma" in combination with Silicea 6x.
Overnight, Lesley settled down and we couldn't believe whe was the
same child. Her diet was still restricted but now we could handle her
and reason with her. From this point on, things got better.

In Jan 1981, Dr. Mesery, a Naturopathic Physician, agreed to
treat Lesley. His remedies included phosphorus, silicea and ar-
senicum in homeopathic doses. These further helped to control the
hyperactivity and then the hair started growing. The patches that
became bald first were the last to fill in. Lesley was very proud to
see her hair growing and of course, we were delighted! The hair was

very dark and wiry initially, but then it began to soften and lighten.

By Nov 1981 Lesley had a bald spot the size of a quarter on the back of her head. It was covered by other hair so was not noticeable and the frontal crown was just starting to fill in.

In June of 1982, Lesley again lost a large patch of hair at the back of her head, but by Oct. it had filled in again. During all this time Lesley continued taking Bioplasma and Silicea 6x as well as being on a sugar restricted diet.

In late 1984 Lesley again had a bald patch appear. As Dr. Mesery had retired I took Lesley to see Dr. Matsen. Besides sugar she tested sensitive to milk and yeast and most grains. These were removed from the diet and a few supplements added. Lesley's hair was soon healthy and silky.

Then on April 1, 1986 Lesley was struck down by a motor vehicle when she ran out into the street. Her injuries were not serious but she did require surgery to close a head laceration. As a result of the accident, her body was subjected to intravenous general anesthetic and antibiotics. The hospital was going to give her a tetanus shot but I refused and explained about the alopecia. They gave her a minute amount and she got an instant reaction to it (a rash on her arm at the sight of the injection) so no more tetanus was given.

About two to three weeks later a bald spot was noticed on the back of her head and within another week, noticeable thinning of the hair as well as loss of hair at the base of the skull. Dr. Matsen put Lesley on caprylic acid which arrested the hair loss and it has now regrown silky as before.

In the last seven years, the medical profession has had no explanations nor solutions to Lesley's problem. Fortunately, we discovered homeopathy and Naturopathic Medicine, and are strong believers in it.

Iris Worbets
North Vancouver, B.C.

PROSTAGLANDINS, FREE RADICALS AND ELECTRICAL ACTIVITY

What is it about a few little toxins generated by poor diet and faulty digestion that can bring about malfunction of an organism that is programmed to run flawlessly? Why should such a powerful self-regulating creature, armed to the teeth with "monsters", fall victim to indigestion? Let's take a closer look at the effects of the toxins themselves.

For hundreds of years, when people got sick they believed that they had poisons in their blood. Modern lab work couldn't find enough toxicity to cause major disease. The discovery of germs led to the ridicule of this toxicity theory. However, recent discoveries in biochemistry have found two missing links that show how small amounts of toxins can cause major problems.

One is the discovery of prostaglandins. Prostaglandins only last a fraction of a second, which is why they have only been discovered recently. In their short lives, however, prostaglandins can have a powerful effect on the body. In fact, they're believed to be the strongest compounds made by the body. In the short time that prostaglandins have been known, an incredible amount of research has been done on them. They have been implicated in dozens of diseases already, and we may expect that number to rise radically. Prostaglandin disorders have been found especially in diseases that involve circulation and immunity. Let's take a closer look at the formation of prostaglandins.

A cell membrane is composed of fats. When a hormone from a gland hits the membrane, it triggers an enzyme to turn some of the membrane fat into a prostaglandin. The prostaglandin in turn stimulates or inhibits the activity of the cell. In other words, it's an off/on switch.

Many different types of prostaglandins can be made, and a slight difference in their structure can dramatically alter their effect on the body in general. The thing that affects the type of prostaglandin the most is the type of fat found in the membrane. That depends on the type of fat in the diet and the climate that the fat was grown in. In general, the colder the climate the more unsaturated the fat. The structure of the prostaglandin changes accordingly. Since climate affects fat types, and fat types affect circulation through prosta-

glindins, obviously the idea of eating according to your climate is important.

Like everything else in life, there is good and bad in prostaglandins. While the "good" prostaglandins can have powerful beneficial impact in regulating the body in homeostasis, "bad" prostaglandins can have an equally powerful but deleterious effect on cell regulation and function. A lot of research has been done on why the harmful ones are formed. Obviously the proper fats have to be found in the membrane. These are called the essential fatty acids. These fats must be in the diet, as the body can't make them. They are found especially in flax and seafood, so these have begun to take a larger role in our diet. However one thing that is often overlooked in esssential fatty acid research is that it is important to have proper bile (liver and gallbladder function) to absorb the fatty acids.

Faulty function of the enzyme that turns the essential fatty acids into prostaglandins, delta-6-desaturase, has been blamed by some researchers as the culprit in diseases involving "bad" prostaglandins. Aspirin blocks the function of this enzyme, stopping the formation of the bad prostaglandins, which gives relief of circulation-induced pain. However, the problem is that aspirin stops the formation of the good prostaglandins as well. Since the good prostaglandins especially influence circulation and immunity, these are the side-effects that you would expect to see with aspirin use. Stomach bleeding and immune deficiencies are well-known problems with aspirin.

Alcohol is known to stimulate the enzyme delta-6-desaturase. Thus the old concept of using hot rum to burn up a cold could be true. The alcohol stimulates the enzyme to produce more prostaglandins, to increase immune function, thus destroying the cold virus overnight.

The problem is that the alcohol has a reverse effect the next day. This may be due to acetaldehyde, the chemical residue from the breakdown of alcohol that can cause hangovers. Acetaldehyde inhibits the enzyme, weakening the immune system further. If the virus wasn't killed overnight, it could come back with a vengeance.

Evening primrose oil and black currant oil were recently found to contain an oil that can become prostaglandins without needing the enzyme. Often good results can be obtained in many diseases.

However, what gives the quickest and deepest results is detoxification. This would indicate that the main interference with proper prostaglandin formation is from toxins. Of the seventy-eight known toxins that originate in the intestine, many are closely related to alcohol (phenols, indol, skatol, etc.), and since one is acetaldehyde itself, it appears that the detrimental effects of the toxins occur by their disruption of the enzyme that turns fats into prostaglandins. Since prostaglandins are so important for smooth physical function it can be seen that disruption of prostaglandin formation amplifies the effect. That is, a few toxins in the blood can result in dramatic problems in the body.

We can expect that further research will verify that this is one of the missing links in understanding how poor diet and digestion can

result in any disease anywhere in the body. Even more important, by reversing this process health may be restored.

FREE RADICALS

Another recent discovery of biochemistry is that of free radicals. Like prostaglandins, free radicals last for only a fleeting moment, but in their short life they can also have a dramatic effect on the body, though in a different fashion.

Let's consider where free radicals come from. The most important nutrient in the body is oxygen. We can live weeks without food, days without water, but only minutes without oxygen. Oxygen comes in many forms. We most commonly identify oxygen as O_2 which is the form it is usually found in in the atmosphere. In this form the two oxygen atoms are bound together by a pair of electrons that they share. O_2 is happy and content. As in a good marriage, both members are fulfilled.

If you split the two oxygens atoms apart, they end up imbalanced. One oxygen atom would have the two electrons and the other would have none.

These are called ions. The one without electrons is positively charged and the one with electrons is negatively charged. Ions are mildly reactive. That is, they are searching for fulfillment. The positive ions are searching for electrons, while the negative ions need to give them away. As they rush around searching for each other, the cell membranes "tease" them by allowing them to rush towards each other, but prevent actual fulfillment. It's this thwarted urge to become more stable that gives action to the body. Ah, the singles bar of life.

Another way to separate O_2 is to break apart the two oxygen atoms in such a way that each one gets one of the electrons. These are called free radicals. 'Radical' is the appropriate word. These molecules are so unstable that they, like prostaglandins, last only a fraction of a second. During their short life they will get an electron from somewhere, anywhere. Since normally there are few free elec-

trons in the body, they usually get them by ripping them out of membranes. Since an area of the body the size of a pinhead can have millions of these free-radical reactions per second, this can have a severely destructive effect on the cell membranes.

Fortunately, the body does have buffers against these reactions. Alpha-tocopherol (vitamin E) works like a Pacman, gobbling up free radicals. Beta-carotene, vitamin C and selenium are a few of the other nutrients in the body that help buffer free radicals.

Now we know that bile has even stronger free scavengers, which gives even more insight into the importance of proper liver and gallbladder function. Since the white blood cells unleash free radicals on invaders to help rip apart their defensive membranes, free radicals aren't all bad. However, it's extremely important that the body keep control over free radicals. If the body loses control of the white blood cells by malfunction of the thymus gland, the extra free radicals can be too much for the buffers to handle, and irritation and eventual damage can result.

The type of membrane damaged by the free radicals determines the seriousness of the damage. The membranes surrounding the more vital internal organs are much more important than surface skin. The most serious long-range damage occurs when the genetic material within the reproductive organs is damaged, as that may be passed on for generations.

It has long been known that damage from exposure to radiation, whether from ultraviolet sun rays or from gamma rays of nuclear fission, occurs from the production of free radicals, which in turn causes the actual physical damage. Sunlight has thus been blamed as the major cause of skin cancer, but we know that moderate exposure to sunlight is healthy. The problems occur when the body is already full of internally-generated free radicals.

Where do these free radicals come from? Any of the toxins from the intestine can probably produce an abundance of them. Whether skatols, phenols, indols, ammonia, acetaldehyde, hydrogen sulphide, neurine, aminoethyl mercaptan, putrescine, cadaverine, histamine, tyramine, formaldehyde or the myriads of others, the common denominator among these physical toxins is their ability to generate large numbers of free radicals. When the buffering system is overloaded, disease occurs.

Many people force-feed the system with anti-oxidant supplements to help buffer these free radicals, and that may give good results.

The dramatic results occur, however, when the production of toxins is stopped at the source, the digestive system.

We have now finished our journey down the digestive system and learned how poor diet and faulty digestion can result in incomplete absorption of nutrients and a build-up of toxins in the blood, which can overload the liver and circulate thoughout the body causing irritation. If the immune system gets overloaded, more serious problems can result.

ELECTRICAL ACTIVITY

Let's go back to the beginning and take another look at this system, but from a different viewpoint. Instead of looking at the physical level, let's look at energy instead.

Remember the mouth makes alkaline juice, the stomach makes acid, the pancreas alkaline and the intestinal flora make acid again. This alteration of acid and alkaline may remind us of batteries. Indeed it is this battery-type system that the body uses, not to make energy but simply to extract energy from food, and to put it into acceptable form for the body to use and store.

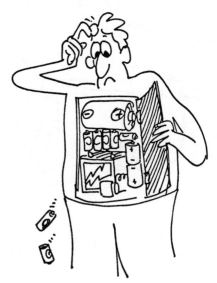

Swedish cancer researcher Dr. Bjorn Nordenstrom has recently discovered that the arteries not only carry cells and nutrients, but also a flow of electrical activity that is critical to both health and healing. He states that it is the alternating flow and ebb of positive and negative ions that carries on the natural healing process in the body. While this concept has been met with extreme skepticism by conventional medicine, alternative physicians would respond with a simple shrug that in effect says, "What took so long?"

Three thousand years ago the Chinese discovered that organs generate biomagnetic energy currents that circulate throughout the body in channels called meridians that distribute the energy to the physical body. They found that the energy is imbalanced long before the organ has problems, so they focused their treatments on maintaining energy balance. One of their insights was that the stomach meridian is one of the most important.

So the digestive system is designed to extract energy, and depends on alternation of alkaline and acid to draw the energy from the crude food mass. The greater the ability of the body to make these opposites, the greater the ability to extract energy. Perhaps we can call this the source of vitality.

The problems in this "digestive battery" occur when the digestive organs function improperly, so that instead of producing a flow of ions in the blood, the electric process "shorts out" so that free radicals circulate through the blood instead of ions. So the blood, which is supposed to nurture the cells with a bath of nutrients, is flooding the cells with a sea of irritants.

The more common digestive deficiencies are of stomach acids and intestinal acids that are supposed to be made by the intestinal flora. The result in disease is an overly alkaline or acidic state. Much has been made of acid and alkaline diets, but they are of less importance if the digestive organs are functioning properly, as the body can then regulate acid and alkaline balances better. In fact, dietary changes will usually result in little long-range improvement in health unless the digestive organs are also improved.

If the liver gets overwhelmed with free radicals and they get passed into the bloodstream, these "sparks" can ignite "spot fires" anywhere in the body if they aren't quickly squelched.

That is the beginning of disease. Disease begins with faulty digestion long before the first aches and pains, long before there are any symptoms.

The real strength of naturopathic medicine is that it includes not only diagnosing and treating conventional physical symptoms, but also interpreting and treating the earlier-stage energy imbalances. A number of energy-testing techniques such as acupuncture pulses, electro-acupuncture devices and applied kinesiology (muscle testing) have been developed to pick up these energy imbalances. Since conventional diagnosis is based on tissue pathology, these more subtle techniques do not diagnose disease as defined by these physical standards. They can be invaluable, however, in finding the true root of a patient's problems.

One hundred and fifty years ago it was discovered that each area of the body has a representative area in the iris of the eye. In effect, the iris works like a colour television screen, the cameras being

found in every cell of the body. By looking in the iris, some of the early preconditions of disease can be seen.

Since we already know that the stomach is the sparkplug of the digestive system and the hub of your body, it should come as no surprise that it is also at the center of the iris, occupying the area just outside the pupil. The intestinal area is represented just outside the stomach. Outside the stomach and intestinal area is a ring which separates these two areas from the rest of the iris, which contains the representative areas for the rest of the body.

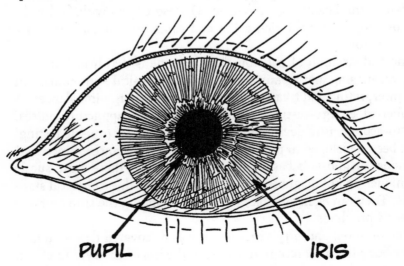

PUPIL   IRIS

If the two internal organs, the stomach and the intestine, are treated with care, it is extremely difficult for the rest of the body to have disease. However, iridology shows how early we fall out of the grace of perfect health. Most Caucasian children are born with bright, deep blue eyes. They usually maintain that clarity during breastfeeding. Once they start eating, however, the eyes often change colour very quickly. Cloudy, murky whites to yellows or oranges start to appear around the intestinal ring as the digestive system begins to get overloaded. Soon the lymphatic system struggles to drain away this metabolic debris and puffy white clouds may show in its representative area towards the outside of the iris. As the elimination organs get overloaded the body may try to push toxins out through the skin which can create a dark ring around the outside edge of the iris. If antibiotics are now used the process can be greatly amplified and what were once blue eyes may now appear any shade of grey, green or hazel. Iridology shows us that the body works like a giant reservoir that has been filling slowly with toxins for years. The childhood diseases often end with puberty as there is a hormonal "boost" of mating energy that increases the vitality. As this begins to wane in the twenties, the toxin load of the body becomes more apparent again. If this reservoir capacity is filled and the person suddenly "catches" a disease, the latest event is blamed as the cause. On looking back, it will be seen that disease is usually a culmination of events, seldom a result of a single stress or disease or infectious organism.

Poor fat handling from a sluggish liver and gallbladder can result in deposits of fat in the arteries. This can be well advanced even during the teens. The consequent poor circulation may show as a haziness around the outer edge of the iris. If minerals settle in these fat deposits they may show as a white crescent around the iris, especially in the top third which represents the head area. This marking has now been recognized by conventional medicine as the "arcus senilis".

Contrary to what some books claim, iridology is not a reliable way to diagnose specific disease, but definite insights into the preconditions of disease can be seen. With improvement of the digestive system, a concurrent clearing of the iris occurs. The sparkle of the eye and glow that exudes from a healthy person is there for all to see and makeup can only struggle to imitate it.

PATIENTS' LETTERS

I am a child care worker and I receive contracts from the Ministry of Human Resources via different private societies to work with problem children and their parents. I have been doing this and other social service work for seven years.

About a year ago, I brought a nine year old, "Robert" to see Dr. Matsen. I had been working with him for about six months with some improvement in his behaviour, but after three or four weeks under Dr. Matsen's direction there was dramatic improvement. At an earlier case conference about Robert the comment was made that he would probably end up in jail. There was general agreement about this then, but there would not be now. Robert went from being an obnoxious and hyperactive child to being a popular and non-hyperactive child. One bit of trouble he did get into after starting to see Dr. Matsen occurred at a summer camp where Robert was able to return to his earlier diet. He was kicked out of camp after five days because he had become so unruly. Robert himself, has now come to understand the importance of his diet, and cooperates accordingly.

"Richard" eleven, and "William" six, are two other children whose families cooperated with Dr. Matsen in following to some reasonable extent his directions.

Richard was years behind his chronological age emotionally and academically. I had been working with him over a two year period. Within about three weeks of seeing Dr. Matsen he lost his hyperactivity. Within three months he began showing very significant academic gains, suddenly learning to read, and rising to the top of his class in problem solving. He is still behind for his age, six months after beginning to see Dr. Matsen, but one can see he is catching up now.

William I immediately brought to Dr. Matsen upon receiving the case. He had previously been on Ritlan for hyperactivity, but his father didn't like the idea and took him off. William also lost his hyperactivity within a few weeks of seeing Dr. Matsen. Now the family says they know immediately when William sneaks anything sweet. Three or four months later Williams teacher tells me he can actually begin to work on academics now, when before his behaviour would not allow this. She is very pleased with the changes. Personally I am very pleased to see the overall family situation improve along with Williams improvement. I suspect that the stress resulting from Williams earlier behaviour could have been enough to break this particular family up.

I cannot bring my clients to Dr. Matsen without parental permission, but when I get it and receive even minimal cooperation from the family, the results are tremendous. Coming from a predominantly counselling background I am surprised, but happy, to find that about fifty per cent of the work I can do with my clients is along nutritional lines.

Tim Head
Vancouver, B.C.

As long as I can remember I've had eczema, on my hands and/or forearms. The biggest offender was dish soap. While in school I was treated with a tar based medicine at night and in the daytime wore a yellow sulphur based medicine. I had to clean my hands and arms with mineral oil.

After graduating, I worked for a medical doctor. With my hands in water a lot, they broke out. He treated me with cortisone and I kept Keri lotion always on my skin. The cortisone kept the "hot" flare ups controlled, though my hands were always a little broken out.

When I married and didn't have time to lavish my hands in lotion, my right hand became almost unuseable, due to the cracked, dry, bleeding eczema. I went to a Dermatologist. He put me on stronger cortisone (said I'd kind of built an intolerance for the other). The stronger medication left my skin damaged and appeared to thin out my skin. When cleared up my skin actually seemed more easily injured -thus the eczema came back stronger.

I gave up all non-essential water contact. (My husband bathed kids, dishes). I even wore gloves to wash my hair. I tried some natural means. Some that I remember were topical vitamin E, aloe vera and "icing" my hands to take the itch away. I started taking oil of evening primrose. It kept my eczema at bay -while not gone it didn't crack and bleed often. It also cost me about $50/month.

A friend suggested I see Dr. Matsen for my eczema. I made an appointment. I discovered my eczema (and chronic constipation) were caused by poor food combining and yeast in my system. He put me on a properly combined diet and a yeast killer for 21 days. My hands cleared up totally and I can toss my high fiber laxatives.

My hands are so clear, I can even wash dishes (and my hair) without gloves. Plus I lost the excess weight I'd gained after three pregnancies and a sluggish system improved greatly.

> *Mrs. L. Floreen*
> *New Westminster, B.C*

We have taken a quick trip through the body and seen some of the things that can go wrong with it. The many different types of diseases can't be covered even in an extensive pathology course. The important thing to remember is that the body wants to heal itself and will do so if the obstacles to cure are removed. There is only one major hurdle to overcome. As that wise Pogo once said, "I have seen the enemy and it is us."

In the next section we will turn your worst enemy back into a good friend by learning how to "tune up your digestive system".

PART II

EATING ALIVE:

"Good dyet is a perfect way of curing:
And worthy much regard and health assuring.
A king that cannot rule him in his dyet,
Will hardly rule his Realme in peace and quiet."
Regimen Sanitis Salernitanum, 11th Century.

CHAPTER 5

Is Disease a Mystery?

There are people who think that to be healthy they must be healed. Doctors, drugs, vitamins, healers, surgery, magic chants, diets, incantations, painful postures, absolutions, strenuous exertions, exotic herbs and expensive potions have been developed to fulfill this need.

It may be true that these will help. It is also true that the body knows how to heal itself. In fact, except for a few genetic and developmental defects, the body knows how to take perfect care of itself.

It is known from research that cells can be kept alive beyond life expectancy with a steady flow of nutrients and, equally important, quick removal of wastes. Cells thrive when given these two conditions: nutrients and elimination of toxins.

Homeostasis is the ability of the body to regulate its cells together as a unit. The body knows just where it should be going and just how to get there.

Isn't it remarkable that everyone in the world has a little internal elf that is flipping switches and turning valves so as to keep the body's temperature at 98.6 degrees F.!

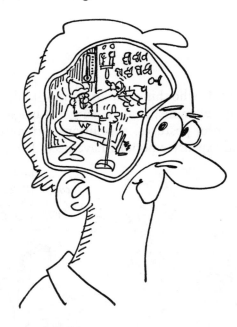

Just think, whether a Bedouin in the sweltering desert or an Eskimo in the freezing Arctic, the body is effortlessly making billions of biochemical adjustments to maintain its equilibrium. Through the most phenomenal of physical stresses this internal intelligence is constantly measuring and balancing, juggling and adapting, always aiming for those common pre-set goals. All of this goes on despite differences of race, sex, nationality, financial status, or political or religious belief.

All who study the body closely must recognize it as living magic.

The following quote is by Nobel Prize winner Dr. Albert Szent-Gyorgyi:

"As a medical student, I learned about those thousand diseases humanity is suffering from. . . . Since then, as a biochemist, I am living in silent admiration of the wonderful precision, adaptability and perfection of our body. Medicine taught me the shocking imperfection, biochemistry the wonderful perfection, and I have wondered where the contradiction lies. Anything that Nature produces seems to be perfect. Should, then, man be the only imperfect creature kept alive in the face of all his imperfections only by means created by his own mind?"

The body can withstand a phenomenal amount of abuse, and homeostasis will maintain internal equilibrium without us even being aware of the process. If homeostasis is pushed harder to maintain order then acute disease exists. High fever helps the white blood cells to be more active. Vomiting and diarrhea can help to flush out toxins. Lack of appetite allows the body to focus on cleansing and repair instead of digestion. Fatigue allows the body energy to be shunted away from motion, inwards to aid healing. Acute disease should quickly and decisively re-establish homeostasis.

If it is unsuccessful in achieving its goals due to a healing capacity that is lower than the disease cause, then the body will slowly surrender its idealistic goals. This is the beginning of chronic disease.

The classical causes of disease such as plague, famine and exposure to the environment have little relevance in modern society, at least in the First World. Medicine has been befuddled by degenerative disease over the last hundred and fifty years or so, and is constantly waiting for future research breakthroughs to shed light on the darkness of disease. In the meantime, patients are "practised" on.

Not everyone has been so reticent to voice an opinion as to disease cause. The following is from Natural Therapeutics, Vol. 3, "Dietetics" by Henry Lindlahr, published in 1914:

" . . . Practically all disease arising in the human organism is caused originally by the accumulation of these effete waste and end-products of digestion and of the tissue changes."

In a similar vain, Thomas Sydenham, the famous seventeenth century English physician, summed up disease with this statement:

"Disease is nothing else but an attempt on the part of the body to rid itself of morbific matter."

In his book "The Wheel of Health" Dr. G.T. Wrench wrote:

"Diseases only attack those whose outer circumstances, particularly food, are faulty . . . The prevention and banishment of disease are primarily matters of food; secondarily, of suitable conditions of environment. Antiseptics, medicaments, inoculations, and extirpating operations evade the real problem. Disease is the censor pointing out the humans, animals and plants who are imperfectly nourished."

The "Father of Cellular Pathology", Rudolph Virchow stated:
"If I could live my life over again I would devote it to proving
that germs seek their natural habitat-diseased tissue-rather
than being the cause of diseased tissue.... "

It is rumoured that even the Master of the Microbe himself, Louis
Pasteur, had a major change of thought on his deathbed and stated
that the resistance of the individual is more important than germs in
the causation of disease.

Chronic disease is simply the inability of acute reactions to
reestablish homeostasis.

Chronic diseases are those little or big complaints that refuse to go
away on their own, no matter how patient you are or how hard you
wish. The important thing to remember is that, except for genetic
problems, your body wants to return to its normal state. Since the
blood is the body's healing agent, where chronic disease exists there
must be "weak blood". Since blood is a product of diet, digestion and
assimilation, these must be improved. Simply improving diet is usually not enough to reverse chronic disease.

The emphasis in this book, as it is my practice, is not on what I
can do for you, but on what you can do for yourself. The word Doc-

tor comes from the latin "To Teach". In Part I we learned that disease is a gradual process beginning in early childhood with physical aggravation of the stomach, which eventually leads to decreased absorption of nutrients and increased formation of toxins that can overload the liver/gallbladder and lymphatic system. Since cells need nutrients rather than toxins to run properly, improving health is simply a matter of improving the nutrient content of the blood and at the same time decreasing the toxins.

Since nutrients get into the blood by proper diet, digestion and absorption, and excess toxins occur due to improper diet, digestion, absorption and elimination. If you can improve diet, digestion, absorption and elimination, then you will both increase nutrients in the blood and decrease toxins. If this increased blood quality is strong enough and maintained long enough, then it may be possible to reverse even chronic disease.

Thus, proper DIET + strong DIGESTION + complete ABSORPTION = STRONG BLOOD + Complete CIRCULATION + Efficient ELIMINATION = GOOD HEALTH.
Your body knows how to heal itself and wants to do it now. Have faith in it but also supply it with the proper physical tools.

PATIENT'S LETTER

Most of my thirty-two years of life have been spent suffering from a variety of "undiagnosed" illnesses. These included digestive problems, gallbladder disorders, chronic colds and sore throats, nerve-related dysfunction, headaches, PMS and for the last year-severe diarrhea and increased weight gain. After visiting countless G.P.s and specialists over the years (four of them alone in the six months prior to Dr. Matsen) not one of them was able to find a "medical" reason for my problems.

After hearing of Dr. Matsen's philosophy and treatment I decided to give it a chance. After four months of his program I am happy to say that I have lost twenty-seven pounds (my desired weight loss) and the diarrhea has long since disappeared!! As well, all the other symptoms that plagued me are long gone as well. I FEEL MAR-VELOUS! I have much more energy along with a great sense of well-being. Thank you Dr. Matsen for changing my health through my eating habits.

> *Maureen Fairfax*
> *Surrey, B.C.*

CHAPTER 6

Diet

Let's begin with DIET. The goal of diet should be to provide all the essential nutrients without aggravating the function of the digestive organs.

Since we have found the stomach of almost everyone over the age of two (and sometimes younger) to be in a state of "shock", the thing to do is to remove the irritants so that the stomach muscle can "de-spasm" and regain proper function.

The reason many people don't get improved stomach function from improved diet is that they haven't eliminated everything that aggravates the digestive organs.

Consider the stomach as being like a young child who has been beaten ruthlessly since birth. It's been hiding in the attic, occasionally whimpering, as you continued to torment it.

So now we've learned the error of our ways and we're going to stop mistreating this sensitive little thing so that it can come down out of hiding and resume useful function. During the first few weeks it's going to still be highly sensitive and the slightest abuse will send it scuttering into spasm again, so care must be taken to avoid every single thing that bothers it. Once it's been fully in operation for a while and is less sensitive, you may give it a little friendly smack once in a while without it going back into complete shock.

In practise I test every person on approximately one hundred things using applied kinesiology (muscle testing) to see what is good and bad for their stomachs. If such testing isn't available to you, there are several general patterns that have shown up after using various testing methods on thousands of patients. Before describing these, I will repeat that a person with a major health problem still must seek out professional guidance, as there are many obstacles to cure in severe chronic disease.

Since some things show up as problems for virtually every person, it can only be assumed that these are not foods. Let's call this . . .

GROUP I. It includes coffee, tea, chocolate, white sugar, alcohol, artificial sweeteners and preservatives and salt and tobacco. It takes little awareness to realize that the effect of most of these is as stimulants, not nutrients. They are used to whip an overloaded liver and/or stressed adrenals into one more round of struggle. Unfortunately their end result is to cause further weakness of these organs as well as thoroughly irritating the stomach.

This is not new information, but it is still largely ignored by the majority of people. It goes without saying that it has only been in the last few years that tobacco has been recognized by western medicine as toxic, in spite of alternative practitioners speaking against it for over a hundred years. The fact that smoking is still increasing in some segments of society only shows our slowness to accept even the obvious. Many of us need to experience the full brunt of major disease before we will accept the need for change. Since disease is really a warning from the body that change is necessary, I find it is more beneficial to encourage some people to eat and drink to excess than to discourage them. Many people need to get to the physical breaking point before they become motivated to make changes.

I find it interesting that when the stomach, intestine, liver/gall-bladder and adrenals have fully recovered from the use of stimulants, there is much more energy than that false energy given by the stimulants. Without eliminating Group I for at least three weeks it

will be virtually impossible to get the stomach "deshocked" and back to work making digestive juices and "sparking" the intestinal tract back to life. Perhaps the one exception to that is tobacco. Tobacco does have a negative effect on the stomach but its worst effects are on the lungs, liver and arteries. It is usually possible to get the stomach back to work without quitting smoking, though the lungs won't recover until smoking stops.

GROUP II. Baking yeast, peanuts, brown sugar, cow products and pork also show up for almost everyone.

GROUP III contains wheat, tomatoes, brewer's yeast and mushrooms which show up frequently.

GROUP IV contains other things sometimes seen as problems, such as lamb, beef, chicken, turkey, eggs, shellfish, fish, soya, lemon, oranges, grapefruit, pineapple, apples, bananas, peaches, currants, raisins, apricots, strawberries, potatoes, squash, rye, oats, rice, corn, alfalfa, eggplant, carrots, cabbage, broccoli, cauliflower, celery, cucumbers, peppers, turnips, walnuts, cashews, brazil nuts, honey, maple syrup, molasses, raw sugar, curry, garlic, vinegar and onions.

One reason why most diets don't actually improve the function of the stomach is that every single thing that irritates the stomach must be eliminated.

If we go back to what we learned in Part I, there are three ways that the stomach can be physically irritated.

The first way is by putting into it things that aggravate it. Everyone's stomach is aggravated by the items in Group I. Group II usually should be avoided as well for a time. A person with any signs or symptoms of disease should also avoid Group III for a few weeks. A person with major disease should be tested to see if any items in Group IV cause problems.

The second way that the stomach can get irritated is from toxins spilling past the liver into the main bloodstream so that every cell in the body is irritated and thus sensitized. This also makes the stomach more sensitive to foods. The goal is to decrease these toxins by speeding up your digestion, slowing down the digestion of the "critters" and improving liver function.

The third way the stomach can be irritated is by toxic bile from the gallbladder being dumped into the base of the stomach (duodenum) which can dramatically cause stomach, esophagus and intestinal spasm and discomfort. Most people who complain of digestive symptoms are actually experiencing them from toxic bile irritation, as the "shocked" stomach that we find almost everyone has since childhood usually is "silent" or symptom free.

To decrease this irritation the bile must be made less toxic by speeding up digestion, slowing down the unfavourable flora and improving liver/gallbladder function. The function of the ileocecal valve is of extreme importance for this, and I must repeat that at least half of the patients I see who are on self-imposed diets have aggravated this valve.

Usually the stomach will spontaneously "de-shock" itself after a period of time without aggravation, and begin to function again. This time period may be anywhere from a few days to a few months. Generally we allow three weeks for the stomach to begin to function properly again.

A person who is in reasonably good health should be able to get the stomach working by avoiding everything listed in GROUPS I, II and III for three to eight weeks, by which time all the digestive organs should be functioning well enough to add back II and III if the other steps outlined are followed diligently. The items listed in the first group are permanently a problem, though once the organs are detoxified and functioning at their best a person may be able to withstand a little occasional abuse.

After about three weeks the foods in GROUPS IV and III become less of a problem as the body detoxifies, and there is usually little problem with them being added back. Anyone with a particular problem should be retested at this point to make sure that improvement is occurring before these two groups are added back.

PATIENTS' LETTERS

I am a sixty-nine year old lady who had been suffering from abdominal pains, periods of great physical weakness, lack of energy and, most distressing, periods of confusion. As I have always been very energetic and clear-headed I found this quite depressing. For some time I had not been driving my car for fear of making mistakes in traffic or of getting lost.

By the time I made my first appointment with Dr. Matsen, I had already seen my regular Medical Doctor and specialists, none of whom could find anything wrong with me. I required my son to accompany me on the bus for my appointments with Dr. Matsen, again because I feared getting confused and lost on my way there.

Dr. Matsen performed several tests and prescribed a diet and naturopathic medicines. I found this difficult because I could not eat many of the foods I have eaten all my life, but I persevered.

Although it took some time, I slowly noticed that my periods of weakness and confusion became fewer and less severe. After several months of treatment I find that although I am not as well as I would like to be, I am very much better than before. I have dared to drive my car around the block a few times, take the bus to go shopping and can again tolerate (within moderation) many of the foods I have missed.

Mrs. K. Hamadan
Vancouver, B.C.

I first saw Dr. Matsen in July of 1984 after giving up on conventional medicine regarding my physical condition. I had chronic indigestion, constant pain and discomfort and a very low energy level. Dr. Matsen after carefully listening to what I had to say and making the tests required, put me on a diet and gave me some supplements. I followed the diet for 6 months very accurately and began to notice changes in the first week. Very soon my energy level changed in such a way that I can honestly say I feel better than I did 10 years ago.

After six months, I did make the occasional mistake with my eating habits, with no negative results at all. Two years have gone by now. I have never again had any problem with my digestive system. Headaches that I thought were related to a previous brain surgery have disappeared as well.

I have just returned from a trip to Europe where for 3 weeks I kept no diet at all and I was amazed to realize that my system did not react in any negative way. The reinforcement that my "special diet" provided me with on the trip encouraged me to go back to the strict diet in order to cleanse myself from what I basically consider "junk food" and food combinations.

I am deeply thankful to Dr. Matsen for my well-being and I have referred many other patients to him and will continue to do so.

Yours truly,
Marianne Haebler
Vancouver, B.C

CHAPTER 7

Digestion

The ultimate truth out of all this is that it isn't the foods at all that are the problem. The real problem is with the digestive vitality of the person.

Think of the digestive system as resembling a flame. If you have a tiny flame then you have to treat it with great care. The fuel must be pure and fine and added slowly, or the fire will flicker and possibly falter.

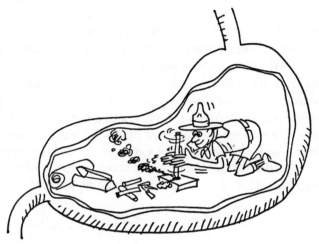

However, if you gradually build up that little flame so that it reaches bonfire proportions, then you can throw the occasional wet log or large chunk on it with only a little smoke being produced. However, many people are busily throwing wet logs on their digestive candles and wondering why their bodies are getting "sooted up".

The confusion over diet is mainly because changing diet by itself doesn't usually improve digestion, so a person remains highly sensitive to many different foods. Sensitivities, or allergies to foods or external substances like pollen or dust, decrease if the digestion is improved and toxins eliminated. If a person can increase digestive vitality, the dietary range can also be increased.

There is no doubt that a person with a strong genetic constitution, healthy intestinal flora (not ravaged by western medicine) and a digestion free from the worries and troubles of life, can eat and drink with abandon for a considerable period of time. However, the prevalence of chronic disease (physical, mental and emotional) in our society indicates that eventually there are limits. However, contrary to what some diet books claim, it's not necessary to be a vegetarian to be healthy. It's also not necessary to eat meat. What is important is that you digest quickly and efficiently whatever you eat.

There is a certain macho nobility to this concept that nutrition is basically a blank cheque. Free of petty restraints, man challenges himself with gluttony: A duel of digestion versus indulgence.

Unfortunately, the only crossed swords in this duel are the scalpels of the surgeons as they remove the gallbladder, uterus, intestine or other casualties. Even the strongest constitution has weak links that must eventually show the strain.

As medicine has gradually assumed responsibility for human health over the last hundred years and disease has become a more and more complex mystery that only big-buck research money can unravel, the stampede to junk food and artificial additives has been allowed to proceed uninhibited, and has perhaps even been encouraged by Big Medicine. Perhaps the ultimate irony is when junk-food franchises sponsor homes for sick children. Is this a conscious or unconscious attempt to ease guilt feelings?

Specific testing that has evolved in the last few decades has helped overcome the confusion that has prevailed around diet. Testing indicates that most people these days have weak digestion and poor intestinal flora, especially children.

Junk food not only feeds the critters their favourite delicacies, but also irritates the digestive organs and reduces digestive speed and efficiency, which of course further aids the intestinal festivities.

Most children show an accumulation of metabolic debris that sensitizes the body. They show reactions to many foods. Any particular food can become a problem as the breakdown of the digestive process and elimination organs continues. While there are certain foods that show up often as problems, anything can show up. Allergies represent only one type of reaction the body can have against specific foods. There are other types that can be lumped together under the general category of food sensitivities.

If people simply stay away from those foods, they may start to feel a little better for a while. However, if the digestive process isn't improved they will eventually develop senstivities to other foods. If they eat in a way that eases the strain on the digestive organs, such as food combining, they will get even better results. However, if they also actually rebuild the digestive organ function, they will slowly detoxify and desensitize the body to the point that the individual foods are no longer a problem. The need for some of the food combinations may disappear as well. As the toxins decrease, external allergies fade away. Aches and pains, fatigue, skin problems, moodiness etc. may disappear as well.

The result of digestive strength is dietary freedom. This is best expressed in the last patient's letter of Chapter 6, as it expresses the ultimate goal of this book. That is to get you so HEALTHY that you have complete freedom to live as you want, but to have you AWARE enough to realize that your health depends on the strength of your digestive system, and to have you MOTIVATED enough that you will WANT to guard this precious resource, and to have you EDUCATED enough so that you will know how to look after it.

Avoiding specific food sensitivities is the first step to rebuilding back the digestive system. The next step is avoiding combinations of foods that are problems.

Mixing certain foods together causes health problems because carbohydrates are first digested by alkaline juices from the mouth, and proteins are digested by acid juices from the stomach. Eating the two foods together results in neutralization of the digestive juices so that the food takes much longer to digest.

Since the digestive time is extended the chances of fermentation and putrefaction toxins being formed by the intestinal flora is increased proportionately. Since there is a race between you and the "Bad Guys" to digest your food, you need all the help you can get.

Separating proteins and carbohydrates from each other allows the mouth and stomach to participate more fully in digestion, thus speeding up digestion and also making it more efficient.

Testing indicates that food combination problems vary from person to person, but as in testing individual food sensitivities, there are certain common patterns that emerge.

In the same way that specific food sensitivities are considered temporary, so are some of the food combinations. Improving function of the digestive organs will decrease the need for certain combinations, as we will learn later. However, on testing over five thousand patients from birth to old age, I have found that nearly everyone who's been off mother's milk for over a year shows weakness of the digestive organs and needs to separate certain foods from each other when eating.

Carbohydrates and proteins should not be eaten together. Anyone who's read Fit For Life will be aware of this. While this need isn't recognized by conventional nutrition, I concur completely with the Diamonds on this. Mixing carbohydrates and proteins together in the average person causes increased toxicity.

The sweeter and the more refined the carbohydrate, such as white sugar, the more it inhibits the digestion of proteins. The heavier the protein, such as red meat, the longer it takes to digest and the more its digestion can be inhibited by carbohydrates.

Proteins are most notable for the nitrogen groups that they contain. The vegetable proteins may take three to four hours to digest, while the animal proteins may take up to six hours. These numbers are extremely speculative; there are many other factors that affect digestion.

Carbohydrates are all made of sugars joined together. The tighter the bond, such as in starches, the less sweetness can be tasted. Holding a starch in the mouth for a short time allows the enzymes of the saliva to break the sugar bonds, and it starts to taste sweet.

A piece of fruit may take an hour to digest. A rice and bean meal may take three to four hours or longer.

Mixing the two groups together greatly increases the production of intestinal toxins in most people, by neutralizing the production of digestive juice and giving the intestinal flora more time to go back for seconds in the intestinal smorgasbord. Their waste products (toxins) are what then foul up the elimination organs and cause most disease.

The sweeter and more refined the carbohydrate, the more it interferes with stomach acid, so whoever invented dessert was way off the mark. The continued use of sweets, even fruit, after protein is the worst of the combinations, and is one of the most destructive to health. This can also be said of most fruit juices combined with protein meals.

Separating the two food groups leads to simpler, quicker, more complete digestion and less party time for the guys downstairs. Less toxin production means more opportunity for your body to absorb nutrients, eliminate cell wastes and maintain homeostasis.

Some books claim that these combinations are rigid, but that's not what I find in practise. For example, there is an exception to this rule for people who are hypermetabolic. These are people who burn up calories extremely quickly. They are very lean, sometimes gaunt if suffering from absorption problems. Testing indicates they will do better mixing proteins and starches or grains together. This helps to slow down their high metabolic rate.

I look at food combining principles more as stepping-stones to improve the function of the digestive organs than as absolute rules. When the digestive organs have regained proper functioning and the intestinal flora are properly reestablished the need for some of these combinations lessens for many people. So there is an option period down the road where you can decide whether to stick to the stricter diet or make additions as improvement in health is made. It is important to follow the stricter diet as closely as possible at the beginning.

The purpose of food combining is to speed up digestion to the point that the intestinal flora have little time to produce new toxins. If digestion can be made so efficient that extra digestive energy is left over, that's what is sent out into the bloodstream to clean out the old accumulated toxins. Thus it's our surplus digestive energy that does the housecleaning in the body.

Since most of us have such overloaded digestive systems, we do little in the way of housecleaning over the years, which is the equivalent of living in a house for many years without vaccuuming it. It's bound to get a little dusty in the corners eventually.

Our ancestors did internal housecleaning whether they wanted to or not, because a hundred years or more ago they were mainly a bunch of starving peasants. They had certain natural advantages over us. Their food was wholesome and natural, their intestinal flora were most likely healthy, and most important, they ran out of food often. In other words they got hungry. When you're hungry your digestive energy goes out into the blood looking for fuel. It starts to digest your body to meet its requirements for energy. Fortunately, at the beginning, it begins to digest a lot of the old debris lying around. So being a little bit hungry actually worked to their advantage by allowing the digestive energy to do a little housecleaning. Of course being too hungry too long eventually leads to starvation and death, but our ancestors never succumbed to this dire fate or we wouldn't be here talking about them.

Thousands of years ago one of those peasants must have realized that he or she felt a lot better during one of those hungry periods, and even when food became abundant again he went without eating occasionally to recapture that good feeling. Thus fasting was discovered.

Fasting became an important part of every culture. Since people tended to not only become more physically healthy as they detoxified but they also felt better mentally, emotionally and spiritually during fasting, it was built into the rituals and traditions of all the religions.

Most people today are so toxic that fasting stirs old toxins up far faster than their already-overloaded elimination organs can handle. Feeling worse is often the result. Once the fast is over, they're also still stuck with the same old run-down digestive system that's going to just go on dumping more and more fresh toxins into the system.

The good news is that you can now get all of the benefits of fasting WHILE YOU'RE STILL EATING.

If your digestion is very efficient, you have surplus digestive juice left over to go out into the blood to do your housecleaning. While our ancestors fasted frequently to accomplish improved health, with the understanding you will get from this book you will be able to get all the benefits of fasting while you're still eating.

The digestive system has highs and lows of energy, as do all the organs of the body. The Chinese have observed these energy flows carefully for thousands of years and have produced a very accurate clock which depicts the times of strength and weakness of the different organs.

The digestive system is strongest between seven and eleven in the morning. The stomach meridian's peak is between seven and nine, and that of the pancreas (spleen meridian) is between nine and eleven. This is the time to eat a big breakfast like the nutritionists have been harping at us to do for such a long time. People who do heavy physical labour such as loggers, construction workers, farmers, and ranchers etc. are famous for their enormous breakfasts.

The problem with eating a big breakfast is, however, that all the prime digestive juice is used up first thing in the morning, so it's virtually impossible to have any surplus digestive juice left for the rest of the day. No housecleaning will be done that day, and if a massive breakfast isn't burnt off by heavy labour (and how many people eat as if they were going to work hard and then they go and sit at a machine or in an office all day?) then that mass of food is going to feed the harmful flora and end up dumping more toxins into the system. Not only is no housecleaning done, but more metabolic debris accumulates.

To get housecleaning done you have to avoid a big breakfast. Well, a lot of people say, "I never eat breakfast so I must be doing housecleaning every morning." Then you find out they run on coffee or tea or chocolate or sugar all morning. Remember, these are all

Group I foods, which means they are all direct irritants to virtually everyone's stomach. So the stomach is so aggravated that it will be tightened up and not make proper digestive juice, and the person will be even worse off. No, there will be no housecleaning done that day either. In fact the liver is going to be even more overloaded, trying to break down the toxins found in these non-foods.

To do housecleaning you have to trick the body in the morning, to make more digestive juice than is actually needed.

This surplus digestive juice will head out into the bloodstream where it will start to clean up a lot of the old debris lying around.

We need something in the morning that will stimulate the production of digestive juice, but it has to be something light that doesn't require much digestion itself. Fruit or vegetable juice or broth are the things that will accomplish this.

Probably the most effective thing that I have found is a variation of the Master Cleanser fasting drink. Squeeze a little fresh lemon (approximately two tablespoons) into a glass of hot water. Add a pinch of cayenne, and a little ginger if you like. The ingredients and proportions can be varied to suit individual taste. If sweetener is necessary add a little maple syrup, honey or molasses.

Lemon, cayenne and ginger are all mild stomach stimulants, so they will stimulate the stomach to make lots of digestive juice. However there is little in this drink that requires digestion, so considerable surplus digestive energy is produced. This goes out into the blood and starts to "vacuum" out the far corners of the body.

Grapefruit or any of the other acid group can be substituted, especially if weight-loss is required. Apple cider vinegar in water is sometimes beneficial, especially in cases of arthritis. Acids before proteins can aid their digestion.

Since we do specific food testing before we work out a diet, we occasionally find that lemon or the other acids aggravate some people. In this case the other fruits might be used. Kiwi, papaya and pineapple are good, due to their protein-digesting enzymes.

Cooking and canning papaya and pineapple neutralizes their enzymes. Raw pineapple enzymes can be irritating to some people. Sub-acid fruits can stimulate surplus digestive juices, though less so than the acids.

The sweet fruits are best used fresh and whole. Juicing and drying tends to amplify their sweetness. Since the sweeter and more refined something is the quicker intestinal yeast can turn it into toxins, it is better to avoid excess sweets.

The fruits should also be used by themselves at this point, so that they don't act as primer for the yeast to ferment starches and grains. You know that if you're baking bread and you mix yeast and flour together nothing happens.

If you want to get the bread to rise, you first must add a little sweetener to the yeast to get it started. As the yeast becomes active it can take the starch of the flour as fuel. The same general thing happens when you mix fruit and grains together. The yeast starts on the fruit and becomes so active that it can then take the grains as well.

Grapes are probably the closest to being perfect fruits as readily-available energy, and they rarely show problems on testing.

However, sometimes all the fruits test as a problem. Then what is recommended first thing in the morning is vegetable juice or broth.

Fresh vegetable juice is preferable. Carrot, celery, beet (usually an ounce or two added to other juices) or cabbage are the most commonly used. Other juiceable vegetables are radish, cucumber, lettuce, garlic, onion, brussels sprouts, asparagus, potatoes and greens. The juices of the common forage plants such as alfalfa, wheat grass and barley grass are extremely important for the severe chronic degenerative diseases, and some day they will probably be as commonplace in stores as milk and bread. For further information on vegetable juices see Norman Walker's book, "Fresh Juices".

Yeast, even when living inside the body like mold, fungi and mushrooms, is much more active in cold wet weather.

This is why some people with asthma or arthritis feel much better when they move to Arizona. In effect, the yeast "dries up" and is less active. The reverse holds true as well. I see many patients who lived happily and healthily in Africa, South America and India but after a winter or two of cold wet Vancouver weather they may suffer from innumerable complaints.

They are told that it's the stress of moving to a new culture that is the problem, but often we find by improving diet, digestion and absorption they feel much better. Often they are on very high carbohydrate diets which are quite suitable for warm climates but which end up feeding yeast during the cold wet winters.

Old Mother Nature obviously had this all figured out, so she made fruit ripe in hot, dry weather. The hotter and drier the weather, the sweeter the fruit. By making sweet fruit ripe at the time the intestinal yeast is least active, she helps you get full benefit from eating fruit. By eating sweet fruit in the winter, we end up feeding the yeast if it is a major portion of the intestinal flora. Of course in extreme cases yeast can even digest fruit in the summer, even if eaten alone. In these cases fruit must be avoided completely until the intestinal critters can be controlled.

If acceptable, we usually recommend fruit first thing, especially the lemon drink in colder climates. The lemon drink and other fruits can be repeated as often as wanted in the morning. Fruit is readily digested and will leave a surplus of digestive juice left over for housecleaning.

However, fruit "stirs up the old toxins" so we don't want to go on fruit all day. There might be more stirred up than your elimination organs can handle.

Since the high mineral content of vegetable juice or broth tends to buffer or neutralize toxins, they would follow fruit very well an hour or two after. The high mineral content also seems to stimulate the body to heal the now-detoxified area.

So we might have fruit in the morning, possibly followed by vegetable juice or broth. Then we want to get a little hungry before we actually eat. It's okay to get a little hungry; that's your body burning up some of the old junk for fuel, like a mini-fast. However, it's important to take it very easy in the early stages. The liver is the major organ for regulating blood-sugar levels. Most people's livers are fouled up with years of toxic accumulation and don't handle blood sugar very well. If you go too long without eating at this point you may experience low blood-sugar symptoms. Since it is the brain that needs blood sugar most, the symptoms may include light-headedness, weakness, confusion. It feels like a curtain of fog descending over the brain. Usually eating quickly relieves the symptoms, but sometimes it takes a little time to get over the symptoms.

The earlier nutritionists used to tell people to carry sugar cubes with them, as sucking on them would quickly raise the blood-sugar levels. This certainly works in the short term but it tends to worsen the problem in the long run, as the refined sugar is released too quickly and the body creates an even stronger rebound effect against this sudden increase in blood sugar.

The newer approach is to eat heavy foods such as proteins, fats or starches often, so that the gradual release of sugar from these slow-digesting foods will slowly raise the blood-sugar level. This approach is more effective at balancing the blood sugar levels, but unfortunately doesn't leave any time when your digestive system is not loaded down with food, and thus eliminates any possibility of detoxification and prevents the possibility of actually curing the problem.

To cure hypoglycemia, the organs have to be detoxified to regain the proper regulation of blood sugar levels. It is therefore important to eat lightly in the morning in order to send surplus digestive juice into the bloodstream, but not so light so long that you actually get low blood-sugar symptoms.

Since this is an individual matter we don't tell anyone to go any particular length of time before actually eating. Ideally one should stay on fruit and/or vegetable juice till eleven or twelve or even one o'clock, but if a person can only go for an hour or two, that's fine.

That hour or two of detoxification might allow the liver to slowly function a little better by the next day, week or month.

People who are younger, weaker or more hypermetabolic, doing heavier work, or experiencing the colder seasons should shorten the time they will go light in the morning.

When one does eat, it's important to avoid mixing the carbohydrates and proteins so as to speed up the digestion and thus reduce the feeding time of the harmful flora. Usually the lunch meal is from the carbohydrate side rather than the protein side, as carbohydrates are clean-burning. When burnt for fuel, the end products are water and carbon dioxide, which are easily eliminated. Protein can also be burnt for fuel, but its nitrogen has to first be stripped off, and it then becomes another burden on the elimination organs.

If the protein is eaten at the end of the day it is more likely that the protein will be used as building material, which is its most important use rather than being burnt up as fuel.

However, there are situations where it is easier or more advisable to have protein at lunch, and that's fine.

No matter whether carbohydrates or protein are used at lunch, the protective foods which are neutral can be used with either. They buffer against putrefaction and fermentation of either proteins or carbohydrates.

Neutrals can be used alone if one doesn't need a high caloric intake. This woudn't be advisable at the start for someone with hypoglycemic tendencies.

Fruit might take an hour to digest, so nothing else should be taken in during that period. A light starch meal such as a muffin might take two to three hours, and again, nothing else should be taken during that time. A heavy carbohydrate meal like rice and beans might take three to five hours to digest.

The lighter proteins like tofu might take three hours, dairy products three to four, fish and poultry four to five, red meats five and pork six hours. Of course these times are purely speculative and can vary with a number of factors, and are given as a general guideline as to how much time to leave between meals.

What we have discussed here is the basic premise of Fit For Life, that not mixing certain foods makes food more rapidly digested and causing less toxins to be formed in the intestinal tract, enabling the body to function better. The newer energy-testing techniques verify

what many alternative practitioners have been saying for decades: that separating food groups aids health.

If this agrees with Fit For Life, why should we have another book that says basically the same thing?

Well, there's a little more to it than that. While the new testing verifies the philosophy of food combinations, there is other testing that shows that dietary changes alone don't usually make a big enough improvement in digestive function to reverse chronic disease consistently. Also when corrections are made to improve digestion, then the need for the stricter food combining is reduced.

PATIENTS' LETTERS

Naturopathic medicine is curative medicine, preventative medicine and family medicine.

We have five children now aged four to twelve and they have all suffered from repeated ear infections and strep throat. They received repeated doses of antibiotics and in October of 1984 alone I spent one hundred dollars in antibiotics that never seemed to work for long. The specialist wanted to have tubes put in the ears of Stephanie. Instead I went to Dr. Matsen and by avoiding certain foods and following food combining we are now down to maybe one infecton per year. I took Stephanie back to the specialist and he now says that her ears are fine. Now their bodies are strong enough to fight infections on their own. By going to a naturopath I saved our family a lot of stress and also saved our medical plan a lot of money that would have gone to repeated visits to specialists.

Sincerely,
Illene Pevec
North Vancouver, B.C.

My wife Joan had been bothered by hot flushes and heart arrhythmia. After starting on your diet she began to lose weight, she felt more energetic and the above problems disappeared. An additional bonus was that her menstrual cycle also stabilized.

My eldest son Julian, who had lived away from home on a poor diet, lost quite a lot of hair, certainly more than would be expected in a twenty year old male. After some time on your recommended diet and supplements his hair regrew in almost all its previous areas.

My second son Adam had been a keen long distance runner with apparently inexhaustible energy. However, three different antibiotics prescribed for him in response to a tooth extraction infection appeared to upset his body chemistry. For almost two years he was very lethargic. In recent times he had to sleep for an hour after a seven hour day's work. After your prescribed diet and supplements he has recovered much of his previous energy and I'm glad to be able to report he is running long distances again.

Because it involved my own body my personal experience was the most striking. I had suffered from migraine headaches for many years. In recent months these became more frequent, e.g. five in the first month of this year, each one lasting two to three days during which I was unable to attend work. I have been to regular doctors and specialists who have assured me that there was nothing seriously wrong but could do no more than recommend avoidance of triggers and prescribe medication to dull the severity of the attacks.

After only three days on your diet and supplements I started to feel better. I awoke each morning with far more energy than I have been used to for years. I lost about eight pounds in body weight and still feel much better for that. But the most significant result for me is that since I started the diet I have not had one minor headache. It feels so good to be out of that recurring cycle of tension and migraine that I had come to expect as unavoidable. In addition, my brain seems to work much better. I am able to remember details and peoples' names much better than I have ever done in the last ten years. To sum it all up, I feel great.

My family and I want to express our gratitude to you for this marked improvement in our health. It worked just as you said it would and we are very grateful to you.

Malcolm K. Smith
North Vancouver, B.C.

CHAPTER 8

Absorption and Detoxification

Getting the stomach working again is an important step towards health. However, getting the intestine working properly is the next step.

More importantly, a very large percentage of people I see who have been following diets have actually worsened their health. I call this "Health Book Syndrome", because usually the worse the blood picture, the more health books the person has read.

There were several events that really opened my eyes to the prevalence and potential seriousness of overdoing anything, even something as apparently innocuous as diet. There was a big strong young construction labourer whom I had started treating. After a few visits to set up a diet for him, he didn't return. Often patients wish to take a slower pace than the one we set out for them, so I never thought anything of it. Several months later he came in and I could hardly recognize him. He was weak, emaciated, physically and emotionally exhausted. He had started on my diet, but had met a local raw-foods advocate who told him to throw away our program and she would have him really healthy in no time. She put him on a rigorous raw-foods diet without any personalized testing. He immediately felt worse and began to lose weight rapidly. Her explanation was that he was detoxifying and would soon feel better. When his physical decline continued and emotional weakness started, she said that the only place that could help him was in Texas. At great expense to him, he flew to Texas where the treatment was continued and his decline went on unabated.

When he finally came in to see me again, his metabolism had become so hyper from his weakened state that he actually tested stronger on mixing carbohydrates and proteins together. Also, he had been given a lot of fruit which he was sensitive to. He also had a severe intestinal flora imbalance which wasn't dealt with. They had eliminated protein from his diet, which was something he had a higher-than-average need for. Most importantly, he was given too much scratchy fiber for his intestine to handle, and his ileocecal valve was malfunctioning and dumping large quantities of toxins into the blood. After altering his diet accordingly he regained his physical and emotional strength within a month.

I find that problems with the ileocecal valve have reached almost epidemic proportions and it can be tragic. Shortly after this experience I had two patients within a week who had both been vegetarians for over twenty years, grew much of their own food organically, and practised a certain degree of food combining. One had cancer of the liver, the other hardening of the arteries requiring bypass surgery. It can be a bit intimidating when a patient has already been following the basis of your program, even if without your guidance, and has suffered from it. While they both showed sensitivities to some of the foods they were eating and both showed intestinal flora problems, the major weakness I could identify was an extreme ileocecal valve problem.

Since that time I have checked for ileocecal valve problems much more carefully, and find that nearly half of the people I see for the first time have problems with this important valve. The most common denominator is that almost all of them have actively attempted to improve their health. They have read widely about health and have tried to conscientiously apply what they have read to their day-to-day lifestyle. The other thing in common is that their blood pictures are generally worse than those of people who've never done a thing for their own health.

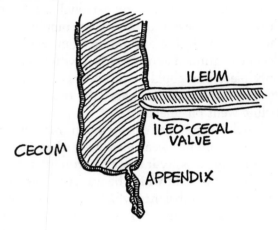

It would appear that health advocates have somehow led people off the road to health. The problem is that fiber is touted as an intestinal broom which can sweep debris from the intestine. Actually the coarser fibers function more as an intestinal rake, irritating the ileocecal valve and thus greatly increasing the quantities of toxins in the blood.

The earlier stages of ileocecal valve problems may not show any signs or symptoms, but as the valve becomes increasingly sensitized a number of things may appear. Probably the most indicative is irregular bowel movements. Every stool may be different. There may be constipation and/or diarrhea. Some of the other indications are tenderness in the lower right abdomen in the area also associated with appendicitis, a sense of fullness after eating small amounts, bloating, and gas. Many of these symptoms may be obviously worse after eating high-fiber foods such as bran or raw vegetables, or irritating spices. The symptoms can be identical to those associated with yeast problems. I find many patients are taking large quanities of yeast killers with little improvement, as the malfunctioning ileocecal valve is the source of their toxicity.

Testing indicates that the main organ to suffer from ileocecal valve problems is the gallbladder, so signs and symptoms may also occur from there.

Poor fat metabolism and the endless list of associated problems, such as acne, hardening of the arteries, strokes and heart attacks, prostaglandin imbalances, weak immunity, stomach spasm and duodenal ulcer from toxic bile irritation, fatigue, and migraines, are sometimes seen with ileocecal problems. Often the person with ileocecal valve problems looks quite healthy, so this barrage of symptoms seems very out of place. It is seldom that anything shows on conventional blood tests, CAT scans, ultrasound or even on physical exam, though a closer look will usually show tenderness deep in the lower right abdomen.

Some patients may have such weakened gallbladder function that they become vegetarians because of their inability to digest fatty foods such as animal proteins. Since many vegetarian diets further emphasize high fiber they can actually make the situation worse. Often a doctor will prescribe more fiber for the bowel problems, or an alternate practitioner will prescribe a raw-food diet, either of which may agrravate the situation. Since the person is now unable to digest the heavier proteins, these are blamed rather than his or her own weakened digestion. I often find the most dogmatic patients have the weakest digestion organs, especially the gallbladder. Sometimes anxiety syndrome is diagnosed, and tranquilizers are prescribed.

To correct an ileocecal valve problem it is important to follow the usual diet and digestion steps: Avoid food sensitivities, especially Group I, do food combinations, avoid scratchy fiber and don't use excessive spice.

Raw vegetables are good for you but it is better to eat the softer things raw, such as leaf lettuce, spinach, avacodoes, sprouts, and tomatoes. The coarser, scratchy vegetables such as celery, broccoli, cauliflower and root vegetables are better juiced if you want them raw, or steamed or otherwise cooked until softened so that their fiber is less irritating.

Grains are dried foods and are quite coarse, irritating to the ileocecal valve. If they are cooked or soaked in water they become softer and less irritating. Oatmeal well-cooked is reasonably soft, while granola is dry and scratchy.

The other way to soften grain fiber is to have it worked over by micro-organisms first. The north European style of making sourdough rye bread by letting bacteria ferment it overnight both softens the fiber and partially predigests the flour, making it easier to digest and preventing any intestinal bad guys from having an easy time on all that fuel. Unfortunately, many sourdough breads these days are made with artificial methods that mimic the action of bacteria but don't have the same beneficial results.

Probably the scratchiest fiber is wheat bran. Baking it, such as in bran muffins, makes it even worse. It's fine if you don't have an ileocecal valve problem, but if you do it has the effect of thousands of little razor blades on a sensitized valve.

If we step back a minute we can see that there is a pattern to this replacement of beneficial creatures. It starts with agriculture.

Fertile soil is a blend of living, dying and dead plants, animals and micro-organisms mixed with the minerals of the earth.

Modern agriculture adds chemicals to boost the minerals available to the plants, and has tried to push the "bad" organisms out of this interdependent environment with pesticides and herbicides.

Similar methods are used in animal husbandry. Antibiotics are considered necessary in the crowded livestock-production environments of today. The residues from those antibiotics and pesticides carry over into the food chain.

Food manufacturing is a major business and its main goal is to get the food to you before the smaller creatures of the planet get a share of it and make a profit. The removal of the choicest nutrients in the food prevents them from getting a crack at it. Of course it also prevents us from getting them. Chemicals are used routinely to prevent the growth of the opposition.

Medicine has a similar approach: Kill the invaders.

The result of all this applied chemistry has been fantastic. More food is grown than can possibly be used for years to come. Mine shafts in the U.S. are filled with wheat and dairy products and farmers can still grow far more. Stores are filled with a variety and quantity of food that the rulers of ancient civilizations couldn't have dreamed of. Hunger is a forgotten word in the mainstream of the industrialized countries. Infectious disease has been under control for decades with antibiotics. Things have never looked so good.

Yet you walk down any street in the U.S. and you see that a third of the population is overweight. Hospitals are overflowing. Patients are backed up waiting for surgery. The governments of countries that have taken responsibilty for their citizens' health are approaching bankruptcy trying to maintain free "health" care, but how much has the real health of the population increased? Allergies have become almost normal in North American children while they're unheard of in "underdeveloped" countries.

It takes little insight to realize that the constitutions of our children, which took thousands of generations to build, are rapidly deteriorating due to poor diet and short-sighted medicine. With the same mentality, the soil that is our true wealth, that has taken perhaps tens of thousands of years to build up, is being rapidly depleted.

Is this another of those gloomy stories of impending doom? Certainly not. The human is such a flexible, resilient creature that we will probably stumble through our present crises like we've managed to stumble through all the other troubles of the past. Out of these potential troubles come tremendous opportunities. Farmers have proven that they can grow quantity. The next step is to aim for quality, which also leaves the soil in a richer state. Organic farming has been proven viable. It just requires consumers to ask for quality first.

It may be necessary for more local producers to supply an area, if we want to get quality without all the preservatives.

The depletion of health in many children can be readily reversed, as shown in the letters from patients. The expense of naturopathic medicine is not high. Few of my patients pay over a few hundred dollars for their care at my clinic. Not only did they receive relief of chronic disease that was considered incurable, but they also received a lifelong understanding, as they now know what caused their health problems and what to do to prevent these from returning. Education, not expensive technology, is the key to health.

This is not to say there is no place for high-tech medicine. There is not a diagnostic device, drug or surgical technique that doesn't have a time and a place to be used to someone's advantage. Remember though that it is the results of disease that are being dealt with, not the causes.

Since no doctor, type of practise or philosophy of healing can help every patient or every type of problem, it's important that there be a variety of approaches to the treatment of disease. A person who slips through the "safety net" of one mode of healing might still have hope that another practioner with different experiences and insights might catch them and help them back to health.

Naturopathic medicine is time-proven. Its therapies are rooted in antiquity. Hippocrates stated, "Let food be your medicine, and medicine be your food". All cultures have used herbs, hot and cold, fasting and diet to maintain health over thousands of generations. Few of the drugs and surgical methods used in western medicine are over a hundred years old, yet during that period of time naturopathic medicine was almost eliminated.

During the last fifty years, "miracle drugs" and surgical techniques were to rescue helpless humanity forever from the perils of disease. As Big Medicine took over the responsibilty for health, the voices that spoke of obvious connections between lifestyle and disease were drowned out by the thundering stampede to junk food and irresponsible lifestyle. During this era of big fin cars, suburbia, ice cream with every meal and a pill for every ill, a purge of "unscientific" medicine began in the political halls and courts of North America. The almost hysterical self-righteousness of the medical profession and its political clout overwhelmed lifestyle-oriented physicians. Rights to practise were withdrawn in state after state, until naturopathy was confined mainly to a few Pacific Northwest states and a few Canadian provinces.

That the demise of alternate practioners in the U.S. has been high-handed is well-documented. The following is the initial decision by Administrative Law Judge, Ernest G. Barnes, Docket No. 9064, dated November 13, 1978:

" The Federal Court determined that the AMA has produced a formidable impediment to competition in the delivery of health care services by physicians in this country. That barrier has served to deprive consumers of the free flow of information about the availability of health care services, to deter the offering of innovative forms of health care and to stifle the rise of almost every type of health care delivery that could potentially pose a threat to the income of fee-for-services physicians in private practice. The costs to the public in terms of less expensive or even, perhaps, more improved forms of medical services are great."

In Canada similar events took place. In his book "Canadian Medicine: A Study in Limited Entry", Ronald Homowy summarizes:

" The following study's conclusions dispute the widely held belief that the various statutes and regulations raising the requirements for medical licensure were, in the first instance, enacted to protect the public from so-called incompetents. The historical data provide substantial evidence that the profession's motives in raising the standards of entry in medical practice and in instituting policies that prohibited advertising or any sort of price competition were almost purely ones of economic self-interest. . . . It is foolish to suppose that their occupation exalts them above using the means at their disposal to act in their own private interests."

Naturopathic training includes as much basic medical science as any health-care profession. Research is an important part of the naturopathic colleges. The quality of naturopathic education and a more open political environment have resulted in the passing of new laws in recent years in Washington, Oregon, Arizona and Alaska that have expanded the rights of naturopathic physicians to practise. Many other states are also considering expanding or relicensing this traditional approach to health care.

Speeding up your digestion by improving stomach function and following food combinations can result in virtual starvation for the intestinal competitors. The less food they digest, the less toxic stress on your system, the less free-radical irritation, the greater your body's inherent healing power. Homeostasis can swing the pendulum away from disease and back to health.

Using inhibitors of the bad intestinal flora, at the same time as speeding up your digestion, can often boost the improvement greatly.

The most important inhibitors of intestinal baddies are lactobacillus acidophilus. These friendly bacteria are the ones that turn milk into yogurt. The bacteria are most active if the yogurt is used when fresh, meaning within a day of making. It should also be used in proper combination.

Since the acidophilus only lives in the intestine for a few hours before it dies, we usually take it in capsules two or three times per day. Taking it after meals results in some of the bacteria being killed by the digestive juice, though some get through. It's a little more effective taking it about half an hour before meals.

We use capsules that also have lactobacillus bifidus with the acidophilus. This is the cousin of acidophilus and is the one that thrives best on mother's milk. It is the most common type of intestinal flora until about seven years of age, when the acidophilus predominates.

There are other species of lactobacillus bacteria used in making sourdough, which is more beneficial than bread that is only raised by yeast.

Some of the other things known to inhibit yeast are garlic, lemon, chlorophyll (found in greens) and oxygen. No doubt there are many more, especially in many of the herbs.

Free radicals and prostaglandins cannot be stored because they only exist for a fraction of a second. However, there is an actual physical storage of toxins that takes place, because in some people one of the first signs of increased vitality is feeling worse, as the body quickly puts its new-found energy into "housecleaning".

Withdrawal symptoms are well-known and are often seen when stimulants such as coffee, tobacco, chocolate or alcohol are removed. Besides the short-term headaches, disorientation, moodiness and fatigue during withdrawal from these drugs, there can be any number of symptoms as the body takes its surplus of digestive energy and tries to eliminate years of stored toxins.

Most of the toxins are stored in the large intestine area, apparently in the membranes. This may be because toxins produced in the intestine irritate the intestinal membrane. The membrane then makes mucous to protect itself. If the toxic irritation continues, then the mucous actually may form a coating over the membranes which can eventually thicken, trapping the toxins in it. As long as the toxins are held in this way they can't get absorbed and generate free radicals and bad prostaglandins, but they can't be eliminated from the body either.

This gradually-thickening mucous coating will reduce the absorption of toxins into the blood. Of course it will also decrease the absorption of nutrients.

As formation of intestinal toxins quickly decreases with speeding up of the digestion, the body may rapidly break up this mucous coating and release its stored toxins. If they are then absorbed into the blood they may cause symptoms to temporarily worsen.

It's not unusual to see strings of mucous in the stool, sometimes blood-tinged, for a short period of time, possibly because of the removal of this coating. To aid this removal of intestinal mucous there are several things that can be used. One is psyllium hulls, which are the seeds of the plantain plant. They are used in powdered form. When water is added it swells into a jelly-like mass. This provides bulk to help bowel movements without the scratchiness of bran. If a large quantity of psyllium is taken at one time, it can form a ball which can block the intestine for a few days, so the better way is to take a small amount at the start, perhaps 1 tsp. two times a day before meals and slowly increase the quantity so that the intestine gradually gets filled.

Clay is sometimes used in conjunction with psyllium. The most common type used is called bentonite. It works as an astringent, pulling the toxins out of the membrane into the intestine rather than releasing them into the blood.

The result of detoxifying the intestine will be increased absorption of nutrients, often very noticeable to a person as an improved sense of well-being. The loss of this membrane coating will, however, also make a person more sensitive, as dietary indiscretions that place even small amounts of toxins in the large intestine will result in greater absorption of them as well. So a person may experience insomnia after one cup of coffee at night, while before detoxification it may have taken several cups for that to happen.

In some ways it makes this approach to health a one-way street. Once you're into it there's no way out. As the organs start working

better most people usually feel much better quickly. Since now the organs tell the person when he or she is making mistakes rather than just staying passively in a state of shock, what a person can get away with is apparently reduced.

This is a bit of an illusion, as the person didn't really get away with anything before. It was just they didn't experience any immediate reaction to whatever they ate or drank, so they may have assumed it wasn't bad for them. In fact the body did have a bad reaction but didn't have the strength to indicate it. It's these many little accumulated suppressed reactions that eventually add up to "sudden" breakdowns such as heart attacks or cancer many years later.

If old toxins are stirred up faster than the elimination organs can handle them, a person can feel worse for a while. This used to be a major problem in my practise, but with a little experience I've managed to greatly reduce the incidences of healing crises.

Anyone who has a chronic disease has already overloaded the elimination organs. It doesn't take very much "stirring up" to overwhelm the already-overloaded organs, especially the lymph system.

Fortunately there is a pumping system to keep the lymph flowing. While the blood has the reliable heart to pump its rich cargo through

the red sea of life, the lymph and veins are pumped by the contractions of the skeletal muscles of the body, through exercise. Exercise
is important for proper waste elimination.

I must add that of all the professional and Olympic athletes I've
seen, none of them tested as having the digestive and lymph systems
working up to par either, so exercise is not a cure-all that can totally
replace improving diet and digestion. Obviously the way to keep the
lymph system clear is to minimize the metabolic debris that it has to
handle, by having quick and efficient digestion.

There are some tricks that can be played on the lymph system as
well. The tonsils are the part of the lymph system that are best
known. They are commonly aggravated in children and can be tremendously swollen. The key to a lasting cure is of course attending
to the digestive system, but short-term improvement can sometimes
be gained with direct physical pressure on them.

The tonsils are normally soft, somewhat sponge-like. They get
harder as they swell with toxic matter. If they are "squeezed",
sometimes this toxic material will squirt right out of the tonsil. This
is achieved by putting a finger down the side of the throat, so as to
reduce gagging. Then when contact is made on the tonsil it is
squeezed against the side of the throat. If good contact is made often

quantities of foul toxins will be squeezed out, and sometimes dramatic improvements in overall health can occur. Since doing this is startling and causes gagging, I seldom do it myself but rather show patients how to do it and let them decide if it's worth it to them. One patient found she gagged less if she used the handle of a long spoon. This usually has to be repeated frequently until the dietary changes start to have an effect.

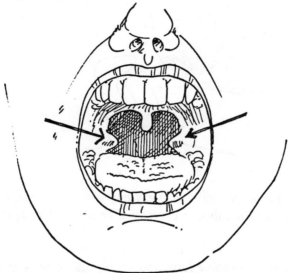

The glands of the neck are often swollen, and can be assisted in draining by massaging the neck in a downward direction. Since specific muscles pump specific parts of the lymph system, stimulation of a muscle will result in greater flow of lymph from its associated organ.

Testing indicates that the muscles most in need of stimulation are the tensor facia latae muscles found on the outside of the thighs. These muscles pump the lymph flow from the large intestine, which of course is where most of the toxins originate. Stimulation is done by vigorously rubbing the leg with a bristly shower brush, loofa or skin brush so that it is lightly irritated. Rubbing the inside of the thigh will also stimulate the small intestine lymph.

Rubbing the chest area will stimulate kidneys, liver, pancreas, stomach and gallbladder. Many of the muscles that pump these organs' lymph drainage are found between the ribs and are associated with breathing, so breath is not only important for its vital delivery of oxygen but also for helping to pump the drainage of toxins.

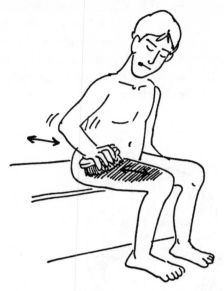

It only takes a few minutes every day while in the shower to give these areas a quick rub and thereby give the lymph system a little boost.

Lymphatic baths can be done several ways.

One way is to dissolve four pounds of Epsom salts in hot water.

Don't stay longer than fifteen minutes, and don't repeat for a week or so.

Also, you can add two pounds each of sea salt and baking soda to warm or hot water, and soak twenty to twenty-five minutes. For more information on baths see "Psychoimmunity and the Healing System", edited by Jason Serinus.

Another way is to draw a warm bath with approximately one cup of Chlorox bleach added. Soak for fifteen to thirty minutes and then follow with a normal shower. Keep head and hair out of the water.

The white blood cells are more active at slightly higher-than-normal body temperatures. The body creates fever as a way to enhance immune system function. The body temperature can be elevated for hours after vigorous excercise, during which period the white blood cell activity is accelerated.

The use of sweat lodges and saunas is universal among cultures in the temperate climates as a means of purification. In most long-term uses of heat, it is important to follow the hot with cold, as excess heat weakens the body while cold stimulates and tonifies.

The Finns are famous for their saunas and also for the high rate of heart attacks. One study showed there was a correlation between the two. Those who went right from the very hot to the very cold were the ones who had the most heart attacks. The sudden exposure to cold stimulates the heart to beat rapidly, but most of the blood still is in the arms and legs, and there isn't enough blood for the heart to function properly. Those who expose their arms and legs to cold first, to put the blood back into the chest before exposing it to cold, don't have such high rates of heart attack.

In the early stages of a cold, a hot bath before bed accompanied by extra covers can induce a fever which might burn up the cold over-night. It is also useful to take two grams of vitamin C about every hour until diarrhea is induced. The vitamin C works both as a buffer of toxins and as a mild laxative if enough is taken. The laxative effect is important, as you will find most acute illness preceded by a period of poor digestion. Bioflavenoids, especially rutin, work with vitamin C to inhibit viruses.

The white blood cells can be stimulated by a number of nutrients and herbs. This is too big a topic to cover in this book. Every naturopathic physician is trained to help boost the immune system as a way to aid a person to health.

Beets, both root and leaf, have been known to aid liver function. As the beet pigments discolor the stool, it's not unusual to have a patient think that there is blood in the stool when they start taking beets.

Dandelion root and leaf are also known to be good for the liver and skin, and are commonly used in liver formulas. Every company that makes nutritional products has its own formula for improving the liver. Methionine, inositol and choline are also common ingredients in these formulas, as they are important tools for the liver to detoxify efficiently.

The most important factor in keeping the stress off the gallbladder is to keep the ileocecal valve working properly. It is critical to not use any more scratchy fiber than the intestine can handle. Black radish tablets are sometimes useful to soothe the membranes of the intestine, so that the ileocecal valve becomes more resistent to abrasion. A long-term calcium deficiency often underlies a sensitive ilocecal valve. Silica extract (from horsetail herb), available from health food stores everywhere, may overcome this deficiency. Chlorophyll also sometimes aids the ileocecal valve to regain proper function as well as being soothing to intestinal membranes.

It is very important to keep the bowels regular during detoxification, even if laxatives or enemas need to be taken for a short time. If one is prone to constipation, it's good to stay away from constipating foods such as cheese and bananas, and to drink plenty of water. Start the day with soaked or stewed prunes, figs and raisins. Remember the stomach juices are the spark for proper functioning of the intestine.

Exercise is also important for proper bowel movements. Our bodies are designed to move. Movement puts pressure on the abdominal organs, including the intestine, and helps stimulate their proper function.

Walking is the cheapest and most available form of exercise. For the last hundred years mankind has put great effort into finding ways to avoid walking, but now we realize how important it is to exercise.

We have seen that exercise is important for stimulating the liver, and gallbladder and intestines, thus helping regular bowel movements, pumping the lymph and vein systems, and raising the body temperature, which in turn aids the immune system.

PATIENTS' LETTERS

I first visited your office, Dr. Matsen, in late December 1986, with symptoms of a virus infection diagnosed by a general practitioner ten years ago. I have had headaches, achy joints and muscles, very low energy and slowed thinking over this period. I had been given everything from aspirin to antibiotics with no improvement.

After your food sensitivity testing I started your diet and supplements. Since last March I had had no further attacks or symptoms!

> *Yours gratefully*
> *Mrs. Dorothy Atwell*

In February of 1895 I went to the Northshore Naturopathic Clinic and saw Dr. Matsen for "unexplained infertility".

After trying for years to have a child and having been to many doctors and specialists and having hormones for ten years, I still did not get pregnant.

Dr. Matsen advised me and changed my diet completely. He prescribed several supplements and within six months I was pregnant.

I now have a beautiful healthy daughter. With Dr. Matsen's help and advice, our long awaited desire for a child became a reality.

> *Yours sincerely*
> *Angela Shemesh*
> *North Vancouver, B.C.*

CHAPTER 9

Three Stages to Health

Let's review what has been suggested so far for the three weeks of Phase I.

First, avoid food Groups I, II and III so the stomach can get back to work making those important digestive juices.

Second, do food combining, separating carbohydrates from proteins and fruit from grains and starches, to speed up the digestion so the intestinal critters don't make so many new toxins. Hypermetabolic people or those with severe metabolic imbalances, such as hypoglycemia, diabetes, epilepsy, narcolepsy, etc., should be under supervision and may be best off to skip Stage I and use the dietary guidelines of Stage III.

Third, take acidophilus and other critter inhibitors such as garlic, chlorophyll and lemon to slow down their digestion, to further reduce their toxin production.

Fourth, eat light foods in the morning as much as possible, so as to have a surplus of digestive juice, which will help clean out the old toxins.

Fifth, exercise regularly, do skin brushing and possibly liver/gallbladder and/or lymph supplementation, to help the elimination organs.

Now a sixth step can be added. In my practise we usually also do eight or nine hydrotherapy treatments, alternating hot and cold, and electronic stimulation. The effect is to gently "jump-start" the digestive organs and aid the elimination organs. Usually by the third or fourth hydrotherapy treatment a person begins to make surplus digestive juice which begins to clean out the old toxins.

How long should these activities be continued? It takes on average about three weeks for the major digestive organs to get "recharged". They are not fully recovered from years of abuse, but there is now "energy" going into them instead of draining out.

People with strong constitutions and high vitality may stir up the old toxins very quickly. If they also have weak elimination organs they may feel worse before feeling better, as they may not be able to eliminate the toxins as fast as they're being stirred up. People with weaker vitality may not experience this worsened feeling, as they usually will not stir things up very quickly. Of course their overall improvement will proceed at a slower rate.

Usually a person feels quite a bit better within three weeks, though it's not unusual to feel a little rough during the first week, due to a combination of withdrawal and detoxification. If cravings for sweets are are too strong, a mineral supplement high in magnesium, iodine and trace minerals will quickly dispel them. Bile salts can also reduce cravings for sweets in some people.

STAGE II

An interesting thing happens to food sensitivities after three weeks or so. On retesting, most people test strong to all Group IV foods and usually to Group III foods, as well as to all Group II foods except baking yeast. Group I usually still tests weak. The necessity for avoiding food combinations remains the same, except in people who are hypermetabolic.

Testing shows that they will do better mixing starches or grains with proteins.

During the three weeks we have succeeded in speeding up and improving the person's digestion and absorption, so that there are now more nutrients in the blood. At the same time digestion by the intestinal bad guys has been inhibited, so less toxins are now being deposited in the blood stream. Consequently, the cells get more nutrients, wastes are removed more quickly, and the body as a whole more readily regulates itself through homeostasis. If the healing capacity of the blood is now greater than the disease process, even chronic disease will quickly disappear.

Although the blood may be strong enough to heal chronic disease, the blood pictures show that it is seldom as good at this stage as it potentially could be. The key to understanding this is the fact that while most other foods now test as being okay, baking yeast will still test as a problem. Even though baking yeast is supposedly dead when baked in bread, it does test as weakening to the body when yeast within the body is a problem.

When after three weeks on the diet the baking yeast still tests weak while most other things are testing stronger, the yeast in the body is still there. However, the big party that the yeast has been having is over. The person is eating less of the foods that yeast thrives on and taking things that inhibit yeast and most importantly, digesting much more quickly. Since the bad flora now have less feeding time at your intestinal trough, they make fewer toxins. With fewer toxins to aggravate them, the function of the organs improves. The usual sequence in which the organs and glands become stronger is stomach, pancreas and parotid, small intestine, large intestine, liver, spleen and thymus, endocrine glands, and gallbladder. This is basically the reverse order in which they developed their problems. The sequence is affected by individual weaknesses, especially if organ damage exists.

This is usually the point where we add to yeast inhibitors the yeast killers. It's important that a person should feel fairly well at this point, or the yeast killer should be delayed. The reason is that as the yeast die off they are quite toxic and can foul up an already-overloaded elimination system, making the person feel considerably worse. By waiting until the digestion is improved and the elimination organs are strengthened before using yeast killer, there are two advantages.

1) You are stronger and the yeast is weaker, making it more certain to die off quickly. Thus you should only need to take yeast killer for a few weeks rather than the months to years that some people end up taking it.

2) Since your digestion is now working much more quickly, there isn't so much undigested food lying around for yeast to regrow on. By killing it off after improving digestion, you should only need to take the yeast killer once.

Compare this approach to dealing with mosquitoes. One can ignore them. This might be called the "Eastern" approach. Another way is to swat them one by one. This might be called the "Natural" approach. A third way is to engulf oneself and the area with poisonous chemicals. Call this the "Western" approach.

"EASTERN"   "NATURAL"   "WESTERN"

The fourth and most effective way may be to drain the swamp that the mosquitos breed in. The same is true of yeast. If you drain the "intestinal swamp" by first improving digestion, you will get rid of the yeast and you need never have a problem with it again, as there will now be no undigested food lying around for it to feast on.

There are a number of yeast killers available. The most consistently effective and readily available is caprylic acid. It is an eight-chain saturated fatty acid usually extracted from coconut fat or butter, and sold mainly through health food stores. There is no toxicity to caprylic acid as such, but because it is fatty it can be stressful to those who have major liver or gallbladder problems.

The effectiveness of caprylic acid is also its main drawback. The yeast often dies off very quickly and can cause dramatic temporary reactions in some people. A way to reduce the impact of these reactions is to start with three capsules with each meal for an adult for two days. If there is no reaction after two days, increase to four capsules twice a day for two days. If there is no reaction, increase to five, and so on until taking eight capsules twice a day. If there is a reaction at (say) five capsules twice a day, go back to four or less until feeling better, then slowly increase again.

I suggest using it twice a day because our program favours two meals a day. If a person has to have three full meals per day due to need for higher calorie intake because of heavier physical exertion or exposure to cold, or as an aid to stabilizing hypoglycemia, then he/she should take the caprylic acid three times per day with meals. Starting with two three times per day for two days, increase to three three times, until gradually working up to five three times per day. Again, if a bad reaction is experienced, reduce the dose immediately.

There are other yeast killers that aren't in a fatty base that can be used in liver/gallbladder problems or by children. Since these aren't readily available, you should consult your naturopath.

Yeast are seldom the only "critters" inhabiting the intestine. However, killing the yeast often will eliminate the toxic environment that these bad guys need to thrive in as well as decreasing the load on the immune system.

Some readily-available products that help inhibit or kill other parasites are pumpkin seeds for tapeworms, garlic for pinworms, and enzymes such as bromelain found in pineapple or papain found in papaya which help to digest a number of different organisms. If enzymes are taken with a meal they help to digest protein. If taken between meals they get into the bloodstream where they help do housecleaning including eating away at critters. Other things are

available through your naturopathic physician to help boost your immune system.

STAGE III

If you've had a puppy with worms, you know the incredible boost in vitality that can occur after they've been removed. When a person is retested after taking yeast killers a similar thing is apparent. Virtually everything tests strong. All Group IV, Group III and Group II foods test strong. Sometimes even some of the Group I non-foods such as sugar test strong, but this usually only lasts for a few days.

Even the combinations change. After the yeast killers, fruit with grains tests okay. Grains or starches with proteins test okay. However, protein tested with sweets, (even with many of the sweet fruits) still tests as a problem. The sub-acid fruits are less of a problem. Sometimes an acid, such as cider vinegar or lemon used with sweet and protein, will antidote the weakness.

How do we explain this? Mixing fruit with grains, or proteins with grains, slows down digestion, but the yeast isn't waiting in the intestine in large quantities now to jump in and make toxins. Mixing the proteins and sweets, however, slows down digestion so much that although the yeast isn't there to make toxins, "good" bacteria switch their white hats to black hats and start to make toxins.

A sub-acid or acid fruit may stimulate the stomach enough to overcome some of the stomach inhibiting effect of the sweet. It may be pushing one's luck to try these combinations. However, there seems to always be a limit to how long food can sit undigested in that dark, damp, warm, germ-infested tube we call the intestine. Before the increase of yeast-related problems brought about by antibiotics and refined carbohydrates such as white sugar and white flour, people could undoubtedly eat starches, grains and proteins together routinely without any adverse side-effects. Since sweets were rare in peasant cultures, they had little problem with mixing sweets and protein, and if they did have problems their elimination organs and immune systems could quickly deal with them.

Civilized diets inevitably offer more and more temptations to the palate. Affections of children are bought with sweets, and dessert with meals becomes routine as income increases. As the elimination organs and immune system become fouled up, medication becomes necessary to "save" the helpless person. The downward spiral in health has begun.

After regaining efficient digestion and THEN killing off the competing intestinal critters, the quality of a person's blood usually improves dramatically, sometimes to perfection. The blood has reached its ideal state: rich with all the necessary nutrients and low in irritating toxins. The cells receive all the raw materials they need and their wastes are readily removed. Homeostasis is in control, and when you reach this state you can virtually feel your blood "purr" through your body.

What happens from this point depends mainly on the vitality of the person. If one has high vitality and few accumulated toxins it isn't too necessary to pay heed to food combinations other than to avoid mixing sweets and proteins. Eating lightly in the morning when possible will usually be enough to continue a gradual detoxification. Of course, remaining on the stricter regime can only add to already bountiful health.

A person with average vitality and a fair amount of toxins accumulated over years of digestive malfunction, but no real chronic disease, should continue to eat lightly in the morning to continue removing the old metabolic debris. Such a person should continue to separate the starches and grains from the proteins. A little starch or grain with protein once in a while usually isn't a problem. For example, barley in chicken soup is no problem. Many of the ethnic ways of eating, using small amounts of protein with starch or grain, are no problem occasionally.

However, a person with weak vitality, large amounts of accumulated toxicity and/or chronic disease will need to remain on the stricter regime much longer. Stage I or II should be maintained as long as necessary so the surplus digestive energy can go out into the bloodstream. It takes time to chip away those years of accumulated fat and metabolic debris. Ideally, such a person should be under the supervision of a naturopath. A sedentary person usually feels best on Stages I and II. Homeopathic remedies can sometimes rebuild depleted vitality. There are also supplements to aid the removal of old accumulated toxins. Every naturopath is experienced in detoxification, as this has been the underlying theme of Naturopathy for hundreds of years. Professional guidance can save a lot of time and money, and prevent complications when intensive detoxification is necessary.

No practitioner or philosophy can help every patient in every circumstance. I have sent hundreds of patients to medical doctors, chiropractors, physiotherapists, massage therapists, psychologists, etc., because they could give better care for a particular problem than I could.

The most important thing that you should have gained from this program is sensitivity. You should now know when you have eaten something wrong, as your once-spasmed and somewhat muted stomach should now be talking back in full voice. Sometimes the message won't come right after eating something. Maybe the message will be in the form of cloudy thinking or moodiness a day or two after, but if you're paying attention you will see now that your digestion is affecting every little nuance of your life. At this point diet books, including this one, will have lost much of their value. Now, instead of being told what you should and shouldn't eat, you can get that information directly from the best teacher you could have, your own body.

Sometimes people stray farther than they should, and regain their old problems or even gain new ones as the digestive strength begins to wane. Sometimes they panic and forget what to do to reverse the problem. Simply start again at the beginning of this program or go to see your naturopath.

PATIENT'S LETTER

I first went to see Dr. Matsen in 1984 for psoriasis as I was dissatisfied with the dermatologist's creams, ointments and impersonal care which seemed to have little or no effect. After about four months of my personalized diet and specific supplements from Dr. Matsen the symptoms disappeared, although the psoriasis reoccurs at times if I go too far off the diet.

In January, 1987, I experienced abdominal pain and frequent blood and mucous in diarrhea. When this continued for a couple of weeks I went to a medical doctor who referred me to a gastrointestinal (G.I.) specialist. He gave me an internal examination and blood tests and x-rays including a colonoscopy. For this ordeal I was an outpatient at St. Paul's Hospital where after several enemas and an injection of barium, a length of hose with a lighting device and microscope was inserted. The doctor, assistant and I could watch a monitor or actually look into the tube and see the colon. I was really impressed with this technology but the pain was excruciating. After this and x-ray results the diagnosis was ulcerative colitis.

The G.I. specialist had prescribed tablets that would control the symptoms, although the side effects included nausea, headaches and possible financial hardship (they cost sixty dollars a month). I asked if a change in diet or lifestyle would help. His response was "Oh, no, it's not uncommon for a person your age (I'm thirty-four) to have colitis, but it is treatable. This is very serious and you'll probably take medication the rest of your life . . . but there's nothing else you can do."

I was not satisfied with this and definitely not interested in taking any prescription for the rest of my life. So I went to see Dr. Matsen again. When I told him the diagnosis, his warm and optimistic response was "We'll have you fixed up in a couple of weeks!" What a relief. He humourously explained what was going on in my digestive system and why my white blood cells were attacking my intestine. With a combination of hydrotherapy, a return to my original diet that I had wandered from, a few supplements and my personal committment to get well, I am now relieved of my symptoms and apparently cured of colitis, and in only five weeks.

Jan Stephenson
Vancouver, B.C.

PART III

MENU PLANS AND RECIPES

CHAPTER 10

Introduction

It is impossible to tell people exactly what to eat and when to eat it. Different people have different metabolisms, affected by weather, type of work, stress and organ function, never mind a wide variety of tastes. People with metabolic imbalances such as hypoglycemia, diabetes, epilepsy, narcolepsy, or are overly metabolic, that is they burn up calories rapidly and have trouble gaining weight, should be under supervision and possible need to start at Stage III.

The Menu Plans are only very general guidelines and are not to be taken dogmatically. The closer you can follow them the better but don't worry if you can't.

In theory a person should be able to go only on water for three days or so with little fluctuation in their energy. However, few people these days have organs that function that well. Detoxifying them will eventually greatly improve their function but at the beginning you may only be able to eat light in the morning for a short period of time. How long that is is entirely up to you. Get a little hungry in the morning before you actually eat a meal but don't leave it so long that you actually get weak and lightheaded. If it's only a few minutes that's okay, that's a few minutes that the body was able to detoxify and the next day you might be able to go a few minutes longer. If you're doing heavy physical labour or sports, especially in cold weather, you might need a large breakfast. Try and make up for it by going lighter on your days off.

Many of the recipes take time and not everyone takes time to prepare their own food. If you use restaurants try to avoid the deep fry places as much as you can. Many of the better restaurants menus are a la carte so food combining needn't be a problem. Many restaurants will substitute to your direction and not use MSG if you ask. If it's necessary to break the combinations, things like soup, even if not combined properly, are often easy to digest. Try to avoid heavy sauces. Most vegetarian restaurants are quite careful as to their ingredients.

The more relaxed you are, the better your digestion works. The more you chew the less strain on the pancreas. Drinking while eating interferes with production of digestive juice. Drinking of most liquids after eating dilutes the digestive juice thus slowing digestion. Water however can get past the food and into the intestine without interfering with digeston. Overeating will bog down the digestive system for hours and certainly prevent any surplus digestive juice being available for detoxifying. Undereating can result in deficiencies of calories, proteins, vitamins, minerals, essential fatty acids, fiber and force the body to cannibalize itself to provide fuel. This is the point where fasting becomes starvation and is seen often because of the emphasis that fashion has placed on leanness rather than health.

In practise it's not unusual to have a person reverse a chronic disease only to return at a future date with the same or similar symptoms. Only rarely has the stomach returned to its earlier "shocked" state even if they have wandered widely from an ideal diet. Occasionally the yeast has returned, usually a result of eating excess sweets. Sweet fruit such as bananas used liberally, especially in winter, can bring yeast back. However, by far the most common problem that people return with is malfuncton of the ileocecal valve and resultant gallbladder problems due to excessive use of fresh fruits and raw vegetables, coarse grains and sometimes spices. This is especially seen in the fall and winter. The reason is that fresh fruits and raw vegetables are hot-season foods that cool the body, especially the kidney meridian. Since the ileocecal valve is on the kidney meridian it gets more sensitive as the weather cools if summer foods are maintained. Thus as fruits pass out of season they should be used less, or, if at all, should be used warm. Therefore, hot applesauce would be better than fresh apples in winter. The hot lemon drink is excellent in cold weather. As salad season ends, vegetables should be cooked more: steamed, stir-fried or in soups and stews. Hot cereals such as oatmeal are great in cold weather.

The menu plans are not designed with a particular season in mind so you will have to adapt them to suit your own needs.

Good eating and great digestion!

STAGE I DIET

7 Days of Sample Menus

DAY 1 — Monday
a.m. Citrus—Lemon Drink
(One half hour to 1 hour before other fruits)

a.m. "Breakfast"
apples

a.m. Snack "Pick-me-up"
(Optional 2 hrs. after fruit.)
vegetable juice (¾ cup carrot juice mixed with ¼ cup beet juice)

Lunch/Dinner
(Anytime from 10:00 a.m.—if snack is omitted—to 3:00 p.m. as desired) Serve about 2 hrs. after snack or 4 hrs. after fruit.)
1. *Spinach Salad* with a vegetable dressing
2. *Lentil Soup*
3. *Sourdough Rye Bread, Flatbreads* or rice or rye crackers

Supper
(any time from 5:00 p.m. to 9:00 p.m.—should be finished at least 2 hrs. before bedtime)
1. Sliced or chopped vegetables with almond or cashew nut butter (as a dip or spread)—try carrot sticks, cucumber sticks or rounds, green or red bell pepper strips, broccoli trees and/or cauliflower flowerets
2. *Broiled Salmon Steaks or Fillets*
3. Steamed Greens—kale, chard, mustard, beet greens or other greens

* Italicized titles of recipes are recipes found within this book.

DAY 2 — Tuesday
a.m. Citrus—Lemon Drink
(One half hour to 1 hour before other fruits)

a.m. "Breakfast"
plums (in season) or pears

a.m. Snack "Pick-me-up"
(Optional 2 hrs. after fruit.)
Carrot Soup

Lunch/Dinner
1. Avocado half stuffed with sunflower seeds
2. *Brown Rice* with *Curried Red Lentils*
3. *Chick Pea or Lentil Chipatis*

Supper
1. Any leafy green salad with dressing
2. *Herb Scrambled Eggs*
3. Baked or steamed broccoli, zucchini or kohlrabi

DAY 3 — Wednesday
a.m. Citrus—Lemon Drink
(One half hour to 1 hour before other fruits)

a.m. "Breakfast"
grapes

a.m. Snack "Pick-me-up"
(Optional 2 hrs. after fruit)
Vegetable Soup

Lunch/Dinner
1. *Rice Salad* with dressing—try *Herb & Oil* or a vegetable dressing
2. *Chick Pea-Vegetable Spread* spread on:
3. Rye or rice crackers or *Flatbreads*

Supper
1. *Wild Salad* with fresh lemon juice OR *Romaine Salad*

2. *Garlic (or Herb Baked) Chicken*

3. Sauteed or steamed carrots, cauliflower and green beans or peas medley

DAY 4 — Thursday
a.m. Citrus—fresh grapefruit halves
(One half hour to 1 hour before other fruits)

a.m. "Breakfast"
unusual fruit—Japanese pears or Japanese pear-apples (if unavailable—use regular pears)

a.m. Snack "Pick-me-up"
(Optional 2 hrs. after fruit
Vegetable Broth

Lunch/Dinner
1. Celery chunks and/or green pepper quarters and/or cucumber rounds spread or stuffed with:
2. *Falafel Spread*
3. *Flatbreads*, rice or rye crackers

Supper
1. *Oriental Salad* with *Lemon-Oil Dressing*
2. *Egg Foo Yong*
3. *Arrowroot Sauce* (Delicious gravy to top Egg Foo Yong with!)

DAY 5 — Friday
a.m. Citrus—Lemon Drink
(One half hour to 1 hour before other fruits)

a.m. "Breakfast"
melon—cantaloupe, honeydew or watermelon

a.m. Snack "Pick-me-up"
(Optional 2 hrs. after fruit
Green Drink

Lunch/Dinner
1. Carrot and celery sticks
2. *Kidney Bean Stew*

Supper
1. Carrot juice cocktail with added broccoli or parsley juice
2. *Beet Treat*
3. *Stir-Fry Vegetables* with one of the following: pre-cooked chunks of beef, chicken or salmon OR raw baby shrimp or tofu chunks

DAY 6 — Saturday
a.m. Citrus —fresh grapefruit halves
(One half hour to 1 hour before other fruits)

a.m. "Breakfast"
berries or cherries (in season) or grapes

a.m. Snack "Pick-me-up"
Miso Soup

Lunch/Dinner
1. *Bean Tacos* on corn tortillas topped with raw, chopped green or red bell peppers,lettuce, spinach or sprouts, zucchini chunks, sliced black olives and diced red or green onions or chives
2. *Guacamole* (to top tacos with)

Supper
1. *Super Sprout Salad*
2. *Broiled or Baked Trout, Sole, Cod* or other fish
3. *Steamed Artichoke* with melted butter

DAY 7 — Sunday
a.m. Citrus —fresh grapefruit halves
(One half hour to 1 hour before other fruits)

a.m. "Breakfast"
peaches or apricots

a.m. Snack "Pick-me-up"
(Optional 2 hrs. after fruit
vegetable juice (½ carrot, ½ celery and 2–3 sprigs parsley)

Lunch/Dinner
1. *Stuffed Green Peppers*
2. *Vegetarian Gravy* (over peppers)
3. *Baked Turnips* or steamed parsnips

Supper
1. *Zucchini Salad*
2. *Shisk Kebabs* with shrimp, chicken, turkey or tofu pieces
3. Optional: leftover soup from the week

ALTERNATE VEGETARIAN SUPPER SUGGESTION

1. *Baked Butternut Squash* with cinnamon
2. *Tofu Spread* with:
3. Rye crackers, corn chips or *Flatbreads*
4. *Split Pea Soup*

EXTRA SNACK SUGGESTIONS

1. Sesame tahini *or* almond *or* cashew nut butter stuffed in celery
2. Sesame tahini on rice cakes or crackers or rye crackers
3. *Tofu Spread* on cucumber rounds
4. *Spinach-Tofu Spread* with cut vegetables
5. Raw almonds or cashews (chewed well)
6. Sunflower seeds and/or sprouts
7. *Pumpkin, Carrot or Zucchini Muffins*
8. *Guacamole* and corn chips
9. *Eggsalad* with vegetable sticks or stuffed in celery
10. Popcorn with butter and sea salt
11. *Falafel or Chick Pea-Vegetable Spread* with vegetables

12. Half an avocado stuffed with *Tofu Spread*

13. Half an avocado stuffed with sunflower seeds *or* almonds or cashews

14. Unsweetened *Applesauce* (homemade)

15. *Soy Cashew Nuts*

16. Leftover soups

STAGE II DIET

7 Days of Sample Menus

DAY 1 — Monday

a.m. "Breakfast"
pears

a.m. Snack "Pick-me-up"
(Optional 2 hrs. after fruit.)
Vegetable Soup
OR
Between 8 & 11 a.m. (Optional 2 hrs. after fruit and 2 hrs. or more before lunch)
Breakfast Cereal or Yogurt
OR
Millet Cereal with a bit of honey, maple syrup or molasses cooked into it *or* served with sea salt and butter

Lunch/Dinner
1. *Rice* or *Romaine Salad*
2. *Cold Bean Balls or Pate*
3. *Sourdough Rye* or wheat bread or crackers (no yeast)

Supper
1. *Spinach Salad* (Optional: add tomatoes and/or possibly a yogurt dressing)
2. Turkey with:
3. *Arrowroot Sauce* (Delicious Gravy)—some of the turkey drippings can be used instead of water in the sauce
4. Sauteed Broccoli with sliced almonds (use oil and tamari soy sauce for sauteing)

DAY 2 — Tuesday

a.m. "Breakfast"
bananas

a.m. Snack "Pick-me-up"
(Optional 2 hrs. after fruit)
Vegetable Broth
OR
Breakfast Cereal or Yogurt
OR
Toast or *Muffins* with butter

Lunch/Dinner
1. Avocado half stuffed with sunflower seeds
2. *Kidney Bean Stew*

Supper
1. *Wild Salad* or other leafy green salad with dressing
2. *Broscht* (Optional: served with buttermilk cheese or yogurt)
3. *Easy Tuna or Salmon Bake*

DAY 3 — Wednesday

a.m. "Breakfast"
melon *or* grapes

a.m. Snack "Pick-me-up"
(Optional 2 hrs. after fruit)
Carrot Soup
OR
Breakfast Cereal or Yogurt
OR
Sweet Rice Cereal with a bit of honey, maple syrup or molasses
cooked into it *or* served with sea salt and butter

Lunch/Dinner
1. Raw vegetables stuffed in
2. *Falafel Sandwiches* served in

3. *Sourdough Rye Bread* or *Flatbreads*

Supper
1. *Super Sprout Salad* (Optional: add tomatoes and/or possibly a yogurt dressing)
2. *Spanish Omelet*

DAY 4 — Thursday

a.m. "Breakfast"
apricots or peaches

a.m. Snack "Pick-me-up"
(Optional 2 hrs. after fruit)
vegetable juice (¾ cup carrot juice with ¼ cup beet juice)
OR
Breakfast Cereal or Yogurt
OR
Wheat Berry Cereal (plain—bit of sea salt optional)

Lunch/Dinner
1. *Beet Treat* with avocado slices
2. *Sweet and Sour Lentils*
3. Crackers, *Flatbreads* or *Sourdough Rye* or Wheat

Supper
1. *Zucchini Salad* (tomatoes may be added)
2. *Turkey Soup*
3. Steamed or baked cauliflower, carrots, green beans or peas medley

DAY 5 — Friday

a.m. "Breakfast"
Lemon Drink

a.m. Snack "Pick-me-up"
(Optional 2 hrs. after fruit)

Miso Soup
OR
Breakfast Cereal or Yogurt
OR
Leftover cereal from the week

Lunch/Dinner
1. Celery and carrot sticks
2. *Split Pea Soup*
2. Corn chips, bread or crackers

Supper
1. Avocado half stuffed with almonds and topped with yogurt
2. Beef Steak or *Salmon Steaks*
3. *Ratatouille*

DAY 6 — Saturday

a.m. "Breakfast"
apples

a.m. Snack "Pick-me-up"
(Optional 2 hrs. after fruit)
Green Drink
OR
Breakfast Cereal or Yogurt
OR
Yogurt with fresh pineapple and/or shredded coconut
OR
Yogurt with chopped papaya or kiwi

Lunch/Dinner
1. *Oriental Salad*
2. *Broiled Tofu Burger* served on:
3. Bread or bun (yeast-free) or with crackers *or* serve with corn on the cob
4. Serve burger with spinach or sprouts and *Super Sandwich Topping*

Supper
1. *Beet Treat Salad* (Optional: with buttermilk cheese)
2. *Shrimp Creole* served over:
3. Steamed cauliflower (broken into flowerets and sliced)

DAY 7 — Sunday

a.m. "Breakfast"
fresh grapefruit halves

a.m. Snack "Pick-me-up"
(Optional 2 hrs. after fruit)
Vegetable Soup or vegetable juice (for juice try: ½ cup carrot, ½ cup celery or broccoli and 2–3 sprigs parsley)
OR
Breakfast Cereal or Yogurt
OR
Cornmeal Cereal with sweetening, cinnamon, sea salt and butter

Lunch/Dinner
1. Green pepper slices or cucumber or celery sticks
2. *Baked Beans*
3. *Sourdough bread* or *Flatbreads* or corn chips or crackers
4. *Baked Butternut or Acorn Squash* with cinnamon

Supper
1. *Greek Salad* (Optionals: use tomatoes instead of red bell peppers, and/or add 2–4 Tbsp. feta cheese
2. Roast lamb or beef or chicken
3. *Cooked Greens* (steamed or sauteed) kale, chard, mustard, beet greens or other greens
4. *Baked Turnips* or steamed turnips

ALTERNATE VEGETARIAN SUPPER SUGGESTIONS

Choose a Lunch or Supper from *Stage I* or repeat a Lunch from *Stage II*.

EXTRA SNACK SUGGESTIONS

1. Any snack from *Stage I*
2. Plain yogurt
3. Yogurt with fresh pineapple and/or shredded coconut
4. Yogurt with cut papaya or kiwi
5. Yogurt with grated cucumber and its juice with paprika or cumin sprinkled on (a bit of lemon juice may be added too)
6. *Buttermilk Cheese*
7. *Spinach-Tofu Spread* with crackers or bread
8. *Tofu Spread* with crackers or bread
9. *Banana or Apple Raisin Bread or Muffins*
10. Yogurt with chopped almonds or cashews

STAGE III DIET

7 Days of Sample Menus

DAY 1 — Monday

a.m. "Breakfast"
plums or grapes

Breakfast
(Optional 1–2 hrs. after fruit)
(Morning soups and cereals may be substituted here as needed or desired)
1. Granola with:
2. Milk or apple juice
OR
1. French toast with:
2. Syrup and/or cooked fruit

Lunch/Dinner
1. Tomatoes, avocado halves or a green bell pepper stuffed with:
2. *Eggsalad* or *Tofu Spread*
3. Pecans or filberts or brazil nuts

Supper
1. *Spinach Salad* (tomatoes may be added)
2. *Spaghetti* or *Lasagna Rice*with tomato sauce and parmesan cheese (browned ground beef may be added to the sauce if desired)
3. Steamed or baked broccoli or zucchini with butter *OR Broccoli or Zucchini Soup*

DAY 2 — Tuesday

a.m. "Breakfast"
peaches or apricots

Breakfast
(Optional 1–2 hrs. after fruit)
1. *Millet* or *Sweet Rice Cereal* with
2. Sweetenings *or* butter and sea salt *Dates, apricots or other dried fruit may be cooked into the cereal for sweetening if desired

Lunch/Dinner
1. *Spinach Salad* (tomatoes may be added, use any dressing)
2. *Vegetable Quiche*

Supper
1. Alfalfa sprouts with a creamy dressing
2. *Spiced Vegetables and Polenta* (4–6 oz. baby shrimp, shredded crab or cubed tofu may be added)

DAY 3 — Wednesday

a.m. "Breakfast"
Lemon Drink

Breakfast
(Optional 1–2 hrs. after fruit)
1. Milk or yogurt
2. 2–3 Eggs—fried, poached or other
3. Toast and jam (or Muffin)

Lunch/Dinner
1. *Romaine* or *Wild Salad*
2. *Lentil Tomato Soup* OR *Sweet and Sour Lentils*
3. Whole wheat pita, whole wheat, rye, eight grain or other bread (yeasted o.k.)

Supper
1. Raw and cooked vegetables (see *Gado-Gado recipe*) and
2. Chopped hard-boiled eggs with:
3. *Gado-Gado Peanut Sauce*

DAY 4 — Thursday

a.m. "Breakfast"
Lemon Drink

Breakfast
(Optional 1–2 hrs. after fruit)
1. Yogurt and fruit
2. Muffins

Lunch/Dinner
1. *Oriental Salad* (2 tsp. honey and 2 tsp. rice vinegar may be added to the marinade) OR *Super Sprout Salad* (tomatoes optional)
2. *Cashew Patties with Mushroom Gravy*

Supper
1. Any green leafy salad (no tomatoes)
2. *Confetti Rice* (Optional: added small chunks of cold ham, chicken, shrimp or marinated tofu)
3. *Arrowroot Sauce* (Delicious gravy to top Egg Foo Yong with!)

DAY 5 — Friday

a.m. "Breakfast"
apples

Breakfast
(Optional 1–2 hrs. after fruit)
1. Milk or yogurt (optional)
2. *Oatmeal* with:
3. Cut fruit or sweetenings and cinnamon and a bit of sea salt

Lunch/Dinner
1.2.3. *Bean Tacos* with everything! (May include tomatoes and be
topped with sour cream and salsa or picante sauce.)

Supper
1. *Fish in Cream Sauce* or *Clam Chowder*
2. *Stir-Fry Vegetables* with almonds or cashews (no meat or tofu)

DAY 6 — Saturday

a.m. "Breakfast"
melon

Breakfast
(Optional 1–2 hrs. after fruit)
Vegetable Soup OR Choose any breakfast

Lunch/Dinner
1. *Zucchini Salad* (tomatoes may be added)
2. *Lentil Burgers*
3. Whole wheat buns or bread on the side (yeasted o.k.)

Supper
1. *Baked Butternut or Acorn Squash* with cinnamon
2. Roast ham, beef, lamb, chicken or turkey
3. *Steamed Artichokes* with butter or a cream sauce

DAY 7 — Sunday

a.m. "Breakfast"
Oranges

Breakfast
(Optional 1–2 hrs. after fruit)
1. Milk or yogurt (optional)
2. Scrambled eggs or omelet

3. *Pancakes* (*Amazing Amaranth* or other) served with:
4. Cooked fruit toppings or applesauce

Lunch/Dinner
1. Optional: any green leafy salad
2. *Pita Pizzas*

Supper
1. *Spinach* or *Romaine Salad* (tomatoes may be used)
2. *Pecan-Cheese Loaf* with *Mushroom Gravy*
3. Cooked (steamed, baked or sauteed) broccoli, zucchini or kohlrabi
4. Optional: corn on the cob

IMPORTANT FOOD TIPS

1. ¾ tsp. sea salt equals 1 tsp. regular table salt. (Regular table salt contains sugar!)
2. When doubling a recipe only use 1½ times the amount of salt. When tripling a recipe—double the salt.
3. When oil is used in recipes, try a light-coloured, natural, cold-pressed variety. As with all natural oil products, (including mayonnaise and salad dressings) refrigerate after opening. This is a must for safety and freshness!
4. Kelp (sea kelp) is an important food supplement. It contains iodine and other minerals and sea salt contains no iodine so kelp and sea salt are almost always used together. Kelp also adds flavour and gives body and depth to recipes. Enjoy it often for its many benefits.
5. All nuts and seeds should be chewed very well for proper digestion. Chew them to powder to mix lots of saliva with them and speed digestion.
6. All types of juices should be sipped very slowly and even swished in the mouth before swallowing to aid digestion and make all the nutrients they contain more easily and completely assimilated. Never gulp juices, savour them.
7. Never under or overcook foods. This may impair flavours and digestion. Don't eat foods reheated more than once as they have lost most of their nutrients but retained their calories!

HOW TO COOK BEANS PROPERLY FOR GOOD DIGESTION
(And No Gas!)

1. Measure the amount of beans (peas/legumes) required and sort through them and remove any misshapen, discoloured or dam-

aged beans. Also remove any dirt balls, gravel, or other foreign objects and discard them.

2. Soak 1 cup of dry beans in 3 to 4 cups of cool or room temperature water and let the beans soak 8 hours or more uncovered. (12 hours for chick peas (garbonzos) and 24 hours for soybeans) Avoid using soybeans as they usually require a pressure cooker.
3. Throw away the water the beans soaked in. (Very Important!)
4. Rinse the beans several times with fresh water.
5. Put the beans in a large pot so that beans fill only ¼ of the pot and add fresh water until the beans are covered by 1 inch or so of water.
6. Bring the beans and water, uncovered, to a boil on high heat.
7. When the beans are boiling, a white foam or froth will generally form on top. Scoop this off and discard it. This is part of what contributes to gas.
8. Add extra water if needed so the beans are still at least 1 inch under water and turn the heat down to very low. Just low enough so the beans are barely bubbling. They cook best at this temperature.
9. Add 1 tsp. ground fennel or preferably 1 tsp. savory to the beans, this also improves their digestibility. (Optional)
10. Cook for 1¼ hours or more until the beans are very tender and a bean can easily be mashed with the tongue on the roof of the mouth.
11. Always chew beans slowly, never eat them fast or when under excessive stress or tiredness.
12. Have some raw foods first in a meal before eating the beans to aid in their digestion.

WHOLE GRAINS

Whole grains are delicious, nutritious and more digestible than refined grains when properly prepared. They are also less likely to aggravate those with allergies, low blood sugar, diabetes, and candida or other health problems. They contain natural fiber and are lower in calories than many refined food products.

The whole grains are divided into two categories: cereal grains; and the main dish grains.

Special Tips About Grains

1. Grains are generally cooked in two cups of water or more per one cup of grain.
2. Cook grains until they are no longer crunchy, but not soggy or mushy.
3. Very few grains need to be soaked before cooking. These include: wild rice (sometimes), whole oats, and rye and wheat kernels (berries).
4. Raw rolled, flaked, or crushed grains must be soaked before eating. Toasted grains may be eaten as they are or with milk substitutes or fruit juices (apple, pear, and peach are excellent for this).
5. Before cooking, check grains for dirt balls, gravel, husks, and other foreign particles by spreading them out thinly and fingering through them.
6. Rice is usually the only grain that needs prewashing, but you may wash any grain if you feel it needs it.
7. It makes little difference if you start cooking a grain in cool or warm water. The exception is ground cereals. These get lumpy when put in warm water unless mixed in carefully with a wire wisk.
8. To prevent grains from boiling over and to distribute heat evenly, water and grains together should never cover more than three-fourths of the cooking pot.
9. Do not add salt or oil to whole grains until the last 10 to 15 minutes of cooking, to make digestion easier.
10. Any grain in *whole* form (does not include rolled or broken whole grains) will never burn during its *first* cooking process as long as the water does not run out and the grain does not become overcooked to the point that it falls apart. (It usually takes 1¼ hours or more for grains to fall apart and burn.) Also they must be cooked on low heat.
11. Never stir whole grains while cooking or they will stick and burn.
12. When reheating whole grains (second cooking), add a little extra water—about ¼ to ½ cup per cup of grain—cook the grain, covered, on a very low heat until warmed. Brown rice can be reheated by steaming in a vegetable steamer.
13. One cup of dry whole grain or cereal makes about four servings.

14. The main-dish grains can almost always be substituted one for the other in different recipes, except wild rice. Grains are similar, but may have slight taste differences.
15. Wheat, rye, barley and oats contain gluten.
16. Cereals may be served with milk on milk substitutes or juices in *Stage III* only.

PREPARATION OF CEREAL GRAINS
See Tip #16

Raw Cereals
Soaked Oats—ORGANIC ROLLED OATS—These are smaller and rounder than regular, natural rolled oats and must be soaked for several hours or overnight before eating, unless they are 'crushed' or chopped after rolling, then they cook as easily as the natural. Use 1 to 1½ cups water per 1 cup of oats. These are usually found only in health food stores and are almost always labelled *organic*. After soaking the oats, drain off excess water (if any) and serve with sweetening, milk substitute and/or fruit.

NATURAL ROLLED OATS—(Regular or Old-Fashioned)—Soak 1 cup oats in 1 cup of very warm water for 10 to 15 minutes. Add flavourings and/or cut fruit and serve.

Rolled Rice or Barley—Use instead of oats in recipes, if available.

Flaked Whole-Grain Cereals—Flaked oats, rye, (wheat), rice, barley and millet may be purchased, but are not always available. Prepare and serve them like soaked organic rolled oats or toast them in the oven like granola. Serve with milk substitute and flavourings.

Puffed Whole-Grain Cereals—These cereals include puffed oats, corn, rice, millet, (wheat), and others. They are usually unsweetened. Serve them as they are with milk substitute and sweetening as desired.

Muesli and Other Raw Cereals—These cereals are usually made with rolled, cracked, or flaked whole grains and ground or chopped nuts and seeds and sometimes shredded coconut, raisins, or other dried fruits. If the cereal is organic or contains very tough, fibrous grains, prepare it the same way as Soaked Organic Oats. If the cereal is just natural and less fibrous, prepare the same way as Soaked Natural Oats.

Granola and Other Toasted Grain Cereals—Made with toasted rolled oats, nuts and seeds, dried fruit, and sweetening, etc. Serve with milk substitute or eat right out of the package. Chew well.

Cooked Cereals

Cooked Oatmeal—ORGANIC OATMEAL—Use 1½ to 2 cups water per one cup organic rolled oats. Bring the water to a boil, then turn down heat and add oats. Stir oats constantly and cook for ten minutes or until oats are easy to chew. Then turn off heat and cover otameal and let it sit 10 to 15 minutes before serving. Add flavouring or fruit.

NATURAL OATMEAL AND CHOPPED, ROLLED ORGANIC OATMEAL—(Regular or Old-Fashioned)—Use 1¼ to 1¾ cups water per 1 cup natural rolled oats. Bring water to a boil and add oats. Stir for 1 minute, cover, remove from heat and let sit for 10 to 15 minutes before serving. Add flavourings.

Cornmeal—Use about 2 to 2½ cups water per 1 cup meal. The coarser the meal, the more water is needed and the longer the cooking time. Start water and meal cooking together in lukewarm water and stir together on a medium heat. Use a wire wisk to make sure the meal and water are well mixed together to avoid lumpy cereal. After the first minute or two, the cereal must be stirred constantly for 10 minutes or more until it is no longer grainy. Add extra water if needed. It should always have a sweetener like honey added to it. Raisins, dates, or coconut and cinnamon cooked into the cereal are also very delicious. Salt is optional. Store cornmeal used for cereal in a cool place, or in the freezer, but never refrigerate it or it will have a damp, musty flavour.

Millet (Cereal)—Use about 3 to 4 cups of water per 1 cup millet. More water is used for the cereal than for the main-dish millet. Bring water and millet to a boil. Dates can be added now if desired—delicious! Use about ¼ to ½ cup dates per 1 cup millet. Then turn down heat to a low bubble, keep pot covered, and cook about 50 to 60 minutes until the millet breaks down and is very soft and mushlike. Before serving, stir the cereal to mix in the dates.

Serve with milk substitute or juice and oil and also honey, if no dates are added. Add salt if desired.

Sweet Rice—Cook and serve like millet cereal above, except use 2 to 3 cups per 1 cup rice and cook it for about 50 to 60 minutes until tender.

Whole Oats—Cook the same as the main dish. Serve plain with salt or with oil and honey, or maple syrup added.

PREPARATION OF MAIN-DISH GRAINS

Short- and Long-Grain Brown Rice—Put rice in a pot and fill it with water. Rub the rice together with hands and swish it around to remove excess starches, dirt, and stray rice husks. Toss out all the water. If water was very cloudy during the first washing, repeat the process once or twice until the water remains relatively clear. Then put 2 to 2¼ cups water per 1 cup rice in the pot on medium heat and bring it to a boil. Then turn down to a low bubble for 45 to 60 minutes. When rice is no longer crunchy, but easy to chew and not soggy, it is done. Onions, herbs, and spices can be added during the last 15 to 20 minutes of cooking time. Keep pot fully covered while rice is cooking, but it won't hurt to peek!

Wild Rice—This is one of the few main-dish grains that sometimes requires soaking before cooking. Wash and then soak 1 cup rice in 2 cups water and let it sit 2 to 4 hours. Only by experimentation can one determine if rice needs pre-soaking. Many varieities can just be cooked, but if they are still hard after 1 to 1½ hours, turn the heat off, let them sit until they cool and then cook them again until tender. Next time—pre-soak if using the same wild rice! Then cook same as brown rice for about 60 minutes or more. Wild rice is very expensive and rich tasting, so it is usually mixed with brown rice. This makes a more delicious, more light-tasting, less expensive dish. Cook the two rices separately and mix before serving, or cook wild rice for 15 to 20 minutes and then add brown rice to it and cook together for another 45 to 60 minutes. Add extra water if needed.

Natural Buckwheat and Pot Barley—Use about 2 cups water per 1 cup grain. Bring grain to a boil, then turn down heat to a low bubble. Cook onions with the grain and add herbs and salt for the last 10 minutes of cooking time. Cook grain 20 to 30 minutes or until no longer crunchy. Add extra water if needed.

Kasha (Toasted Buckwheat)—Cook the same as natural buckwheat for only 15 to 25 minutes. Use a bit less water for cooking.

Millet (Main Dish)—Cook the same as rice, but use 2½ cups water per 1 cup dry millet. It usually does not need pre-washing. Cooks in 40 to 55 minutes. Serve like rice and use interchangeably with rice in recipes calling for rice. This is the best of grains, highest in vitamins and very alkaline.

Whole Oats or Whole Wheat Kernals (Berries)—These must be soaked in 2½ cups of water per 1 cup grain for several hours or overnight before cooking. Then change the water and cook for about 45 to 60 minutes. They will still be slightly chewy, but not crunchy when done. This grain can be cooked separately or together with other whole grains.

Whole Rye—Soak and cook this the same as oats above, but use it sparingly because it is strong and bitter. Mix it with oats and cook them together using only 1/6th to 1/10th part rye. Rye adds zest to simple meals, but its flavour does not appeal to everyone.

STAGE I RECIPES

ALSO FOR USE IN STAGES
II and III

BEVERAGES

Lemon Drink
1 cup of water
Juice of one lemon
Several dashes of cayenne red pepper
Optional: 1–2 tsp. honey, maple syrup or molasses (The later is best for those with low blood sugar or diabetes.)

Mix the sweetening with the water and heat it just enough so the sweetening will dissolve. Remove from heat and add the remaining ingredients and serve warm *or* Chill the water and sweetening, then add the juice and cayenne and drink.

Lemon Drink with Ginger
Using the above ingredients, simmer 1–2 tsp. of finely grated ginger in one cup of water for about 6 minutes. Then strain and add sweetening if desired while it's still hot. Then chill or serve warm with the added juice and cayenne. (A large batch may be made for each week and refrigerated. Make sure to add the lemon juice and cayenne to it fresh daily though.)

Green Drink
6–8 leaves of green leafy vegetables (spinach, chard, mustard, parsley, etc.)
½ cup spring or distilled water (if possible) or regular water

Blend thoroughly and strain and drink for lots of chloryphyll and vitamins. Drink no more than ½ cup per day. ½ tsp. or more barley green powder may be used in carrot juice or with other greens as a variation.

Herb & Oil Dressing (Lemon-Oil Dressing)
(For Meat Meals)

1¼ cups oil
1–3 Tbsp. lemon juice (fresh)
1–2 tsp. wheat-free tamari soy sauce OR 1 tsp. sea salt
1 tsp. each: parsley and paprika
½ tsp. basil
¼ tsp. each: marjoram, thyme and kelp
Several dashes cayenne red pepper
Optional: ½–1 tsp. vegetable broth powder *or* onion powder

Mix together all the ingredients and beat well. Refrigerate for a couple hours so the herbs and flavours can mingle. Serve chilled or at room temperature on salads.

Herb & Oil Dressing with Garlic
(For Starchy Meals)

Eliminate the lemon juice and add 1–2 cloves of fresh crushed garlic to the above recipe.

Blended Lemon-Oil Dressing with Garlic
(For Meat Meals)

1 cup oil
2–4 Tbsp. lemon juice (fresh)
2–3 cloves garlic—minced
¼ cup fresh parsley—chopped

½ tsp. sea salt
Several dashes each: cayenne red pepper and kelp
Optional: ½ tsp. of one or more of the following: dill weed, oregano
  and/or basil

Blend, chill and serve. (A food processor may also be used.)

Cucumber Dill Dressing
(Makes about 1½ cups)

1 large cucumber—peeled and seeded
2 tsp. dill weed
½ cup oil (water may be used instead with some loss of flavour)
Few dashes of kelp
Several dashes of cayenne red pepper
Sea salt to taste
Optional: 1–2 cloves garlic—crushed

Blend all ingredients well, chill and serve. Best used within 5 days.
Great dressing with any meal in Stage I or on:

Avocado Dressing
(Makes about 1 cup)

2 medium avocados
3–4 tsp. fresh parsley—chopped
½ cup green onion tops—chopped
½ cup oil (or ¼ cup water & ¼ cup lemon juice for meat meals)
⅛–¼ tsp. sea salt
Few dashes of kelp
Cayenne red pepper to taste

Blend all ingredients well and serve. Best used within 3 days. Good
for any *Stage I meal OR* if lemon juice is used, only use with meat
meals in *Stage I or II*, anytime for *Stage III*.

Romaine Salad
(Serves 2)

6–8 leaves romaine lettuce (or other lettuce except crisp-
head)—torn in bite size pieces
1–2 stalks celery—chopped thin
1 small turnip, parsnip or new potato—grated very fine
½ cup red cabbage—shredded very fine OR 1 red bell pepper—in
thin strips
Optional: green onions or chives—chopped

Wash, dry, chop and mix all ingredients. Toss and serve with a favorite dressing.

Spinach Salad
(Serves 2)

1 small or medium bunch spinach—torn
1 large beet or carrot—grated
1 zucchini—if small, slice in rounds, if larger use ½, quarter & chop
1 large avocado—in thin wedges or chunks
Optional: *Starchy Meal*—1–2 Tbsp. sunflower seeds—pre-soaked
　　　　　Meat Meal—1–2 Tbsp. raw, sliced almonds—unsoaked

Wash the spinach by swishing it in cold water to remove the sand.
Remove the stems, dry it and tear it into bite-sized pices. Scrub the
beet or carrot and zucchini and grate and chop. The sunflower seeds
should be soaked in water 1–2 hours, then drained to soften them
and make them easier to digest. Mix all the ingredients and toss
lightly. Be gentle with the spinach as it bruises and spoils easily with
too much handling or squeezing. Use lemon juice, *Lemon-Oil, Herb
& Oil, Cucumber or Avocado Dressing* depending on the type of
meal.

Zucchini Salad
(Serves 2)

2 small *or* 1 large zucchini—grated
½ regular *or* ¼ English cucumber—grated
8–12 red radishes—sliced in paper thin rounds (if none, used sliced
    carrot)
1 green bell pepper—cut in ¼ inch strips
1 leaf of lettuce (any kind but crisp-head)—torn very small
Optional: 1–2 floweret(s) of cauliflower—grated
Optional: 1–2 green onions *or* chives—chopped

Wash, dry, chop, grate and toss all ingredients. This lovely salad is
suprisingly light and delicious! Serve with dressing.

Super Sprout Salad
(Serves 2)

1 cup alfalfa sprouts
½ cup other sprouts
1 avocado—chopped
6–8 spinach leaves—torn small
½ red bell pepper—chopped small
¼ cup or less broccoli flowerets—bud tips only, break very small

Prepare and toss gently and serve. Tastes great with a tahini or
cashew-nut or *Cucumber or Avocado Dressing.*

Greek Salad
(Serves 2)

1 small cucumber—cut in chunks
1 red bell pepper (instead of tomato)—cut in chunks
½–¾ cup black olives—cut in half lengthwise
Optional: 1 small white or red onion—chopped small
Lemon-Oil Dressing OR Herb & Oil Dressing

Wash and peel the cucumber with a potato peeler (if waxed) and chop. Mix with the other ingredients and dressing, toss and refrigerate for 30–60 minutes before serving. Stir every 10–15 minutes while it marinates.

Oriental Salad
(Serves 2)

8–10 stalks asparagus—pre-steamed 10–15 min. until tender
10–14 snow peas (edible pea pods)—pull ends and top string off
1 small carrot—cut in shoe strings (see below)
1 stalk celery—cut in shoe strings
½ can bamboo shoots—rinsed and dryed
½ can water chestnuts—sliced thin
Starchy Meal: add 1–2 Tbsp. raw or toasted sesame seeds
Meat Meal: add 1–2 Tbsp. home roasted (or raw) sliced almonds
Optional: green onions or chives—chopped

Prepare salad and marinate 1–2 hours before serving in fresh lemon juice OR *Lemon-Oil Dressing* OR *Herb & Oil Dressing.* To cut into shoe strings, chop vegetable into 2½ inch lengths. Then slice into very thin, long sticks. To roast raw almonds: Heat in a dry pan in a toaster oven at 400° for 10 minutes, until some of them pop and they are lightly browned. Use 425°–450° in a regular oven. This salad is especially nice when it is arranged artistically on a plate.

Beet Treat
(Serves 1–2)

1–3 grated beets
1–2 lemons—juiced

Mix beets and juice together and serve on a lettuce leaf or in or around an avocado half. Delicious! The lemon juice makes the beets taste sweet.

Beet Treat Salad
(Serves 2)

2–4 beets—grated (keep separate)
1 avocado—chopped
6–8 lettuce leaves (leaf, red, bibb or boston)—torn
1 green bell pepper—in rings, sliced
¼–½ cup lentil, mung, alfalfa or other sprouts

Prepare and toss all the ingredients together except the beet. Dish out the salad and spread the beets over the top. Use lemon juice or *Lemon-Oil Dressing.*

Rice Salad
(For Starchy Meals Only)
(Serves 2–3)

Use the *Spinach, Wild* or *Romaine Salad* as a base. Add ½–¾ cup pre-cooked, cold, brown rice and toss. (Fluffy, cooked millet may be used instead of rice.) Serve with a starchy meal type of dressing. *Cucumber, Avocado* or Tahini *Dressings* are suggested.

Wild Salad
(Serves 2)

Note: Please be aware of *what* you are picking and eating. Get experienced advice. Some wild plants are poisonous. Never pick salad greens from lawns or highly cultivated areas. Choose a wild, unpolluted area.

2–3 cups salad greens—may include: lamb's quarters, young &
   small dandelion greens, sorrels, fiddleheads, young-wild
   strawberry or raspberry leaves (vit. C)
8–16 wild mint leaves—torn

16–30 flower heads—(for colour & vit. C) may include: wild-purple violet blooms, blue-pea vetch blooms, white or red wild clover blooms, and/or pink-wild rose petals (petals only)

Sort and wash all leaves and flowers. Dry gently. Tear leaves for salads. Toss everything together and serve with lemon juice OR *Lemon-Oil OR Herb & Oil Dressing.*

VEGETABLES

Artichokes (Globe)

Choose firm, dark green (with no purple or 'fuzz'), well-rounded, unwrinkled artichokes. Wash 1–2 and cut off all the stalk except for about ¼ inch. Pull off and discard the first row of leaves around the stalk. With a sharp, serrated knife, cut ¾–1 inch completely off the tip end of the artichoke and discard. Snip ¼–½ inch off the tips of each remaining whole leaf. Place the vegetables upside down (top down, stalk up) in a vegetable steamer (over low boiling water) and steam for 30–40 minutes until very tender. When a knife pokes in and out easily it should be done.

Melt some butter for dipping the leaves into. Starting with the bottom row of leaves nearest and stalk, pull off one leaf at a time and dip it in the butter. With the inner part of the leaf facing upwards, pull the base of the leaf between your teeth, pulling off all tender, easy-to-chew parts. (The easy parts are the edible parts.) Discard the rest of each leaf. As you get closer to the center, you can eat more of each leaf as it keeps getting more tender until you reach the 'choke' which is a stringy, kind of prickly part that you scrape off with a spoon and discard. What's left over is *entirely* edible. Dip it in butter and savour the best part—the 'heart.' A delectable treat, and good for the liver too! For *Stage III, Citrus Butter* may be used.

Baked Turnips
(Serves 2)

Choose firm, bright coloured, white/purple turnips. Scrub 2–3 medium turnips with a good scrub brush and cut off the tip root and the stem end. Slice in ¼ inch rounds and bake on a lightly oiled baking sheet about ¼ inch apart. Bake at about 400° for 9–14 minutes until very tender, but not dry. Delicious plain or see below.

Herb Baked Turnips
(Serves 2–3)

3–4 medium turnips—sliced ¼ inch thick
¼ cup oil
1 tsp. dried parsley—crushed
½ tsp. dried basil—crushed
⅛–¼ tsp. sea salt
Few dashes each: cayenne red pepper and kelp

Mix all ingredients together well (except the turnips.) Dip the turnip slices in the mixture and bake as above.

Cinnamon Baked Squash
(1 Squash Serves 2–4)

1 Butternut, buttercup or acorn squash
Water
Cinnamon

Cut one squash in half lengthwise and scoop out and discard all the seeds. Fill the hollowed out section with water and sprinkle the entire squash generously with cinnamon. Place each half in a bread or loaf pan (to help it stay upright) with 1 inch of water in the bottom of the pan to keep the squash moist. Prick the squash all over the top surface with a knife to speed its cooking time. Bake at 400° for about 60–70 minutes until tender and a knife goes in and out easily. Serve hot with added sea salt and butter if desired. Butternut squash is naturally sweet and less stringy than the other varieties. It is beige and kind of pear-shaped, though much larger.

Honey Baked Squash
(Stage III only)

1 Squash (as above)
Water
Honey (or maple syrup)
Butter
Sea Salt

Prepare as above only fill the hollowed out section of the squash with sweetening and butter and sprinkle the entire squash with sea salt. Bake as above in water. Use the honey-butter sauce from the hollow of the squash to baste the squash with when serving. Added cinnamon is optional.

Vegetable Soup
(Serves 6–8)

6 cups water or stock
1 cup peas or chopped green beans
1 cup corn
1–2 potatoes—unpeeled, small and cubed
2–3 stalks of celery or 1 green bell pepper—chopped
2 carrots—sliced thin
1 large onion—chopped small
1 small zucchini—sliced thin or chopped
Optional: 1 stalk broccoli—chopped small

1–2 Tbsp. oil
1 Tbsp. wheat-free tamari soy sauce
3–4 tsp. vegetable broth powder OR 3–4 vegetable boullion cubes
2 tsp. parsley

1½ tsp. sea salt
½ tsp. each: basil, oregano and kelp
Several dashes cayenne red pepper
Optional: bit of honey
Optional: dark miso—keep separate

Steam the hard vegetables like potatoes and carrots for 10 minutes
before making the soup. Saute the onions in the oil in a large pot until the onions are slightly transparent. Then add the water, steamed
vegetables, and all the rest of the ingredients. Cook the soup on a
low-to-medium heat for 40–60 minutes until all the vegetables are
tender but not soggy and the flavours develop. Then take 1–2 cups
of water with vegetables from the soup and blend it or use a food
processor to liquify and add it back into the soup. This adds flavour
and depth and gives the soup a natural thickness. Correct the soup's
spices according to personal taste and add a bit of honey to balance
flavours if needed, or extra water to thin the soup. After the soup is
finished cooking, 1–2 Tbsp. miso can also be added to one cup of the
broth and then to the soup for more taste and nutrients. Serve the
soup hot and let it cool before refrigerating leftovers.

Miso Soup
(Serves 4–8)

6 cups water or stock
4–6 oz. seaweed (wakame or kombu is best)
1 large onion—chopped
2 carrots—sliced thin
2–3 stalks celery—chopped
1–2 vegetable bouillion cubes OR 1–2 tsp. vegetable broth powder
1–2 Tbsp. oil
1 tsp. parsley
½ tsp. sea salt
Several dashes kelp

⅓ cup dark miso

Saute the onions and vegetables in the oil in a large pot. Use a pot big enough to hold all the soup. When the vegetables are tender and slightly transparent, add the water, seaweed and all the rest of the soup ingredients except the miso. Let the soup cook on low heat and keep it covered and hot. Remove 1 cup of broth from the soup and mix it with the miso. When the miso is dissolved into the broth, mix it with the rest of the soup and let the soup sit covered about 5–10 minutes so the flavours can mingle. Do not cook the miso; that would destroy valuable vitamins and enzymes. Serve the soup immediately when ready. Leftover soup can be reheated slightly, but never let the soup come to a boil.

Vegetable Broth

Use 1–2 cups leftover *Miso* or *Vegetable Soup* and liquify in a blender or food processor. Add extra leftover steamed vegetables if desired. Add extra water to thin the broth to a desired consistency. Add additional flavourings if needed. Heat on low-medium heat for 15–30 minutes and serve hot or cold in a bowl or in a glass.

Carrot Soup
(Serves 4)

4 cups carrots—sliced and steamed until tender
1 1⅔ cups water or vegetable stock
2–3 Tbsp. butter 2or 1–2 Tbsp. oil (for flavour)
2 Tbsp. wheat-free tamari soy sauce
2 tsp. parsley
1 tsp. dill weed
½ tsp. sea salt
Several dashes of kelp
Cayenne red pepper to taste
Optional: several dashes of onion or garlic powder *or* a few crushed
    mint leaves

Liquify all ingredients until smooth in a blender or food processor. Then heat the soup in a saucepan on low-to-medium heat just up until a boil. Do not boil. Serve hot. Garnish with chopped chives or green onions or fresh parsley if desired.

Lentil Soup
(Serves 4)

4 cups water or stock
1 cup brown lentils
4–6 stalks celery (or broccoli)—chopped
2 carrots—sliced
1 large onion—chopped
1–2 cloves garlic—minced
2 Tbsp. butter or oil
2 Tbsp. wheat-free tamari soy sauce
3 tsp. parsley
1 tsp. sea salt
½ tsp. each: basil, oregano and thyme
⅛ tsp. cayenne red pepper
Several dashes of kelp
Optional: ½ tsp. dill weed

Bring the lentils, vegetables and water or stock to a boil on high heat, then simmer for 1 hour on low heat or until the lentils are very tender. Add the remaining ingredients and simmer another 15–20 minutes, stirring occasionally. Serve hot and enjoy. Keeps 7 days in the refrigerator or may be frozen for later use.

Split Pea Soup
(Serves 8–10)

1 lb. (2¼–2½ cups) green split peas
7–9 cups water or vegetable stock
2 medium onions—chopped small
¼ cup oil or butter

3–5 tsp. wheat-free tamari soy sauce
2 tsp. parsley
1½ tsp. sea salt
1–2 tsp. honey (to balance out the flavours)
1 tsp. each: basil, oregano and mint leaves
½ tsp. each: thyme and kelp
¼ tsp. each: marjoram and savory
Several dashes cayenne red pepper to taste
Optional: 1–2 potatoes and/or carrots—chopped small and presteamed

Cook the split peas and water in a large pot for about 1½ to 1¾ hours on medium heat or until the peas totally dissolve into the liquid. Then add the onions, herbs and vegetables and cook over a medium-to-low heat for about 20–25 minutes more to develop the flavours. Stir the soup occasionally, keeping the heat low so it does not stick or burn, just simmers. Each bowl may be topped with a bit of chopped green onion or a small handful of alfalfa sprouts.

Kidney Bean Stew
(Serves 10–12)

1 lb. dry kidney beans—soaked
1 lb. (6–10) carrots—sliced in ⅓–½ inch pieces
1 small or medium eggplant—chopped in ½–¾ inch chunks
8–20 stalks celery—chopped in ⅛–½ inch pieces
6–8 medium potatoes—in one inch chunks (leave the skins on)
3–4 medium onions—chopped
2–3 green peppers—in chunks
Optional: 6–10 jerusalem artichokes—chopped
Optional: 1–2 cups fresh or frozen corn and/or peas

2–3 Tbsp. wheat-free tamari soy sauce
1–2 Tbsp. vegetable broth powder OR 2–4 vegetable bouillon cubes
1 Tbsp. parsley
1½ tsp. sea salt
1 tsp. each: sea kelp and basil

½ tsp. paprika
⅛ tsp. or less cayenne red pepper
Optional: ⅛ tsp. cumin powder OR dill weed

Drain the soaking water from the beans and discard. Wash the beans thoroughly and cover 1 inch above them in water. (See "How to Cook Beans.") Cook the kidney beans until tender. Pour off and save all the cooking juice from the beans except for 2 cups. (Save extra juice for *Vegetarian Gravy*!) Leave 2 cups of juice with the beans.

While the beans are still cooking and nearly finished, in a separate pot steam the hard vegetables like potatoes, artichokes, carrots and eggplant for 10–15 minutes. Then add the rest of the vegetables to the hard vegetables and cook them together for another 7–10 minutes until the vegetables are tender, but still slightly crunchy.

Then add all the drained vegetables to the beans along with all the herbs and spices. (Save the steaming water for stock or *Vegetable Broth*.) Simmer everything together on low to medium heat for 20–30 minutes until the flavours mingle.

Stir-Fry Vegetables
(Serves 2–4)

½ head or less Chinese cabbage—chopped fine OR regular white or
    savoy cabbage may be used
4 stalks celery *or* bok choy—¼ inch thick, sliced on a long slant
2–4 green onions—chopped in small slanted pieces
1–2 carrots—⅛ inch thick, sliced on a long slant
1 green pepper *or* 1 stalk broccoli—chopped in long thin pieces
1–2 cloves garlic—sliced or minced
¼ cup stock, water or broth—cool
¼–⅓ cup tamari soy sauce (wheat-free)
3 Tbsp. oil—use toasted sesame oil if available
3 tsp. arrowroot powder
1–3 tsp. ginger root—peeled and finely grated

Optional: 1 cup edible pea pods and/or large, white mung bean sprouts and/or a few sliced water chestnuts

An oriental wok is preferred for this recipe, but a frying pan can be used instead. Slowly heat the oil in the wok with the garlic and be sure the sides of the wok are oiled. Add all the vegetables and ginger except for the pea pods and sprouts and cook until almost tender. Stir the mixture continuously to coat and cook the vegetables completely. Add the remaining vegetables and continue to stir.

Separately mix together well: 3 tsp. of arrowroot with ¼ cup liquid as suggested. Then mix it all together with the vegetables, heat everything another minute or two, add the tamari and perhaps several dashes of cayenne red pepper, stir and serve. Meats or tofu can be added to the stir-fry *or* it may be served over hot, whole grains like brown rice.

Shish Kebabs
(Serves Any Amount)

Use ½ – ¾ inch thick pieces about 1 to 1½ inches long of several of the following vegetables and foods: (Use about 2–3 cups per person.)
Pineapple chunks
Green pepper
Red bell peppers
Zucchini
Onions
Broccoli (pre-steamed 5 minutes)
Cauliflower (pre-steamed 5 minutes)
Tofu or marinated tofu
Baby shrimp
Chicken or turkey pieces (pre-cooked)

Use 2 or more skewers about 1 foot long for each person. Bamboo (from an Oriental store) or stainless steel skewers (spears) may be used. Use a variety of vegetables and other foods. Place the foods on the spears alternately, filling each spear completely. Place the skewers in a long flat baking pan with ½ inch high edges, with 2 cups of water in the bottom of the pan. Pour tamari soy sauce (wheat-free) generously over each kebab before placing right under the hot broiler of your oven. Broil 5–12 minutes, depending on the type of oven, until tender and juicy and well-browned. Serve immediately before they cool.

Bean Tacos
(Serves 6 or More)

1 dozen taco shells or corn tortillas or round rice wrappers (from Chinese stores)
Use some of the following:
Lettuce or spinach—shredded
Sprouts, any kind, alfalfa are best
Green onions or chives—chopped
Black olives—sliced
Green or red bell peppers—chopped
Cucumber—chopped
Avocado—chopped
Taco Beans (See Recipe)
Optional: Guacamole

Heat oven to 350° and place the corn tortillas on the oven racks separately for 1–2 minutes until they are firm but not brittle. Corn tortillas should be taken directly from the freezer (if frozen) and separated with a butter knife and placed right away in the oven to avoid the edges curling up. Cover each corn tortilla (or shell) with a layer of Taco Beans, assorted chopped vegetables and guacamole. If using a tortilla, eat it like a tostada (or pizza—flat) and enjoy. (If rice wrappers are used, dip them for a few seconds in hot water before filling with *hot* taco beans and vegetables. They may be wrapped and baked if desired.)

The Beans
2 cups dry pinto beans—soaked and cooked
1–2 onions—chopped

2–3 Tbsp. tamari soy sauce (wheat-free)
1 tsp. each: paprika and cumin and sea salt
½ tsp. oregano
¼ tsp. or less cayenne red pepper
⅛ tsp. each: coriander and ground cloves
Several dashes of kelp
Optional: a bit of sweetening to mellow the flavours

Cook the pinto beans until tender. Add the onions and cook another 15 minutes. Drain and save most of the water from the beans. While the beans are still hot, mix in all the herbs and spices. Mash about half the beans (leave some whole but do not separate them) with a masher or fork with a little of the drained liquid from the beans. Discard the rest of the liquid or save for other recipes or soup stock. Use the beans hot for Bean Tacos. They can also be used cold on tortillas, by spreading them on warm tortillas with some vegetables and heating under the broiler until hot, then topping with guacamole after.
In *Stage III*, sour cream may also be added.

Guacamole

1 large, ripe avocado—peeled and mashed
1 tsp. onion—crushed or minced or powder
½ tsp. paprika
Several dashes each: cayenne red pepper, cumin and kelp
Few drops of wheat-free tamari soy sauce
Vegetable salt to taste
Optional: 3–4 tsp. fresh lemon juice (*Stage II and III*)
Optional: 4–6 black olives—chopped fine

Mix the ingredients together and chill ½ hour before using to keep it fresh. Use on Bean Tacos or as a cracker or vegetable dip. (Lemon juice may be used by Stage I if the Guacamole is used as a vegetable dip for snacks. If used for a dip, bury the avocado pit in the bottom of the dip bowl to help keep the dip fresher longer!

Stuffed Green Peppers
(Serves 4–6)

1 cup dry brown rice or millet
4–6 green peppers—cut in half lengthwise and seeded
2 large or 4 small carrots—minced very small or grated
2 medium onions—chopped small
2 tsp. parsley
1 tsp. sea salt
½ tsp. each: basil, oregano and paprika
⅛ tsp. each: marjoram, thyme and kelp
1–2 Tbsp. sesame seeds *or* chopped sunflower seeds
Several dashes cayenne red pepper
1–2 Tbsp. oil

Cook the brown rice or millet for 50–60 minutes until the grain is tender and fairly dry. In a large skillet heat 1–2 Tbsp. oil and saute the onions and carrots and all the herbs until they are slightly tender. Then add the cooked grain to the skillet and saute for 5 minutes more so the flavours can mingle. Place the raw green peppers in a large uncovered baking dish (about 1½ inch sides), but side up. Fill the pepper shells with the grain-vegetable mixture. Fill the bottom of the baking dish around the peppers with about ⅓ inch of water. Bake the peppers at about 350° for 15–25 minutes until the grain is lightly browned and the peppers are tender but still a little crisp. Serve hot with *Vegetarian Gravy* or *Arrowroot Sauce* in a pinch. A half cup pre-cooked chick peas may sometimes be added to the grain in the frying pan if desired for added nutrition.

Vegetarian Gravy
2 cups kidney bean cooking juice
3 Tbsp. wheat-free tamari soy sauce
1 Tbsp. oil
2 Tbsp. arrowroot powder
½ cup millet, rice or oat flour (*Stage II or III* whole wheat may be used)

¼ – ½ tsp. of *one* of the following: curry powder or vegetable broth
   powder (*Stage III*, chili powder is optional)
¼ tsp. each: sea salt and kelp
Cayenne red pepper to taste

Cook ½ – 1 pounds of kidney beans and drain off and save all the liquid, or use leftover liquid from the *Kidney Bean Stew*. Use 2 cups of
the "muddiest" part of the liquid for this recipe. Use the beans in
another recipe or freeze them for later use. Mix all the ingredients
together and stir over medium-low heat until thickened. Correct
herbs and spices according to your own taste and use the gravy on
Stuffed Green Peppers, burgers, rice, vegetables and in other recipes
as desired. A wonderful gravy to use often.

Cold Bean Balls or Pate
(Serves 2– 4)

1 cup pre-cooked beans—mashed (chick peas, pinto, aduki or
   kidney beans)
1 cup steamed vegetables—mashed (carrots, broccoli, zucchini or
   greens)
2 Tbsp. sesame tahini
2– 4 tsp. fresh parsley—chopped fine
2 tsp. tamari soy sauce (wheat-free)
1 tsp. each: sea salt and paprika
½ tsp. each: basil and cumin
¼ tsp. each: marjoram and thyme
⅛ – ¼ tsp. cayenne red pepper
Several dashes of kelp
Optional: Toasted sesame seeds or toasted sunflower seeds—ground

Mix all the ingredients together and shape into balls. Use 1– 2 Tbsp.
of arrowroot powder if needed to help keep the balls firm or shape
into a small loaf and slice. Use other favourite seasonings if desired.
Chill before serving or serve at room temperature. The balls or pate
may be coated with ground sesame or sunflower seeds. This is a
great recipe to use up leftover beans and vegetables on! Try them

hot too, covered in *Vegetarian Gravy*. They may be browned in a frying pan.

Curried Red Lentils
(Serves 2–4)

3–4 cups water
1 cup red lentils
1 onion—chopped small
2 Tbsp. butter (or oil)
2–3 tsp. honey to balance flavours (maple syrup or molasses can be used)
2 tsp. curry powder
1 tsp. each: sea salt and turmeric
1/8–1/4 tsp. each: cayenne red pepper, cominos (ground cumin) and coriander
Several dashes each: cinnamon and ground cloves

Begin cooking the lentils and onions in the water. Lentils (red) will take 20–30 minutes to cook fully. Do not cook them until they fall apart, just until they are tender. About 5 minutes before the lentils are finished cooking, add the spices and butter and sweetening and cook everything together another 5–10 minutes so the flavours can mingle. Correct the spices according to your own taste. Add extra water if necessary so the legumes will be contained in sauce. Enjoy with brown rice, millet or another whole grain.

Middle Eastern Falafel Spread
(Serves 4–6)

1 cup dry chick peas (garbanzos)—soaked and cooked
1/2 cup sesame tahini
2–3 tsp. fresh onion—grated or minced fine
2 cloves garlic—crushed
2–3 tsp. wheat-free tamari soy sauce
2 tsp. each: dried parsley and cumin seeds or powder (cominos)

½–1 tsp. sea salt
½ tsp. each: oregano and celery seed
¼ tsp. kelp
⅛ tsp. coriander
⅛ tsp. or less ground cloves
⅛ tsp. or more cayenne red pepper to taste

Cook the chick peas until tender, then drain and save the liquid. While the chick peas are still very hot, mash them together with the onion and all the rest of the ingredients. Herbs and spices may be altered according to personal taste. Use the falafel spread as a sandwich spread or to stuff celery with. (Extra liquid from cooking the beans may be added to the mixture if it is too dry.) Leftover spread may be refrigerated up to 7 days or frozen. The spread is tastiest when hot.

Falafel Sandwiches

Use pocket bread, *Flatbreads* or sliced bread and spread the falafel spread on one piece, topping it with sliced green pepper, cucumber rounds, green onions, chopped zucchini, avocado and/or other vegetables. Top with mayonnaise and/or mustard (Try the *Super Sandwish Topping*) or *Guacamole* and the 2nd piece of bread. Enjoy!

SNACKS AND SPREADS

Soy Cashew Nuts
(Makes 2 cups)

2 cups "raw" cashew nuts—whole if possible
2 Tbsp. butter or oil
2–4 Tbsp. wheat-free tamari soy sauce
Optional: several dashes cayenne red pepper

Heat the butter or oil in a heavy frying pan; then add the nuts and saute them for a couple of minutes. Add the soy sauce and a little cayenne if desired for a zesty taste. Stir them for a few more minutes over low heat, being careful not to burn the nuts. Blanched almonds or other nuts may be used instead, but cashews have the richest flavour. Serve like mixed nuts, either hot or cold.

Spinach-Tofu Spread or Dip
(Makes 1½ cups)

2 cups spinach (firmly packed)
6–8 oz. regular, firm tofu—mashed
2 tsp. dried parsley
1–3 tsp. wheat-free tamari soy sauce
½ tsp. basil
¼ tsp. each: oregano and marjoram
Several dashes kelp
Sea salt to taste
Cayenne red pepper to taste

Use fresh, large-leafed spinach and swish it in cool water to remove the sand. Discard the tougher spinach stems. Rinse the tofu and squeeze out the excess water. Steam the spinach 8–12 minutes until tender. Place the spinach and tofu with all the herbs in a food processor with the cutting blade. Wiz until smooth. Or add a few tsps. of water and blend a few seconds on high speed in a blender, then stop and stir. Blend and stir until smooth.

Serve with cut vegetables or fill celery with it. *Carrot, broccoli, zucchini and other vegetables may be used instead of spinach.

Tofu Spread
(Makes about 2 cups)

12 oz. tofu
1–2 stalks celery or ½ green bell pepper—chopped very fine
½ red bell pepper—chopped very fine
1 bunch of green onions (green part only) or chives—chopped very fine
¼–½ tsp. garlic powder

¼ tsp. paprika
Several dashes cayenne red pepper and kelp
Vegetable sea salt to taste

Wash and drain the tofu and mash it together with all the herbs and spices. Then mix in the remaining vegetables. Serve with vegetable sticks or stuff it in celery or ½ green pepper for elegant serving. (Mayonnaise may be added if desired.)

EGGS AND MEAT

Herbed Scrambled Eggs
(Serves 2)

6 eggs
6 Tbsp. water
½ tsp. parsley
⅛ tsp. each: paprika, basil, thyme
Several dashes each: kelp, sea salt, cayenne red pepper
1 green pepper—chopped small
Oil (or butter)

Saute the green pepper in a little oil until tender. While sauteing, beat all the other ingredients together well with a wire wisk until the eggs are foamy. Add the egg mixture to the green pepper and make sure the pan is hot. Stir occasionally for about 5 minutes or so until the eggs are somewhat solid but still very tender. (Overcooked eggs become rubbery.) Serve immediately.

Egg Foo Yong
(Makes 12 small—Serves 3–4)

6 eggs—beaten until foamy
2–3 tsp. oil

1 Tbsp. wheat-free tamari soy sauce
1/8 – 1/4 tsp. sea salt
1/8 tsp. paprika
Several dashes of cayenne red pepper and sea kelp

6–8 oz. tofu (firm, regular type)—mashed
3–4 oz. mung bean sprouts
Optional: 2–4 oz. shredded crab or baby shrimp
Optional: 1/4 cup chopped green onion tops
Extra oil for sauteing

Beat all the liquid ingredients and herbs together well. Then mix in the mashed tofu, bean sprouts and seafood if desired. Moderately oil a large skillet or griddle and heat it until fairly hot. Drop about 3–4 Tbsp. (or 1/4 cup or less) of the mixture in one side of the skillet. Make 2–3 more as room permits. Fry until the bottoms are browned, about 1–3 minutes. Turn over with a metal or plastic spatula (turner) for about 1 more minute until cooked through but still tender. Re-oil the skillet for each batch.

Serve hot immediately or keep in a warmed oven until serving. Make sure to stir the mixture well before making each egg foo yong pattie. (Each pattie will be as big around as a large pancake.) Serve with egg foo yong sauce (*Arrowroot Sauce*) or wheat-free tamari soy sauce.

Arrowroot Sauce (Grain Free)
(Delicious Gravy)

1½ cups water
3 Tbsp. wheat-free tamari soy sauce
5 tsp. arrowroot powder
2 vegetable or chicken bouillion cubes OR 2 tsp. vegetable broth
   powder
Several dashes of cayenne red pepper and kelp

Mix the arrowroot thoroughly with the water in a saucepan and add the remaining ingredients. Mix well. Cook over a medium heat, stirring constantly, until thickened. Keep warm over a low heat. Keeps refrigerated up to 7 days or may be frozen.

Easy Tuna or Salmon Bake
(Serves 2–3)

1 can tuna or salmon—drained
3–4 Tbsp. mayonnaise
Vegetable salt to taste
Several dashes each: cayenne red pepper and kelp
Optional: ¼ cup green onion tops—chopped fine

Mix everything together and pat it into one or two small, oiled baking dishes about ½–⅓ inch thick. Bake at 350° for about 10–15 minutes or until browned on top. Serve immediately. Easy and delicious!

Eggsalad
(Serves 2)

4 eggs—hardboiled
2–4 tbsp. mayonnaise
⅛ tsp. paprika
Several dashes each: cayenne red pepper and kelp
Vegetable salt to taste
½ stalk celery or ¼ green pepper—minced very fine

Mash the hard-boiled eggs with the mayonnaise and spices until mashed very fine. Then add the finely chopped vegetable, mix and serve or chill for later use. Use it to stuff celery with or eat with vegetable dippers as a nutritious, high-protein snack or part of a meal.

Garlic Chicken (or Herb Baked Chicken)
(4 Pieces—Serves 2)

4 pieces chicken
3–4 Tbsp. wheat-free tamari soy sauce
4 large or 6–8 small garlic cloves
Lots of dried parsley and paprika
½ tsp. each: basil and thyme
Sea salt

Put the washed chicken in a baking dish (round, 8"–9" Pyrex suggested) with about ¼ to ⅓ inch water in the bottom. Pour the tamari over the chicken pieces. Sprinkle each chicken piece very generously with crushed, dried parsley, covering the entire surface of each piece. Next, sprinkle on just as much paprika. Sprinkle on about ⅛ tsp. each of basil and thyme over *each* piece of chicken and add sea salt as desired. Crush the garlic and place it in the water surrounding the chicken. Bake at 350°F for 30–40 minutes. After the first 10 minutes, baste the chicken with the garlic and juices from the bottom of the dish. Baste every 10 minutes until crispy and done.

Broiled Salmon or Other Fish

Wash the fish steaks or fillets and place in a Pyrex dish with about ¼–⅓ inch of water. Rub each piece with a bit of soft butter. Add a few splashes of tamari to each piece, then squeeze 1–2 tsp. of fresh lemon juice over each piece. Sprinkle with sea salt or vegetable salt, cayenne and a bit of kelp. Broil the steaks for 7–12 minutes on the first side and 3–6 minutes on the second. Broil the fillets for 3–7 minutes on the first side and 2–5 minutes on the second. Serve with butter, lemon wedges and fresh-chopped parsley.

BREADS AND MUFFINS

Sourdough Rye Bread

Starter Recipe
(Makes About 8 Cups)

In a jar with a tight fitting lid, (enough to hold 8 cups) mix 1 packet of sourdough culture with 1 cup of whole rye flour. Add ⅔ to 1 cup or so of warm water. Just enough to make a thick, stirrable batter. Cover tightly and place the jar in a warm place for 12–18 hours. Repeat this process twice more until the mixture contains 4 cups of whole rye flour and water and then let it sit for another 12–18 hours more. The mixture will then contain some bubbles and smell a bit sour. Keep the mixture refrigerated for use in recipes. It will keep for several months.

Bread Recipe
(Makes 1 Large Loaf or 2 Small)

2½ cups whole rye flour (or other Flour(s))
1–1½ cups warm water
½ cup sourdough starter
1–2 Tbsp. honey, maple syrup *or* molasses
Extra flour

Mix the warm water with the flour and sweetening and mix well. Add the starter and enough extra flour to make a stiff dough. Knead in more extra flour until the dough is no longer really sticky and does not separate. Shape it into a loaf (loaves) and place in a large, oiled loaf pan. Cover loosely with tin foil and put in a warm place for 12–18 hours. After it has doubled in size, bake it (still loosely covered in foil) at 375° for 50–60 minutes. When browned and done, let cool 10 minutes, remove from pan(s) and let *cool completely* for several hours *before* serving or wrapping for storage. This bread is more wholesome and easier to digest for those with allergies, candida or digestive problems.

Use a 'true' starter culture for sourdough breads. These are available at some health stores or order culture from:

PLAZA AMARANTHIA
Sourdough Starter - Detmold 83
P.O. Box 647, Port Coquitlam
British Columbia, Canada V3B 6H9

or

PLAZA AMARANTHIA
Sourdough Starter - Detmold 83
P.O. Box 127, Gardner
Colorado, U.S.A. 81040

Flatbreads
(A Wheat or Gluten-Free, Pita-Like Bread)
(Makes 8 Breads)

½ cup rye, barley, buckwheat, millet or amaranth flour
½ cup brown rice, oat or tapioca flour
2 tsp. arrowroot powder
½ cup water
2 tsp. oil
⅓ – ⅔ cup extra flour for kneading

Sift the flours together and keep separate. Mix the oil and water together and add to the dry ingredients. Work it together with a fork and then with your hands. Knead a bit and roll into a ball. Divide into 8 parts. Roll each in a ball and pat flat. Use a rolling pin and extra flour and roll each bread between 2 sheets of waxed paper. Turn over frequently while rolling and use enough flour so the dough does not stick. Lightly oil a frying pan and heat fairly hot. pre-heat the oven to 400°F.

Put one, somewhat rounded, about ⅛ inch thick, flatbread at a time in the frying pan. heat 15–20 seconds on each side. Then put it immediately into the oven for 3 minutes on the 1st side and then turn it over for 1½–2 minutes on the 2nd side. The breads should 'puff-up' a bit in the oven, though they will not completely puff-up like traditional pita, because pita is yeasted. Re-oil the frying pan before heating each bread. A paper towel dipped in oil may be used for re-oiling. Cool the finished breads before storage in plastic bags. Breads taste great hot too!

Chick Pea Chipatis (or Lentil)
(Makes 8–10)

1 cup chick pea flour (garbanzo flour) or lentil flour
⅓ cup water
½ tsp. oil
½ tsp. sea salt

Mix everything together well and roll into one-inch balls and pat flat. Use a rolling pin to roll out pastry-like rounds of dough. Heat a lightly oiled frying pan until very hot. Then, on medium-high heat, warm each side of the round bread for 1–2 minutes on each side until warmed and slightly browned.

Serve hot or store in the refrigerator for later use, lightly toasted or cold. Chick pea flour is sometimes called chana or besan, especially in East Indian stores. These stores also sell ready-made lentil chipatis that can be heated in a moderate oven until crispy. (Approx. 350°) for about 1–2 minutes.

Applesauce
5 to 10 lbs. baking apples, Spartan and MacIntosh are best
3 to 6 Tbsp. water

Peel the apples. (Apple peels make the sauce bitter and require blending which greatly lessens the flavour and nutrients in the sauce. It is not worth using apple peel unless the apples are organic. See below.) Chop the apples in 1 inch pieces and put in a pot with a good fitting lid. Use 3 Tbsp. water (or a bit more) for every 5 lbs. of apples. Turn the heat on high for only 1 minute. Stand close by and turn the heat down low and simmer the apples for 50–60 minutes or a bit more. It depends on the amount and type of apples. Simmer until they are tender enough to mash with a small holed hand masher. Stir the apples every 10–15 minutes while cooking. Optional sweetening or cinnamon may be added in *Stage II or III* to the finished apples but they are unnecessary if the apples are not overheated, overcooked or if too much water is not added. Eat the applesauce hot or chill for eating plain or cooking with in recipes.

Organic Applesauce

Use the above recipe, but choose organic apples. Wash and cut off any blemishes on the skin, but do not peel them. Remove the cores and chop in ½–¾ inch pieces. Cook as above, cool the apples, and blend bit by bit in a blender or food processor. Add a bit of sweetening, cinnamon and a dash of sea salt if desired, in *Stage II and III* only.

Banana Bread or Muffins (Stage II or III)
(Makes 1 Large Loaf)

2 cups flour:
1 cup regular whole wheat flour *and* 1 cup whole wheat pastry flour
    OR 1½ cups regular whole wheat flour *and* ½ cup unbleached white flour
2 medium bananas
½ cup honey *or* ⅓ cup maple syrup
⅓–½ cup apple, peach or pear juice
¼ cup oil
4 tsp. no-alum baking powder
2 tsp. vanilla extract
¼ tsp. sea salt

Cream the oil and sweetening together. Mash the bananas separately and beat them into the oil mixture. In a separate bowl, sift all the dry ingredients together and add them to the wet mixture. Add the ⅓ cup juice and vanilla and beat well. Add extra juice only if the batter is too stiff. Scoop the mixed ingredients into an oiled and floured pan and bake at 350° for 55–65 minutes until nicely browned on top and a toothpick comes out fairly clean. Do not remove the bread from the oven while testing or until completely baked. Let the bread cool before slicing or it will be doughy. See: How to Make Muffins.

Pumpkin Bread or Muffins (Stages I or II or III)
Follow the Banana Bread recipe except for these changes:
Instead of bananas use 1 cup of cooked and mashed pumpkin
Increase the honey to 1 cup *or* maple syrup to ⅔ or ¾ cup
Add 1–1½ tsp. cinnamon
Add ⅛ tsp. each: nutmeg and ginger

Apple Raisin Bread or Muffins (Stage II or III)
Follow the Banana Bread recipe except for these changes:
Instead of bananas use 1 cup applesauce or stewed apples (peeled)
Use apple juice
Add ½–1 cup raisins
Add 1 tsp. cinnamon
Add several dashes each: nutmeg and ginger

Zucchini or Carrot Bread or Muffins (Stage I or II or III)
Follow the Banana Bread recipe except for these changes:
Instead of bananas use 1 cup of small zucchini *or* carrots—grated very fine
Increase the honey to ¾ cup *or* the maple syrup to ½ cup
For Zucchini Bread, 2 Tbsp. grated orange rind may be added
For Carrot Bread, 1 tsp. cinnamon may be added

How to Make Muffins

The above recipes make about 10–12 muffins. Fill lightly oiled and floured muffin tin cups (or use paper cup inserts for muffins) ⅔ to ¾ full of batter and bake about 25–40 minutes at 350°. Fill any left-over, empty muffin cups with water before baking. Refrigerate all homemade breads and muffins.

STAGE II RECIPES

ALSO FOR USE IN STAGE III

SALAD DRESSINGS

Yogurt Garlic Dressing

1 cup plain yogurt
1–2 cloves garlic—crushed
1–2 Tbsp. fresh lemon juice
Dash or two of sea salt
Optional: bit of cayenne red pepper

Mix together very well. Do not blend. Chill before serving.

Yogurt Dill Dressing

1 cup plain yogurt (preferably a tart variety)
2–3 tsp. dill weed (to taste)
1–3 tsp. fresh lemon juice
Optional: ¼ cup or less chives or green onion tops—chopped fine

Mix (don't blend) all ingredients together well. Add a bit of sea salt
if desired. Serve at room temperature or chilled if preferred.

Yogurt Green Onion Dressing

1 cup plain yogurt
½ cup green onions (white and green parts)—chopped
2–3 tsp. fresh parsley—chopped
1–2 tsp. tamari soy sauce
¼ tsp. each: sea salt, paprika and basil (may use fresh)

Blend all ingredients thoroughly for a better blend of flavours and a green coloured dressing. Chill before serving.

CHEESES

Buttermilk Cheese
(Makes about 1 cup)

1 litre buttermilk

Pre-heat the oven to 225°. Pour the buttermilk into a 9"×12" baking pan and bake for 1½ hours. The buttermilk will separate. Strain the "cheese" in a colander lined with cheesecloth or a fine strainer. Let it strain for about 1 hour while gently stirring the cheese every 15 minutes or so to help remove the whey. Then chill the "cheese" and use in recipes. (This makes a lovely cheese similar to cottage cheese in texture and flavour, but without the additives found in cottage cheese. J.M.M.) It keeps 1–2 weeks refrigerated.
*Original Recipe by Joyce Cherry

Cheese and Chives
1 cup buttermilk cheese
⅓ cup chopped chives or green onions (finely chopped)
1–3 tsp. fresh lemon juice
Sea salt to taste

Mix all ingredients and enjoy stuffed in celery or avocado or in *Stage II*, stuffed in a tomato.

Buttermilk Cheese Spread

Follow the recipe for the *tofu spread* but use Buttermilk Cheese instead of the tofu. Delicious!

Borscht
(Serves 8–10)

4 cups water from steamed vegetables
4 cups cabbage—shredded
2 cups beets—chopped or sliced
1 cup potatoes—chopped in small cubes
1 cup tomato puree
½ cup carrot—sliced thin (about 1 medium)
2 large onions—chopped small (about 1½–2 cups)
1½–2 Tbsp. apple cider vinegar
1½–2 Tbsp. honey (same amount as vinegar)
1 Tbsp. vegetable broth powder OR 2 vegetable bouillon cubes
1–1½ tsp. sea salt
3 bay leaves
¼ tsp. dill weed
cayenne red pepper to taste
3 Tbsp. oil or butter
Optional toppings: chopped tomatoes, or chives or fresh parsley
    and/or sour cream or yogurt

Steam the beets, potatoes and carrot until tender and save the steaming water. Add extra water if needed to equal 4 cups stock and put aside. In a soup pot, saute the onions in hot oil or butter until semi-tender. Add the cabbage and saute another 5–8 minutes until the cabbage is fairly tender. Add the 4 cups steamed vegetable water and the steamed beets, potatoes and carrot. Add the rest of the ingredients (except the toppings), stir, cover and let simmer on low heat for about one half hour. Remove the bay leaves and adjust the flavour if desired. Serve hot with topping(s).

Turkey Soup
(Serves 10–16)

12–16 cups water or stock
Bones of 1 turkey
1½–2 cups turkey pices—cut small

4–6 stalks celery—chopped
2 zucchini—chopped
2 large onions—chopped
2–3 cloves garlic—minced
3 tsp. vegetable broth powder
2 vegetable bouillon cubes
4 Tbsp. tamari soy sauce
2 Tbsp. parsley
2 Tbsp. butter or oil
1–2 tsp. sea salt
1 tsp. basil
½ tsp. thyme
⅛ tsp. each: cayenne red pepper and kelp

Bring the water and turkey bones on high heat to a boil, then turn down low to medium until the water is barely bubbling and simmer for 2–4 hours to make flavourful turkey stock and draw the calcium from the bones into the water. Then strain and save the water (stock) and discard the bones, retaining any leftover, wholesome bits of meat.

Saute the onion, garlic and vegetables in the oil or butter until somewhat tender, in a large skillet and add this to the turkey stock along with the remaining ingredients. Simmer everything together for 1–2 hours. Serve or save until the next day. Soup is best the 2nd to 7th day as the flavours have developed more. Leftovers may be frozen.

Sweet and Sour Lentils
(Serves 3–4)

2 to 2½ cups water
1 cup brown lentils
1 small onion—chopped
3–4 Tbsp. apple cider vinegar
3–4 Tbsp. honey
1 Tbsp. oil

1 tsp. sea salt
1 tsp. basil

Bring the water and lentils to a boil on high heat and immediately turn the heat to low so the lentils are bubbling slightly. Cook them covered for about ½ hour, add the onions and cook another 15 minutes. After 45 minutes, if most of the water is not cooked out or absorbed by the lentils, remove the lid of the pan and let the lentils finish cooking for another 15–20 minutes until most of the liquid is gone and the lentils are fully cooked and very tender. then add the oil, seasonings, and extras and cook the lentils for another 5–8 minutes or so covered, until the flavour of the spices mingles with the lentils. When finished cooking, the lentils should look like a very thick soup or stew. Serve hot or cold. Great for lunches.

Ratatouille
(Serves 4)

1 medium eggplant—peeled and cubed
1 cup tomato juice
1 large onion—chopped small
4–6 cloves garlic—minced
¼ cup oil
2 bay leaves (remove before serving)
2 tsp. dried parsley
1½ tsp. sea salt
1 tsp. each: basil, marjoram and oregano
⅛ tsp. rosemary
Cayenne red pepper to taste

3–4 medium tomatoes—in small chunks

2 large green peppers—in strips
2 medium zucchini—in chunks
2 Tbsp. tomato paste

Optional: fresh, chopped parsley or green onions or chives

Heat the oil in a large cooking pot and saute the onion and garlic until slightly tender on fairly high heat. Add the eggplant and salt it lightly. Continue to saute until the eggplant is a bit tender and the onions and garlic are somewhat transparent. Then add the tomato juice and herbs, stir, cover and simmer on low heat for about 12–15 minutes until the eggplant is very tender. Then add the peppers and zucchini, tomatoes and tomato paste. (The tomatoes may be added earlier with the eggplant if more tender tomatoes are desired.) Stir and simmer 5–10 more minutes until the new vegetables are a bit tender but still retain a bit of crunchiness, or are as tender as you like. It can be topped with fresh parsley or green onions or chives. (*In Stage III* it may be served over rice or other grain.)

Baked Beans
(Serves 6–8)

2 cups dry white pea or navy beans
½ cup molasses
⅓ cup tomato paste
1 medium onion—chopped fine
2 Tbsp. tamari soy sauce
2 tsp. apple cider vinegar
1½ tsp. sea salt
1 tsp. each: curry powder and dry mustard
½ tsp. sea kelp

Cook the beans until tender. Drain off all the water except 1½ cups. Use the 1½ cups water to mix with the beans and remaining ingredients. Scoop the mixture into a lightly oiled 1 or 1½ quart (or litre) baking dish. Bake for 1 hour in the uncovered dish at 275°–300° and then serve. Leftovers reheat easily in a saucepan.

Broiled Tofu Burgers
(Serves 4–6)

1½–2 cups water
¼–⅓ cup tamari soy sauce, *Quick Sip* or teriyaki sauce

½ tsp. curry powder
¼ tsp. each: cayenne red pepper and cumin
Several dashes of kelp
14–16 oz. regular plain tofu—in one block

Freeze the block of tofu (packaged or in a plastic bag) overnight or until it is frozen solid. Defrost it by putting the package of tofu in hot water. When it is defrosted, remove the package, rinse the tofu and gently press out all the excess water. Slice the tofu into slabs about ½ inch thick.

Simmer the tofu slices in the marinade for 15–20 minutes. Then drain the tofu slices and broil them for 2–3 minutes on each side before serving with *Super Sandwich Topping* or plain mustard or another topping. Enjoy it with a hearty salad or steamed or sauteed vegetables.

Spanish Omelet
(Serves 1–2)

4 eggs—separate yolks and whites
4 Tbsp. hot water
½ tsp. sea salt
⅛ tsp. paprika
Several dashes cayenne red pepper
2 tsp. butter (or oil)
1 batch of Spanish Sauce (kept hot)

Beat the egg whites until stiff and peaks are formed. Set aside. Beat the yolks thoroughly until foamy. Melt the butter in a hot omelet pan while heating the broiler in the oven. Mix the water, sea salt, paprika and cayenne with the egg yolks. Then slowly fold the stiff egg whites into the yolk mixture. Pour the eggs into the hot buttered pan and cook, unstirred on medium heat until the omelet sets and is brown underneath. Then place the pan under the broiler to brown the top of the omelet. After it begins to brown, put 2–3 spoonfuls of the Spanish Sauce in the centre of the omelet and fold it over. Finish cooking the omelet 1–2 more minutes if needed, then serve it topped with the rest of the Spanish Sauce.

Spanish Sauce

2 Tbsp. butter
1–2 green onions—chopped
8–10 black olives—sliced
½ green pepper—chopped small
4–6 mushrooms—sliced OR ¼ cup eggplant—pre-cooked & finely chopped
¼ tsp. each: sea salt, dried & crushed red peppers, and paprika
Cayenne red pepper to taste
2 cups tomatoes—seeded and chopped

Melt the butter in a saucepan and saute the onion and green pepper until fairly tender. Add the tomatoes and simmer uncovered for 12–20 minutes until they are very tender and have broken apart and much of the liquid from the tomatoes has evaporated. Add the rest of the ingredients, simmer another 5 minutes covered and use according to the omelet recipe to fill and cover the omelet or serve the sauce over brown rice or another whole grain in *Stage III* only.

Super Sandwich Topping

1 Tbsp. mayonnaise
1 Tbsp. grey mustard
Several dashes each: cayenne red pepper and kelp
Optionals: ½ tsp. miso *or* tamari soy sauce
Optionals: ⅛–¼ tsp. vegetable salt *or* onion or garlic powder

Mix everything together well and use as a spread on *Tofu Burgers*, *Falafel Sandwiches*, Vegetable Sandwiches and others. Adds a delicious kick to any sandwich.

Shrimp Creole
(Serves 2–4)

½ cup green pepper—chopped small
½ cup green onions—chopped (white & green parts)
¼ cup celery—chopped small

1 medium carrot—diced very fine
2 Tbsp. oil
1–2 cloves garlic—minced
1 cup mushrooms—sliced OR 1 cup eggplant—diced and pre-cooked
    tender
2–3 Tbsp. fresh parsley—chopped
3 cups tomatoes (canned or fresh)—chopped
½ tsp. basil
¼ tsp. thyme
Several dashes cayenne red pepper
Optional: sea salt to taste if desired
½ lb. or 200–300 gms. fresh baby shrimp (use more if desired)

On medium-high heat, saute the onions, garlic, pepper, celery and carrot for a few minutes until somewhat tender. Add the mushrooms (or pre-cooked eggplant) and parsley and cook for 3–5 minutes more. Then add the tomatoes and herbs, stir and simmer on low heat for 30 minutes, covered. Lastly, add the shrimp, stir and simmer an additional 3–5 minutes. Serve over steamed, chopped cauliflower for *Stage II* or over brown rice, pasta or another whole grain in *Stage III*. This lovely delicate flavoured dish should be eaten the first day if possible. However, leftovers may be eaten the 2nd day or the 3rd day at the latest.

PANCAKES

Amazing Amaranth Pancakes
(Grain-free)
(Makes 8 or 10 — 3 inch pancakes)

1 egg, beaten
¼ cup apple juice*
1 tsp. oil
¼ cup amaranth flour
¼ cup tapioca flour

3 Tbsp. arrowroot powder
¼ tsp. cinnamon
¼ tsp. baking powder (wheat-free)
⅛ tsp. sea salt

Beat the egg until light and foamy. Mix in the juice and oil. Lightly
oil a frying pan and heat it until very hot. Lower the heat to medium
high. While the pan is warming add the remaining dry ingredients
one by one and beat thoroughly. Once the batter is ready, make the
pancakes immediately. Use 2–3 Tbsp. batter per pancake and keep
the pan hot. Once the bottom browns, flip the pancakes over. Watch
carefully as the pancakes cook quickly. Lightly re-oil the frying pan
with a napkin or paper towel *before* each new batch.

*Other sweet fruit juices may be used instead of apple, such as:
mango, papaya, peach, pear or apricot.

Millet and/or Rice Pancakes
(Gluten-free)

1 egg, beaten
1½ cups milk substitute
1 cup millet flour*
1 cup brown rice flour*
½ cup tapioca flour
Several dashes of sea salt

Follow the directions for *AMAZING AMARANTH PANCAKES.*
These make light, thin pancakes. To thicken add ¼ cup extra flour
(your choice) and/or ¼ tsp. baking powder.

*Instead of 1 cup each millet and brown rice flour, 2 cups of millet
or brown rice flour may be used. Makes about 1½–2 dozen—3 inch
pancakes.

Buckwheat Pancakes
(Wheat-free)

2 eggs, beaten
1–1¼ cup milk substitute*
1½ cups millet or brown rice flour
¾ cup buckwheat flour
Several dashes sea salt
Optional: ¼ tsp. cinnamon

Follow directions for the *AMAZING AMARANTH PANCAKES*. *A sweet fruit juice may be used instead of milk substitute. If desired, try: apple, apricot, peach, pear or tropical fruit juices. Makes about 1½–2 dozen—3 inch pancakes.

STAGE III RECIPES

DRESSINGS

Citrus Butter for Artichokes
(For 1 or 2)

¼ cup butter—melted
¼ tsp. fine grated orange rind
2 Tbsp. orange juice (fresh)
1 Tbsp. lemon juice (fresh)

Mix the rind and juices with the melted butter and serve with steamed artichokes for dipping the leaves in. *Stage III* only.

Easy Thousand Island Dressing
1 cup natural mayonnaise
1-2 Tbsp. tomato paste
2–4 tsp. apple cider vinegar *or* fresh lemon juice
⅓ cup chopped pickles *or* relish
1–2 tsp. or more honey *or* maple syrup to taste
Several dashes each: sea salt and cayenne red pepper

Beat all ingredients together well and adjust the flavourings if needed. Chill before serving with *Stage III* salads.

SOUPS

Broccoli or Zucchini Soup
(Serves 3–4)

3–4 stalks broccoli (4 cups)—chopped for steaming OR 3–4
   zucchini (4 cups)—chopped
1½ cups cashew or almond milk
2–3 tsp. parsley
½ tsp. basil
¼–½ tsp. sea salt
¼ tsp. each: thyme and paprika
Several dashes cayenne red pepper

Steam the vegetables until tender, then blend them with the "milk"
and herbs. Put the soup in a saucepan and heat it just to boiling on
medium heat. (Do not boil or overheat!) Serve immediately. This is
a wonderful, creamy type soup, more flavourful than soups made
with cow's milk which actually detracts from the flavour of the vegetables.

Nut Milk
2–3 Tbsp. "raw" cashew pieces or raw blanched almonds
1½ cups water

Blend thoroughly in the blender or a food processor for 2–4 minutes
until the water becomes white with the blended nuts. (At highest
speed.) Strain and use in many recipes instead of cow's milk.

Tomato Lentil Soup
(Serves 8–10)

8 cups water or stock
2 cups lentils
13 oz. can of tomato paste

3–4 medium tomatoes—chopped OR 1 large can (28 oz. or 795 ml) tomatoes with juice—chopped
2–3 stalks celery—chopped
1 large onion—chopped
2–4 tsp. tamari soy sauce
2 tsp. parsley
1–2 tsp. honey (to balance the flavours)
1 tsp. each: sea salt, basil and oregano
½ tsp. each: kelp, marjoram and thyme
Several dashes cayenne red pepper

Cook the lentils and water for 30 minutes in a large pot on medium heat. Add the onions, tomatoes, and vegetables and cook these all together for another 30 minutes. Add the remaining ingredients and continue cooking everything on low heat for about 20–25 minutes or until the tomatoes have turned into liquid, the vegetables are tender, and the lentils are very soft. Stir the soup occasionally.

Clam Chowder
(Serves 8–10)

2 cans whole baby clams with juice (approx. 5 oz. clams & 5 oz. juice)
2½ cups water
2 cups milk or 1½ cups milk & ½ cup cream
2–3 Tbsp. butter
1 medium onion—chopped small
3 cups potatoes—unpeeled, diced
6 Tbsp. whole wheat flour (or millet or arrowroot)
1–2 tsp. sea salt
¼ tsp. paprika
Several dashes cayenne red pepper

Carefully melt the butter (so it won't burn) in about a 1 gallon pot and saute the onion in it until slightly tender, then add the flour and saute until browned to add flavour. Next, add the water and potatoes (rinse the potatoes well in cool water before adding to the soup) and simmer on low to medium heat for 15–20 minutes until the potatoes are fairly tender. Then add the clams with their juice and the spices and simmer 25 minutes more. In a small saucepan heat the milk until hot but not boiling. Add the hot milk to the soup and simmer 10 minutes more. Keep the soup covered at all times and be careful not to burn it using too high a heat. Serve and enjoy when ready. It's delicious the 1st day or the next. Keeps 5–6 days refrigerated and may be frozen if defrosted slowly.

MAIN DISHES

Lentil Burgers
(Serves 6)

2 cups dry lentils — cooked until tender and drained (see Sweet and Sour Lentils for how-to)
1–2 eggs — beaten foamy
1 medium onion — diced
½ cup cracker crumbs
1 tsp. tamari soy sauce
½–1 tsp. sea salt
⅛ tsp. kelp
Cayenne red pepper to taste
Tomato juice

Mix all the ingredients together and use just enough tomato juice to hold the mixture together and shape into burgers. Fry like other burgers in a skillet or on a griddle that is oiled and hot. Cook about 12–20 minutes on the first side and 6–12 on the second side, or until nicely browned. These are best served without a bun, with ketchup or a sauce or gravy. Try *Arrowroot Sauce* or *Mushroom Gravy*.

Pecan-Cheese Loaf
(Serves 8)

1½–2 cups pecans—crushed very small
1½ cups cooked brown rice
1 cup wheat germ
1 cup mushrooms—sliced thin
1¼ lbs. aged cheddar cheese—grated
1 large onion—minced
2 cloves garlic—minced or crushed
1–2 tsp. tamari soy sauce
1/16–⅛ tsp. cayenne red pepper
Several dashes kelp
4 extra large (or 5 large) eggs—beaten foamy

Combine all the ingredients except the eggs in a large bowl. Mix thoroughly, add the eggs and mix again. Pack the mixture into a heavily oiled 9" or 10" square baking pan. Bake at 350° for 45–50 minutes or until firm and browned. Cut into pieces and serve with hot *Mushroom Gravy*. It has a meatloaf consistency and tastes terrific!

Mushroom Gravy I
1¾ cups water
1 cup mushrooms—sliced thin
½ cup whole wheat flour (or millet)
2–3 Tbsp. tamari soy sauce
2 vegetable bouillon cubes
3 tsp. vegetable broth powder
Cayenne red pepper to taste
Several dashes kelp

Mix all the ingredients together and heat in a saucepan on medium heat, stirring constantly until very hot, then simmer on lowest heat about 15 minutes until thickened and the mushrooms are tender. Serve hot over nut loafs, burgers, grains or vegetables. Chill leftovers for later use. Delicious!

Mushroom Gravy II

1 cup milk
1 cup sliced mushrooms
1 large onion—chopped fine
1 clove garlic—minced
4 Tbsp. arrowroot powder—mixed in ¼ cup water
2 Tbsp. butter
1 Tbsp. tamari soy sauce
Sea salt to taste
Several dashes cayenne red pepper and kelp

In a saucepan saute the onions and garlic in the butter until slightly tender. Add the mushrooms and continue to saute until the onions and garlic are fairly transparent and the mushrooms are tender. Add the arrowroot mixture and stir until thickened. Then add the remaining ingredients, stir a minute or two longer and serve. Use as above.

Cauliflower Patties
(Makes and Serves 6–8)

1 cup raw cauliflower—grated
1 cup cashew pieces—crushed
1 cup medium or sharp cheddar cheese—grated
1 cup bread crumbs
1 small onion—chopped very fine
1 clove garlic—crushed
1 Tbsp. whole wheat flour
1 Tbsp. dried parsley *or* 2–3 Tbsp. fresh parsley—chopped
1 Tbsp. butter or oil
½ tsp. each: sea salt and thyme
Several dashes each: cayenne red pepper and kelp
2 extra large eggs—beaten foamy

Mix all the ingredients together except the eggs. After mixing, add the eggs and mix again. Form into patties and cook like burgers in an oiled skillet or on a griddle. In the hot pan (or griddle) broil each pattie for about 10 minutes on the first side and a bit less on the second until browned. Serve with *Mushroom Gravy.*

Spiced Vegetables and Polenta
(Serves 4–6)

1 medium eggplant—peeled and cubed
1 cup tomato juice
1 large onion—chopped small
4–6 cloves garlic—minced
¼ cup oil
1 tsp. each: cumin, ground coriander and chili powder
1½ tsp. sea salt
Hot sauce and/or Cayenne red pepper to taste
3–4 medium tomatoes—in small chunks
2 large green peppers—in strips
2 medium zucchini—in chunks
3 Tbsp. tomato paste

Optional: fresh, chopped parsley, or green onions or chives

Cook the above in exactly the *same* way as the Ratatouille. (The vegetables are the same but the herbs and spices are different.) Serve over hot Polenta as soon as prepared. Both may be reheated again if needed.

Polenta
3½–4 cups water
1½ cups whole yellow corn meal
1½ cups medium cheddar cheese—grated
1 tsp. sea salt

Mix the cold water and corn meal together in a large sauce pan and stir over medium heat until it thickens and is no longer grainy. Turn the heat down low and keep stirring while adding the cheese and sea salt. As soon as the cheese is melted the polenta is done. Scoop ½ cup or more onto a warm plate and top with the spiced vegetables. Top with parsley, green onions or chives and enjoy! A little sour cream or yogurt is also nice with this.

Gado-Gado Spicy Peanut Sauce with Vegetables
(Serves 6)

2 medium onions—chopped small
2–3 cloves garlic—minced
2 Tbsp. butter or oil
2 bay leaves (remove before serving)
2 tsp. fresh ginger root—grated fine

2–2½ cups water
1 cup natural peanut butter
¼ cup fresh lemon juice
1 Tbsp. honey
1 Tbsp. apple cider vinegar
1 tsp. tamari soy sauce
½–1 tsp. sea salt
⅛–¼ tsp. cayenne red pepper to taste

Saute the onions, garlic, bay leaves and ginger in the butter or oil until slightly tender, about 2–3 minutes. Add the remaining ingredients, mix thoroughly and simmer on the lowest possible heat for 30–35 minutes, stirring occasionally.

Serve Over:
2 cups shredded cabbage—raw or steamed
1 cup raw carrot—grated
1 cup raw celery—sliced

1 cup marinated tofu chunks
3–6 hard boiled eggs—sliced
3 Tbsp. toasted sunflower seeds or nuts

3 cups mixed steamed vegetables—broccoli, zucchini, and/or mushrooms, etc.

On one large platter, or separately on each plate, first arrange a layer of raw ingredients, then one of steamed, then the egg slices and tofu, nuts or seeds. Top with the sauce and enjoy!

Pita Pizzas
(Serves 2)

4 whole wheat pita breads
2–3 cups tomato sauce—warmed
2 cups medium cheddar, swiss or mozzarella cheese—grated
2–4 Toppings: sliced black olives, chopped green peppers, tomato slices, zucchini or mushroom slices, chopped onions, pineapple chunks, and/or chopped meats

Heat the breads in the oven for 1–2 minutes to warm them and cover them with hot tomato sauce (heated in a saucepan). Cover with toppings and broil for 1–3 minutes until hot and crispy. Enjoy these fast, easy and scrumptious pizza treats as a meal or quick snack. They are great hot and taste good cold in lunches too.

Spaghetti
Whole wheat or other whole grain noodles
Tomato sauce
Parmesan Cheese

Add the noodles to already boiling water and keep the heat just high enough so it continues to bubble (though not furiously.) Use a large cooking pot and at least 1 gallon of water per pound of noodles. Cook the noodles until tender outside and still a bit firm inside, not mushy but not chewy. Noodles may take from about 5 to 20 minutes to cook depending on the type of noodle and what it's made from. Do not always trust package instructions as they are sometimes incorrect. When ready, drain the noodles in a colander and serve immediately with tomato sauce (or other sauce) and Parmesan cheese.

Lasagne Rice
Brown rice
Tomato sauce
Medium cheddar cheese (undyed)—grated
Parmesan cheese

Cook the brown rice and during the last 10 minutes of cooking time, sprinkle the grated cheese over the rice so it can melt. When ready, serve with tomato sauce and sprinkled Parmesan cheese. Enjoy this delicious and more nutritious version of lasagne.

Confetti Rice
(Serves 2–3)

2 cups cooked brown rice—still hot (about 1 cup dry)
1 large avocado—chopped
2 medium tomatoes—chopped
½ cup mushrooms—sliced
4–5 tsp. tamari soy sauce
½ tsp. vegetable salt
½ tsp. vegetable mixed seasoning like: Spike, Herbamare, etc.
1/16 tsp. cayenne red pepper
Dash or two of kelp

Cook the brown rice and add the mushrooms on top the last 10–15 minutes of its cooking time. While the rice is still hot, mix in the raw tomato and avocado along with the herbs according to taste. Serve immediately as it cools quickly and should be eaten hot. This dish does not reheat or store well. It's best to eat fresh, right after preparing. Delicious!

Terrific Tomato Sauce
(Makes about 5 cups)

13 oz. tomato paste
1–1½ cups water

4 medium tomatoes—chopped
1 large onion—chopped small
1 small eggplant or 1 cup mushrooms—chopped
2–3 cloves garlic—minced
3 bay leaves (take out later)
2 Tbsp. tamari soy sauce
2 Tbsp. oil
2–3 tsp. parsley
2 tsp. each: basil and oregano
1 tsp. each: sea salt and honey (or maple syrup)—to balance flavours
½ tsp. each: marjoram, thyme, kelp and rosemary
⅛ tsp. or less cayenne red pepper

Heat the oil in a large pot (dutch oven) on medium-high temperature. When the oil is hot, add chopped onions and garlic and eggplant or mushrooms and saute until they are tender. Then add the
tomatoes and cook until they turn to liquid. Add the tomato paste
and water and mix everything together thoroughly. Lastly, add all
the herbs and spices and simmer the sauce on very low heat for
40–60 minutes with the lid covering the pot, stirring occasionally.
A little extra water may be added for a looser consistency. Correct
the herbs and spices if needed. When the sauce is finished, remove
the bay leaves. Then use the sauce in recipes or refrigerate it no
longer than 7 days or freeze for later use. The recipe can be doubled
or tripled for larger batches. Be sure to use less sea salt when increasing recipe sizes.

EGGS AND MEAT

Vegetable Quiche
(Makes 2 Pies—Serves 8–12)

Optional: 2 9″ or 10″ pie crust shells (see recipes)
12–16 oz. swiss cheese—grated (half cheddar may be used)
4 extra large or 5 large eggs—beaten until foamy

½ lb. mushrooms—sliced
2 cups broccoli—chopped
2 medium onions or 6–8 green onions—chopped fine
2 green peppers—chopped
2 Tbsp. oil
2 tsp. tamari soy sauce
1½ tsp. sea salt
1 tsp. parsley
½ tsp. each: paprika and basil
Several dashes each: cayenne red pepper and kelp
1½ to 2 cups milk

Sauté the onions and vegetables in oil along with the sea salt and herbs. Pour off any excess liquid. When the vegetables are tender, mix them with the tamari and set them aside until the cheese sauce is ready. Heat the milk. (Use more milk if more cheese is used.) Take the milk off the heat *before* if comes to a boil and in the grated cheese.

Stir the sautéed vegetables and spread ¾ of them in the unbaked pie crust shells. (To avoid using a pie crust—just lightly oil a pie pan.) Mix the beaten eggs into the melted cheese and milk and pour-scoop them over the vegetables in the pie pan. Do not leave the cheese or eggs in the milk for more than a minute or two, or the eggs will harden and the cheese become rubbery. Top the pie with the remaining vegetables, spread out evenly over the milk mixture. Bake immediately in a pre-heated oven at 350° for 35–45 minutes or until the pie is slightly browned, golden in colour and firm. (¼–½ lb. or 100–200 gms. shredded crab or baby shrimp may be added as a variation in some quiches.)

Fish in Cream Sauce
(Serves 2–4)

1 lb. fresh or frozen fish fillets (try sole, cod, haddock, etc.), (defrost if frozen)
1½–2 cups milk or milk substitute
2–3 tsp. butter (or oil)

½–1 cup mushrooms—sliced
¼ tsp. each: basil and paprika
1 tsp. dried parsley
Several dashes each: sea salt, cayenne red pepper and kelp

Place the fish in a lightly oiled low-sided baking dish. (Pyrex is a good choice.) Pour the milk over the fish and around it. Then sprinkle or pour on the rest of the ingredients and place little dabs of butter on top. Broil for 7–12 minutes on the first side and 5–7 minutes on the second side, until tender but not dry. Serve with lemon wedges and/or tartar sauce.

DESSERTS

Carob Frosting

Sift together:
½ cup milk powder—non-instant is best
½ cup roasted carob powder (dark)
Optional: 2–3 tsp. instant coffee substitute (for a more chocolatey flavor)

Add:
⅓–½ cup honey
6 Tbsp. milk
2 Tbsp. light oil
1–2 tsp. vanilla
4–6 drops peppermint extract
Optional: ¼–⅓ cup coconut—shredded, unsweetened to sprinkle on top of cake

Mix the carob powder with the non-instant milk powder. Mix all the other ingredients and slowly add dry ones to them and mix thoroughly until smooth. (If noninstant milk powder is not available, mix instant milk powder separately with the milk, then add rest of the wet ingredients and mix. Lastly, add carob powder. Instant milk powder tends to stay lumpy when mixed differently. Double the frosting ingredients if lots of frosting is wanted.

Add extra milk if thinner frosting consistency is wanted. Frosting will thicken and harden as it chills. Chill frosting for 1–2 hours before using on the cake.

Carob Cake
(Makes 1—9"×13" or 1—2-layer 8" round cake)

Wet Ingredients:
1½ cups honey
1–1½ cups milk
½ cup light oil or softened butter
3 extra large eggs—beaten
2 tsp. lemon or orange rind
2 tsp. vanilla
1–2 tsp. lecithin—liquid

Dry Ingredients:
2½ cups w.w. flour—half pastry, half regular
½–⅔ cup roasted carob powder
2–4 oz. walnuts or pecans—chopped
3–4 tsp. baking powder—low or no-alum
½ tsp. salt
Optional: 1–2 Tbsp. gluten flour
Optional: 3–4 tsp. instant coffee substitute

Mix all the wet ingredients together well with a fork or wire whisk. In a separate bowl mix the dry ingredients by sifting them together once and stirring. Begin by using only 1 cup milk and add the extra ½ cup if the mixture is too dry. The mixture should be thick but able to be poured into the baking pan(s). Beat the cake batter 100–200 strokes until smooth and then mix in the nuts. Lightly oil and flour the pan(s), pour in the cake batter, and bake at 325° for 45–60 minutes until lightly browned and a toothpick comes out clean. Cool the cake before removing the cake from the pans and adding frosting. Frost with carob frosting for the best tasting cake, although cream frosting may also be used.

24 Karat (Carrot) Cake
(Makes 1—9"×13" or 1—2 or 3 layer 8" round cake)

Wet Ingredients:
6 medium carrots—grated fine (about 2 cups)
1½ cups honey
¾—1 cup milk
⅓ cup oil
3 extra large eggs—beaten
2 tsp. vanilla

Dry Ingredients:
2½ cups w.w. flour—half pastry, half regular
2—4 oz. walnuts or pecans—chopped
3—4 tsp. baking powder
1 tsp. cinnamon
½ tsp. nutmeg
½ tsp. salt
Optional: 1—2 Tbsp. gluten flour

Mix the wet ingredients together thoroughly. In a separate bowl mix
the dry ingredients together. May be sifted. Add the dry mixture to
the wet and beat 100—200 strokes. Then add the nuts and mix them
in. Lightly oil and flour the pan(s) and scoop the thick mixture into
the pan(s). Bake at 350° for 50—60 minutes until golden brown.

Cool the cake before removing from pan(s) and frosting. Frost
with cream cheese frosting.

Cream Cheese Frosting
16 oz. cream cheese
½—1 cup honey or add honey to taste
2 tsp. vanilla
Optional: coconut—to sprinkle on top

Leave the cream cheese at room temperature for 1—2 hours until
very soft. When the cake is done and cooling, the cream cheese
should be soft enough to whip. Use a mixer and slowly mix the

honey and vanilla into the cream cheese until smooth. Chill the frosting for an hour or so and then frost the cake. Sprinkle coconut on top if desired.

Dessert Pie Crusts

Add 1 tsp. honey to any of the following recipes if they are to be used for dessert recipes. These recipes may be used for Quiche without the added honey.

Double Pie Crust Recipe
(Makes 1—10" double crust)

2 cups sifted w.w. flour (at least half pastry flour)
1 tsp. salt
⅔ cup light oil
¼ cup cold milk or cold water
1–2 tsp. liquid lecithin

Mix the wet and dry ingredients separately. Add the dry ingredients to the wet and use a fork or pastry blender to mix. Knead the dough for a couple of minutes and divide it into 2 parts. Roll one part between 2 pieces of wax paper. Roll the dough until it is about ⅛ inch thick and 11–12 inches in diameter. While rolling out the dough be careful to turn it upside down once in a while and lift the wax paper on each side occasionally so it will not stick permanently to the dough. Lightly oil the 10" pie pan. Remove one layer of wax paper from the rolled dough and turn it upside down over the pie pan. Gently remove the top, last layer of wax paper and shape the pie crust to the pan. Push the dough into the corners of the pan; do not stretch the dough or it will shrink and grow smaller while the pie is baking. Use a fork to poke air holes in the dough.

After shaping the bottom crust, fill it with pie filling and cover it with the second rolled-out pie crust. Flute the edges together, make a few slits on the top crust, and then bake at 425° or 30–40 minutes until golden and flaky. Serve pie hot or chilled.

Single Pie Crust #1
(Makes 2 single crusts)

2 cups sifted w.w. flour (at least half pastry flour)
1 stick butter or margarine—softened but not melted
¼ cup cold water
1–2 tsp. lecithin—liquid
1 tsp. salt

Single Pie Crust #2
(Makes 2 single crusts)

2 cups sifted w.w. flour (at least half pastry flour), or 1¼ cups millet
   flour and ¾ cup rice flour
½ stick butter or margarine—softened but not melted
¼ cup oil
¼ cup cold water
1–2 tsp. lecithin—liquid
1 tsp. salt

Add the mixed flour and salt to the butter and lecithin and mix as well as possible. Add the water and continue mixing. Knead a few minutes and continue making the dough the same as the double crust recipe except use 2 pie pans and make 2 single crusts. Also bake the crust 3–5 minutes at 325° *before* adding the filling and then bake it all together according to the filling recipe. Use this for pies or quiche.
Note: Crusts made with butter or margarine tend to shrink a little more, so be careful not to *stretch* the dough.

Pumpkin for Recipes

There are several ways to prepare pumpkin for use in recipes. A small pumpkin can be boiled whole then seeded and peeled before mashing and draining off the excess liquid *or* a large pumpkin can be cut into large pieces, seeded and baked till tender before peeling and mashing it. (Bake pumpkin about 375° to 400°F for 45–70 minutes.) Canned pumpkin may be used although it is not as fresh or nutritious.

*Some kinds of orange winter squash may be substituted for pumpkin.

Pumpkin Pudding

Blend:
2 cups cooked pumpkin (see recipe)
1–1¼ cups nut milk
⅓–⅔ cup honey *or* maple syrup
2 large eggs
2 Tbsp. arrowroot powder
1 Tbsp. instant milk powder (may be omitted)
2 tsp. vanilla extract
½–1 tsp. cinnamon
¼ tsp. ginger
Several dashes nutmeg and sea salt
Optional: 1 Tbsp. molasses

Blend all ingredients and taste the mixture. Make any changes according to taste. The mixture will be somewhat thick, but very pourable. Lightly oil 1–2 baking dishes and pour the mixture into them about 1½ to 2 inches thick. Bake the pudding at 325°F for about 30 to 45 minutes until the mixture becomes firm and turns golden brown. Chill thoroughly before serving.

Pumpkin Pie

Use a pie crust of your choice. Use the *Pumpkin Pudding* recipe as the filling and bake the same way. One pudding recipe makes 2 to 3 pies. Each piece of pie may be sprinkled with extra cinnamon.

Apple Pie
(1 medium or large pie)

6–8 large baking apples, cored and chopped (peeled, if desired)
½–¾ cup honey *or* ⅓–½ cup maple syrup
2½ Tbsp. arrowroot powder
1½ to 2 tsp. cinnamon
¼ tsp. sea salt
Optional: ½ cup raisins or currants or chopped nuts

Use Rome, Spartan, MacIntosh, Jonathan, Newton, Lodi or other baking apples. Simmer the apples and raisins or currants with ¼ cup water on medium heat for 8 to 10 minutes or until tender. Drain the apples and save the liquid. When the liquid cools, mix it with the arrowroot powder and sea salt. Add 1–2 Tbsp. extra water if needed. Heat it in a saucepan until it thickens, stirring constantly.

Mix the apples, arrowroot mixture and the remaining ingredients together and scoop into 2 pie custs. 1 or 2 Tbsp. of ground nuts may be sprinkled on top for extra flavour and attractiveness.

Bake at 375°F for 25 to 40 minutes, until browned and set. (The larger and thicker the pie, the longer the baking time.)

Pumpkin Cookies
(makes 4–6 dozen)

Dry Ingredients: Sift together
2 cups whole wheat, millet flour or rice flour
½ cup soy, buckwheat, amaranth or whole wheat pastry flour
3 tsp. baking powder
2 tsp. cinnamon
½ tsp. sea salt
½ tsp. nutmeg
¼ tsp. ginger
Optional: 1–2 cups raisins or currants
             1 cup chopped nuts

Wet Ingredients:
½ cup oil (or soft clarified butter)
1–1¼ cup honey *or* ¾ cup maple syrup and ⅓ cup pumpkin liquid
    or water
¾ cup brown date sugar *or* barley malt powder
2 eggs beaten
1 Tbsp. molasses
Optional: 1–2 tsp. vanilla extract

Add: 1½ cups pumpkin (cooked & mashed)

Stir the dry ingredients into the wet. This makes a thick but pourable batter. Bake medium sized cookies for 12–14 minutes at 400°–425°.

Tapioca Treats
(Wheat-free)
(makes 1½ dozen)

¼ cup tapioca flour
¼ cup brown rice flour*
¼ cup barley malt powder*
½ cup crispy brown rice*
½ cup dried, unsweetened coconut* (fine grated)
3 Tbsp. maple syrup
1 tsp. pure vanilla extract

Mix the flours and malt powder together well. Add the maple syrup and vanilla extract and mix thoroughly. Carefully stir in the crispy brown rice, then lastly, mix in the coconut. Shape a teaspoonful of the mixture into a ball and flatten it to about ⅜ inch thick on a lightly oiled cookie sheet. Bake at 350°F for 8–10 minutes. Remove from the oven while they are still soft, but lightly browned. They will harden as they cool. Once cooled (approx. ½ hour), store in a tin with a small crust of bread inside to keep the cookies moist and absorb excess moisture.

*Variations: These may slightly alter the flavour, but not the consistency of the recipe.
*Instead of: Use:
rice flour   millet flour
coconut   ground nuts or seeds
crispy rice   chopped nuts
barley malt   *fine* brown date
              sugar (can be ground in blender or food processor or
              grinder)

Oatmeal Cookies
(Makes 4–5 dozen)

Mix well together:
⅔ cup brown date sugar
½ cup (1 stick) butter or margarine—softened
½ cup honey or ⅜ cup honey and ⅛ cup molasses

Add:
2 cups rolled oats
1 cup w.w. flour
½ cup pastry or unbleached white flour
2 eggs—beaten
1 tsp. cinnamon
1 tsp. vanilla
½ tsp. baking powder (no-alum)
¼ tsp. salt
Few dashes nutmeg

Mix the dry ingredients separately and gradually add them to the wet ingredients.
    Make sure the batter is fairly stiff and hard to stir. Add a bit more honey or flour if needed. Drop a spoonful or two of batter per cookie on an oiled cookie sheet. Make sure the cookies are one inch or more apart. Bake for 10–14 minutes or until lightly browned (but tender) at 400°.

Carob Chip-Nut Cookies
(Makes about 4–5 dozen)

Mix well together:
⅔ cup honey
½ cup butter or margarine—softened
½ cup brown date sugar
¼ cup milk powder—non-instant
1 egg—beaten
2 tsp. gluten flour or arrowroot powder
1 tsp. vanilla
¼ tsp. salt

Add and mix in well:
1 cup w.w. flour
¾ cup carob chips (purchase at health food store)
½ cup w.w. pastry or unbleached white flour
½ cup chopped walnuts, pecans, or almonds

Drop a spoonful or two of batter for each cookie on a lightly oiled cookie sheet. Bake for 1–12 minutes or till very lightly browned at 375°. These cookies can also be made into *bar cookies* by spreading the batter about ½ inch thick on a cookie sheet and baking at 350° for 15–20 minutes. Then cool a few minutes and cut into squares or bars.

Rice Pudding
2 cups pre-cooked brown rice, cold (about 1 cup dry)
½ cup milk, nut milk or sweet juice (apple, pear or peach are best)
½ cup honey *or* ⅓ cup maple syrup plus 2 Tbsp. extra juice or milk
2 large eggs—beaten foamy
2 tsp. vanilla extract
1–1½ tsp. cinnamon
⅛ tsp. sea salt
Optional: ½ cup raisins or currants

Plain, leftover rice may be used or sweet, brown rice, if it is available. Mix all the ingredients together and pour them into a lightly oiled casserole pan about 9"×9" and bake 35–45 minutes uncovered at 375° until 'set' and somewhat firm. Served hot or cold, this makes a delicious easy and nutritious dessert.

Date Squares
(Makes 1 9"×9" Pan)

1 CRUNCHY CRUST RECIPE
1 DATE SPREAD RECIPE

Press ½ or more of the crust recipe onto the bottom only of a lightly oiled 9"×9" pan. Next, spread all the date mixture on. Lastly, evenly 'sprinkle' the remaining crust mixture over the top of the dates and pat them together gently as a top crust. Bake around 350° for 25 to 40 minutes until the top is lightly browned, but still tender. The crust will harden as it cools, don't let it harden in the oven or it will be *very* hard! Cut it into pieces before it cools completely or it will be difficult to cut. A rich dessert or snack!

Date Spread
1 to 1 1/6 lb. dates—pitted (up to 500 gms)
⅔ cup water
Few dashes salt
Optional: 2 Tbsp. lemon juice, fresh
            1–2 Tbsp. lemon rind—grated fine

Put all ingredients in a saucepan and cook on a low heat to medium-low heat until the dates get soft and mix easily with the water. (About 30 minutes or more.) When the date mixture can be stirred into a pastelike texture, take it off the heat and let it cool before using for Date Squares.

Crunchy Crust
(For Date Squares or Apple Crisp)

Mix:
¾–1 cup honey *or* ⅔ cup maple syrup
½ cup oil
¾ tsp. sea salt

Mix Separately:
2½ cups rolled oats
1 cup whole wheat or oat flour
Optional: 2 Tbsp. lemon rind—grated fine

Slowly add the dry ingredients to the wet and mix well. Use for Date Squares or as a crust for other recipes.

PART IV

STRESS AND DIGESTION

"I learned this, at least, by my experiment;
that if one advances confidently in the
direction of his dreams, and endeavours to
live the life which he has imagined, he will
meet with a success unexpected in common hours."

Thoreau-Walden

CHAPTER 11

Fright to Fight or Flight

We have come a long way in our trip through the body and we can see how disease has a connection, direct or indirect, to sluggish or inefficient digestion. Yet we still have more to learn about digestion. Our trip has started at the mouth and gone down through the muscles of the stomach and intestine, into the blood to the liver and gallbladder, throughout the main bloodstream to the lymphatics and the immune system. To understand how this group of systems and organs works together as a unit we have to leave the microscope and stand back a bit. The parts that we have explored, together form the central core of the body, and they get their nerve energy primarily from the parasympathetic nervous system.

There is another part of the body that is energized primarily by a different nervous system. This is the skeletal muscle system, which gets its nerve energy from the sympathetic nervous system. While the stomach juices are the "spark" for proper digestion, the "sparkplugs" of the sympathetic nervous system are the adrenal glands. The adrenals normally secrete hormones which help maintain mineral and sugar levels. In emergencies, however, they secrete a powerful hormone called adrenalin or epinepherine which shunts energy away from the parasympathetic nervous system (digestive and lymphatic systems), and sends it outwards via the sympathetic nervous system to the skeletal muscles so that you can fight or flee from danger. Obviously, this is called the fight or flight response.

To see how it works in action, picture a zebra out in an open grass-land. He can see that there is no danger in the vicinity, so his main energy is concentrated in the central core of his body. The parasympathetic nervous system is dominant, so the digestive and lymph systems are fully activated. He is chewing and the grass goes down into the stomach, which makes digestive juices that stimulate the intestinal tract. In the intestine, the friendly bacteria are busy baking little grass pies. In the lymph system, the thymus gland is orchestrating the white blood cells which quickly deal with any viruses, yeast, fungi, bacteria, parasites or abnormal cells. The skeletal muscles of the legs are used at the moment for little more than props.

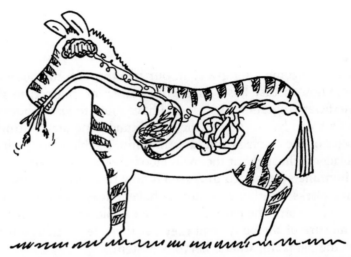

Now picture that same zebra with a massive lion barreling through the tall grass directly towards the zebra, drool pouring from his jaws and a hungry glint in his eyes. Does this zebra care whether there's a little undigested grass in his intestine? Does he care if there's a virus or two hiding out somewhere in the lymph system? Emphatically, NO! Forget about those trivialities, let's get these legs moving, fast! So the adrenal glands fire up, and the energy switches from the central core of the body to the skeletal muscles, and the zebra either kicks the lion in the chops or "hightails" it out of there.

Within minutes, it's almost all over one way or the other. Either the zebra made good his getaway, or he's become dinner for Leo and

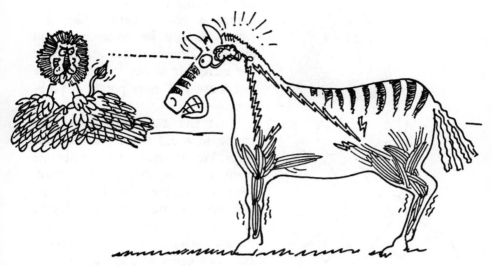

friends. If he got away, within a short time the adrenal glands would stop making fight or flight hormones. The adrenal hormones in the blood would be broken down and the energy would slowly shift away from the skeletal muscles and back to the digestive and lymph system. Within a short time he would be back to grazing. Even if the lion was still within sight, as long as he was outside the zebra's "safety zone", the zebra would continue peacefully grazing.

Real physical danger is a rarity in our society. The wild beasts have long since been exterminated from populated areas or locked up in zoos.

However, we have a built-in video screen in our minds on which we are constantly projecting pictures. This has great uses for we can take experiences from the past and present and then project them into the future on our mental screen. From this information we can then anticipate what problems and/or opportunities might arise in the future so that we can best prepare for them.

The problem is that when you project a picture of a potential problem in your mind your body doesn't know that it is not a real problem, that it is merely an imaginary potential problem. The body reacts exactly as if you were in extreme physical danger. The body energy shifts away from the digestive organs and lymph system and out to the skeletal muscles so that you can run from or fight with

this "roaring lion" of the mind. In nature a real situation like this would usually be resolved within minutes. However, our minds have the incredible ability to create more and more and more potential problems.

We spend a great deal of time trying to avoid these problem pictures. We can temporarily obliberate them by using drugs and alcohol. We can avoid them briefly by taking holidays, going fishing, playing cards, sports or other games, watching t.v., sleeping in, being too busy, etc., but often as soon as we stop these activities the mind begins to fill again with all the potential troubles that might occur.

Outside sources often contribute to a sense of danger and trouble. Newspapers and T.V. news exaggerates the amount of real danger that exists in our communities.

WE INTERRUPT THIS PROGRAM FOR AN IMPORTANT BULLETIN!

Also we even pride ourselves when we use our minds to our best advantage. If we use our mind to see a situation sooner or clearer than someone else so that we can make a quicker or better deal, then this is something that we boast or brag about. There is, however, a very fine line between practical use of the mind's creative abilities and using it as a scheming machine.

Even a small real problem can turn into a major health problem by constantly thinking about it rather than doing something constructive to resolve it. Problems should be quickly and decisively dealt with or, if they can't be dealt with summarily, they should be consciously put aside until they can be dealt with.

Talking about a problem with a good friend or a counsellor may help to shrink it back to its proper size after a runaway mind has exaggerated it out of proportion.

Since during stress the body is shunting energy into the skeletal muscle system for fight or flight why not follow through with some vigorous exercise. Running, aerobics, cycling, martial arts, swimming, etc., are good ways to burn up accumulated stress and help remove the sense of powerlessness that often accompanies it.

There are softer forms such as tai-chi and yoga, relaxation classes, meditation and breathing excercises that can help rebalance the mind and body.

Water therapy can be very effective at de-stressing. Since the skin is the major sense organ of the body, immersing it in water can give a sense of nurture. Water temperature above body temperature is relaxing for a short period of time. Excess heat can be weakening however so heat is best followed by cold.

There is a simple technique that can be used to disengage the mental activity from having a negative impact on the body. You touch three fingers from each hand on the corners of the forehead and then pull the skin lightly apart so the skin in the center of the forehead is slightly stretched. With muscle testing it has been found that if you now think about a particular problem it won't weaken the body. Holding these points seems to work as a clutch to effectively disengage the mental activity from the physical body. If these points are held for a few minutes it takes the "sharper edges" off the problem for hours.

If having a "bad" picture in the mind has a bad effect on the body, even if the picture is not real, then a good picture in the mind should have a good effect on the body, even if it's not real. This has proven true in many clinical studies. Children with cancer play a game like Pac-Man but on the screen it uses white blood cells chasing cancers cells. The result is increased activity of their own white blood cells.

Creative visualization is a rapidly growing form of therapy and can be done easily. Sit or lie down in a comfortable position. You can start by thinking about a particular problem. However you have unlimited tools available. You can visualize anything from a machine gun and hand grenades to a magic wand and fairy dust to change the picture on your mind's video screen from that of a problem into one with a happy ending. If you create an improved picture in your mind your subconscious will immediately swing all its powers into having that picture expressed into physical reality. Jules Vernes imagined undersea travel and that made the submarine virtually inevitable.

Positive thinking is a form of creative visualization. If what comes out of our mouth is indicative of what goes on in our minds then let us speak words of support and encouragement. This is especially important with young children as they are forming much of their self image from feedback from those around them. Everything seen and heard is recorded as reality so until the ability to discriminate is learned it's especially important to avoid continually berating a child.

PRICELESS PEACE OF MIND

There may be a point where everything we do becomes futile and pointless. The more we struggle the more mired we become. This is the point where surrender may be more beneficial than furthur struggle.

There is a certain wisdom behind peasant philosophy. What is beyond your control is simply shrugged off. "C'est la vie", "That's life" indicate surrender to greater forces. However, the point where you should fight and where you should flee is not always easy to know.

> "God grant me the serenity to accept
> the things I cannot change,
> courage to change the things I can
> and wisdom to know the difference."
>
> Anonymous

While physical pain and disease are messages from your body that something's wrong and change is necessary, despair is God's message that something is not right spiritually. We take joy and pride when we mentally and physically force our way through life's problems. Depression and despair, however, are the rewards for our failures. We get so caught up in our little skirmishes that we often miss the bigger picture.

If we lay back on the grass on a clear summer night we can see what appears to be endless numbers of twinkling stars. The universe seems immense. Actually you can only see a few thousand stars with the naked eye, but it is now known that there are over two hundred billion stars in our galaxy, the Milky Way. Also, there are approximately one hundred billion known galaxies.

Our life's dramas of victory and defeat begin to pale in comparison with the gigantic stage on which they are being played out.

With such immensity it would seem that our lives must be lonely and insignificant.

"One night a man had a dream. He
dreamed he was walking along the
beach with the LORD. Across the sky
flashed scenes from his life. For each
scene, he noticed two sets of footprints
in the sand; one belonging to him, and
the other to the LORD.
When the last scene of his life flashed
before him, he looked back at the
footprints in the sand. He noticed that
many times along the path of his life
there was only one set of footprint. He
also noticed that it happened at the very
lowest and saddest times in his life.
This really bothered him and he
questioned the LORD about it. "LORD,
you said that once I decided to follow
you, you'd walk with me all the way. But I
have noticed that during the most
troublesome times in my life, there is

only one set of footprints. I don't
understand why when I needed you
most you would leave me."
The LORD replied, "My precious,
precious child, I love you and I would
never leave you. During your times of
trial and suffering, when you see only
one set of footprints, it was then that I
carried you."

Anonymous

We worry and struggle because we feel alone in life and our alone-
ness makes us fearful. All of this weakens us however and it is not
what God intended for us.

"I came that they might have life, and
might have it abundantly." (John 10:10)

Could the promise of abundant life apply to every little lost soul in
this vast universe?

"Behold, I stand at the door and knock;
if any one hears My voice and opens the door,
I will come in to him." (Revelation 3:20)

How do you open the door to God? By prayer. Do you need a degree or a course to pray or authorization from someone else? No, all
you need is desire. Here is a sample prayer titled "The Difficulties of
Praying."

" Why, O Lord, is it so hard for me to keep my heart
directed toward you? Why do the many little things I
want to do, and the many people I know, keep crowding
into my mind, even during the hours that I am totally free
to be with you and you alone? Why does my mind
wander off in so many directions, and why does my heart
desire the things that lead me astray? Are you not enough
for me? Do I keep doubting your love and care, your

mercy and grace? Do I keep wondering, in the centre of my being, whether you will give me all I need if I just keep my eyes on you?

Please accept my distractions, my fatigue, my irritations, and my faithless wanderings. You know me more deeply and fully than I know myself. You love me with a greater love than I can love myself. You can offer me more than I can desire. Look at me, see me in all my misery and inner confusion, and let me sense your presence in the midst of my turmoil. All I can do is show myself to you. Yet, I am afraid to do so. I am afraid that you will reject me. But, I know-with the knowledge of faith-that you desire to give me your love. The only thing you ask of me is not to hide from you, not to run away in despair, not to act as if you were a relentless despot.

Take my tired body, my confused mind, and my restless soul into your arms and give me rest, simple quiet rest. So I ask too much too soon? I should not worry about that. You will let me know. Come, Lord, come. Amen."

(Author Unknown)

EPILOGUE

YOUR RIGHT TO KNOW

Health care is a personal topic these days. We are beginning to take an interest in our bodies. We don't leave it all up to the physicians. More and more people are curious to know not only how their bodies work, but how they can get—and keep— their bodies working at peak performance. That's the theory behind this book. We believe you not only have the right to know how your body works, but it is essential for good health. Only when you fully understand it, can you treat your body with the respect and the proper nutrients it deserves.

Perhaps you're one of the many who have gone to a doctor knowing that your body wasn't working "just right." Either you didn't have the energy you used to, or you complained of constant or continued headaches. The doctor routinely examined you, found nothing wrong and dismissed your complaints. But you—knowing your body better than any doctor—still felt something was not quite right.

Chances are you were hesistant, after an experience like that, to go back to the doctor with an illness. You probably felt he would dismiss it and leave you feeling foolish again.

PREVENTION IS PREFERABLE

We feel that any complaint about your body—no matter how minor it may seem—is not foolish. You know what your optimum performance is. You are the first to recognize when you're running a little slow. By the time it is recognizable to others— "Gee, you've been looking a little pale lately"—whatever is wrong is pretty well advanced and will require a great deal of care to fix. By giving your body that care before an illness sets in, you can not only avoid feeling under the weather, but maintain your body's top performance. It's really not that hard.

The wise old adage—"An ounce of prevention is worth a pound of cure"—is still very true today, even with all the wonder drugs and high tech medicine available. We believe you deserve to treat your body to that ounce of prevention.

NATURAL IS BEST

We also believe that "the natural way" is the best. Just look at the death rate in this country from heart attacks. Then look at the shelves in the grocery stores. They are filled with over-processed and over-refined foods of all kinds. These foods are literally killing us. That's why we believe that we need to "detoxify" our bodies. We need to return to the basics. Even many of our vitamin supplements are filled with artificial flavorings and colorings.

IT'S EASY TO GET STARTED

Dr. Matsen uses specific natural supplements to aid the body's organs in regaining their proper functioning. Here's a list of some of them:

YEAST INHIBITORS
(Used from Stage I through Stage III)

<u>Garlimed</u>—Garlic capsules. Take one to three capsules two or three times daily.

<u>Lactobacillus Acidophilus and Bifidus</u>—Available in powder or capsule. Take one or two capsules twice a day. Refrigerate the product if possible.

YEAST KILLERS
(Used during Stage II)

<u>Capricin</u>—A strong yeast killer. Its fatty base may bother those with liver or gallbladder problems. Three capsules twice a day. If there is no reaction, then increase as directed in the book (page 163).

<u>HoBoN FY</u>—A mild yeast killer in liquid form. It's easy for children to take. Take one teaspoon twice daily.

<u>Zymex</u>—A middle strength yeast killer. Take two to three times a day.

OTHER SUPPLEMENTS
(Taken at any stage, as needed)

A.F. Betaris—Improves bile. Take one to three capsules with meals.

Black Radish—Aids Ileo-cecal valve. One or two capsules with meals.

Cal-Amo—Helps to decrease allergic sensitivity. One or two capsules with meals.

GLYCO-MED—Helps to stabilize blood sugar.

Immu-Plex—Helps the immune system. Two capsules, two to six times daily.

Min-Tran—Reduces cravings and nervousness. Two capsules, two to six times daily.

SILICAMED—Remineralization Supplement. Two to five capsules daily.

VARICOSAN—Helps varicose veins and poor circulation in the legs. One tablet daily.

VITAMED—Multi-Vitamin-Mineral Supplement. One tablet three times daily.

Vitamin C with Bioflavonoids

Whole Dessicated Adrenal—Helps adrenal function. One to three times daily.

HERE'S TO YOUR HEALTH

Some of these items are available at your local health food store and others can be obtained through your naturopathic physician.

If for any reason, you have additional questions or comments concerning any of the materials found in this book, feel free to write our:

Editorial Department
FISCHER PUBLISHING CORPORATION
P.O. BOX 368
CANFIELD, OH 44406

We wish you the best of luck in your pursuit of good health.

INDEX

Other Outstanding Books
on Health And Natural Healing From

Fischer Publishing Corporation
Canfield, Ohio 44406

How To Fight Cancer And Win by William L. Fischer

It clearly spells out real cancer preventives and cures, many never before published, with strong scientific documentation and stories of miraculous cures. They are all presented in a concise, easy-to-understand style. You can put this vast knowledge into practice to ensure that this deadly disease never strikes home.

ISBN 0-915421-07-0 ....$14.95

The Mircle Healing Power Through Nature's Pharmacy by William L. Fischer

Now you can learn how to treat virtually every disease or condition known to man—naturally! A comprehensive guide to help you and heal you...the most complete...most useful...and most up-to-date work of its kind. Complete with many documented case histories and 32 full-color illustrations.

ISBN 0-915421-04-6 ....$19.95

Hidden Secrets Of Super Perfect Health At Any Age Book II by William L. Fischer

Contains never-before-published health-related information with an incredible number of alternatives for treating everything from cancer to insomnia, from prostrate problems to male impotency, from varicose veins to migraine headaches. Brings hope to sufferers of colitis, arthritis, bronchitis, asthma, heart problems, poor circulation and more. 288 pages.

ISBN 0-915421-05-4 ....$14.95

Mysterious Cause Of Illness and How To Overcome Every Disease From Constipation to Cancer Eating Alive by Jonn Matsen, N.D.

Famed Canadian doctor uncovers the mysterious *REAL* cause of illness—and shows you how to overcome every disease from constipation to cancer. Dr. Matsen's acclaimed food-based "miracle cures" use *no* drugs, *no* surgery. They simply turn on the natural "internal healing power" built into every human body. Here is a safe, easy approach to health and longevity that has cured many "hopeless" cases after conventional medicine has failed! If you read nothing else, read Dr. Matsen's new revelations of secret remedies.

ISBN 0-915421-09-7 ....$16.95

Secrets To Healthy Eyes by John MacKay

This revolutionary new book deals with the natural remedies from Glaucoma to Cataracts, Nearsightedness, Night Blindness, Impaired Vision and More...Explains the very latest in medical technology and shows how a new procedure can cure common sight defects forever.

ISBN 0-915421-08-9 ....$14.95

The Dr. Rinse Formula by Dr. Morton Walker, DPM

This is the important book that tells how this world-famous Dutch doctor conquered a serious heart condition with his world-famous super nutritional formula. It can add many years to your life while reversing or preventing poor blood circulation—atherosclerosis—high/low blood pressure—stroke—arthritis—bursitis—angina—high cholesterol—glaucoma—low energy—and other cardiovascular-related ailments and allergies.

....$ 9.00

Body Secrets For Perfect Health And Fitness by John Orsini

Anyone who wants to become totally fit will find this book invaluable. *Body Secrets* reveals countless secret methods and shortcuts. John Orsini has trained and advised Olympic Medal Winners and provided nutritional counseling to high school athletes, movie stars, business executives, and weekend sports enthusiasts. *Body Secrets* is your chance to cash in on John Orsini's highly successful proven methods, to be fit and stay fit.

ISBN 0-915421-10-0 ....$14.95

How To Survive In The Hospital by Joan Haas-Unger, R.N.

There are too many procedures, performed by too many doctors, in too many places, with too high a stroke-and-death rate. This landmark book can help you lower your risks and increase your chances of survival in the hospital.

ISBN 0-915421-06-2 ....$12.95

Shipping/Handling $3.00 for one book.
Additional books $1.00 each.

Fischer Publishing
425 w. main street   box 368
canfield, ohio 44406
(216) 533-1232